IRS Form 1023

Tax Preparation Guide

Jody Blazek CPA

John Wiley & Sons. Inc.

Library of Congress Cataloging-in-Publication Data:

ISBN-13 978-0471-71525-2
ISBN-10 0471-715525

Printed in the United States of America

10 9 8 7 6 5 4 3 2 1

About the Author

Jody Blazek is a partner in Blazek & Vetterling LLP, a Houston CPA firm that focuses on tax financial services for exempt organizations and the individuals who create, fund, and work with them. Blazek & Vetterling LLP provides tax compliance, auditing, and planning services to over 250 nonprofit organizations, including schools, churches, museums, human service organizations, business leagues, private foundations, garden clubs, fraternities, research institutes, civic associations, cultural organizations, and others.

John began her professional career at KPMG, then Peat, Marwick, Mitchell & Co. Her concentration on exempt organizations began in 1969 when she was assigned to study the Tax Reform Act that completely revamped the taxation of charities and created private foundations. From 1972 to 1981, she gained nonprofit management experience as treasurer of the Menil Interests where she worked with John and Dominique de Menil to plan the Menil Collection, the Rothko Chapel, and other projects of the Menil Foundation. She reentered public practice in 1981 to found the firm she now serves.

In addition to this book, she is the author of five books in the Wiley Nonprofit Series: *IRS Form 990 Tax Preparation Guide for Nonprofits*; *Tax Planning and Compliance for Tax-Exempt Organizations, 4th Edition* (2004); *Financial Planning for Nonprofit Organizations* (1996); *Private Foundations: Tax Law and Compliance 2nd ed.* (2003) and *The Legal Answer Book for Private Foundations* (2001), coauthored with Bruce R. Hopkins.

Jody serves on the Financial Accounting and Transparency Group created by Independent Sector to support the Panel on the Nonprofit Sector evaluating 2004 proposals of the Senate Finance Committee. She is immediate-past chair of the AICPA Tax-Exempt Organizations Resource Panel and a member of the 990 and 1023 Task Forces. She serves on the national editorial board of Tax Analysts' *The Exempt Organization Tax Review* and the AICPA *Tax Advisor*. She received the "Most Creative" award for 2003 from the Houston Chapter of Certified Public Accounts. She is a founding director of Texas Accountants and Lawyers for the Arts and the Houston Artists Fund and a member of the board of the Gulf Coast Institute, the Anchorage Foundations, and the Main Street Coalition Council. She is a frequent speaker at nonprofit symposia, including those sponsored by the Conference of Southwest Foundations, the Association of Small Foundations, the AICPA, the Arizona, New York, Washington, Maryland, and Texas Societies of CPAs, The University of Texas School of Law, United Way of the Texas Gulf Coast, Professional Education Systems, and the Nonprofit Resource Center.

Jody received her BBA from University of Texas at Austin in 1964 and took selected tax Cources at South Texas School of Law. She and her husband, David Crossley, nuture two sons, Austin and Jay Blazek Crossley.

Contents

CONTENTS

Preface

Helping people to create a nonprofit organization and achieving IRS approval for tax-exempt status is my goal for this book. From start to finish, it addresses the process for seeking recognition of tax exemption for a nonprofit organization with the filing of Form 1023, *Application for Recognition of Exemption* under §501(c)(3) of the Internal Revenue Code. Advice is provided for successfully preparing the form, choosing the right alternative to contest a negative IRS determination, monitoring the ongoing reporting requirements for public charities, and seeking state exemption. Readers will find explanations of the rationale behind the information that the IRS requests—and these explanations will aid in the decisions that shape the prospective tax-exempt charity into an acceptable form. For complex issues, references to my other book, *Tax Planning and Compliance for Tax-Exempt Organizations*, are provided.

Even those familiar with the form should review first Section 1.1 of this book, Before You Begin, and read its subsections on what's good, missing, and challenging about the revised form. The first chapter also describes the procedural issues. It is critical that the process begin with a consideration of whether the proposed entity can satisfy both the organizational and operational tests set out in the Federal income tax code. Before embarking on the arduous task of submitting Form 1023 and responding to the form questions regarding qualification, the Suitability Test can be used to evaluate the viability of the plans to create a new charitable nonprofit.

Once a decision is made to go forward with submission of Form 1023, its careful preparation is imperative. The application must be provided to and/or copied for anyone that asks to see it in the future. For many organizations, the highest scrutiny it will ever receive from the IRS occurs when the application is reviewed. Due to its limited resources, the IRS examines only a small portion of the U.S. exempt nonprofits after they have been initially approved. This situation will undoubtedly continue—at least until the Form 990s are all electronically filed several years from now.

Form 1023 encompasses a wide range of information about how the organization intends to accomplish its mission. Chapter 2 considers the form line-by-line and explains the import of the information requested to supplement IRS instructions. The application should paint a well-defined picture of the new organization as it will operate, in both words and numbers. The newly revised form delves deeply into those plans with its long series of questions. Applicants need to carefully consider the depth of information to be provided in its explanations for *Yes* answers. There will be a temptation to provide more details than necessary. For some questions, it may be suitable to simply say plans are not yet developed. Bruce Hopkins, author of *The Law of Tax-Exempt Organizations*, writes, "There is a considerable overreaching by the IRS by means of this form."

The process of completing these forms is actually a healthy exercise for a new organization's creators. The gathering of the necessary information provides a good opportunity to do strategic planning for the proposed organization. Organizers can focus on realizable goals that can be described and discard any ill-conceived or potentially nonexempt projects. All aspects of the organization's structure, mission, finances, and relationships are explored in the process of answering the questions. Why the organization was created and whether it evolved from a previous life are explained. The prospective nonprofit is asked to evidence its qualification for tax-exemption by describing its planned activities including:

- Types of programs it will conduct
- Who will participate in programs and receive benefits (sometimes referred to as its *exempt constituents*)
- How contributions will be solicited
- How money will be spent, including—in great detail—compensation and other financial transactions with persons who create and manage it

Successful preparation of Form 1023 involves weighing the material facts that should be submitted against their potential for generating controversy with the IRS. While the facts must be accurate, there is room for judgment in the presentation of a potentially nonexempt activity. Another important aspect to consider is the possibility that the organization could be somewhat constrained to operate in the manner presented in Form 1023. The organizers must look to the future and the possibilities must be thoroughly considered before the application is submitted. Any future "substantial change" in operations necessitates resubmission or communication with the IRS.

Form 1023 provides eight specialized schedules for certain applications. Chapter 3 explains the information requested on those schedules for churches, schools, scholarship awards, and others. Strategies for solving problems, such as denial of the application or late filing, are explored in Chapter 4. Chapter 5 considers the special issues for public charities seeking an advance versus a definitive ruling as a public charity. Chapter 6 addresses future reliance on the original determination letter. Lastly, Chapter 7 illustrates state exemption filing requirements.

I applaud Cindy Westcott, Marvin Friedlander, Janet Gutterman, and other IRS personnel who crafted the new Form 1023 to incorporate guidance that should bring about more complete and acceptable applications. Some applicants will undoubtedly complain. A majority of the existing organizations exempt under §501(c)(3) have revenues less than $250,000 annually and do not engage the services of knowledgeable professionals to prepare the form. For them the 38 pages of instructions alone will be daunting. A Form 1023-EZ deserves future consideration for such nonprofits, particularly those without plans to compensate or enter into other financial transactions with their officials or to conduct international programs or other activities the IRS deems requires additional information.

Readers of this book can also access its companion web site, located at: http://www.wiley.com/go/blazek_1023

In addition to Form 1023 for a Public Charity and Form 1023 for a Private Foundation, you will find many other helpful checklists, letters, and procedures (some of which are included in the Appendices to this book). These forms can be customized or printed and used repeatedly as needed.

Acknowledgments

I thank the philanthropists and volunteers who share their dreams with me. The experience I have gained assisting them in the birth of their new non-profit organizations was invaluable to me in preparing this book. I also thank my wonderful associate, Amanda Adams, for her careful and insightful editing and invaluable assistance in evaluating the new Form 1023.

Jody Blazek
December 2004
Houston, Texas

CHAPTER 1

Form 1023: Application for Recognition of Exemption under IRC §501(c)(3)

This book is a strategic guide for obtaining IRS recognition of tax-exempt status as a charitable organization. A charitable organization must by law request Federal approval for tax-exempt status by submitting Form 1023, *Application for Recognition of Exemption Under §501(c)(3) of the Internal Revenue Code*, to the Internal Revenue Service (IRS) and paying the applicable user's fee, The desired result is a determination letter describing the category of qualification for exemption and public or private status granted.[1]

By taking you step by step through Form 1023 this book provides a blueprint for seeking this result. It includes specific suggestions for answering each question on Form 1023 and navigating the steps involved in the approval process. Practical advice on the alternatives available in contesting an adverse IRS determination is also provided—as well as strategies for solving problems such as denial of the application or late filing. (Comments and suggestions regarding Form 1024, which is submitted by business leagues, civic associations, unions, and other categories of §501(c), are not included in this book because this form is currently under revision.)[2]

---

[1]Model filled-in Form 1023s are shown in Appendix B and C. Determination letters are reproduced in Appendix I.

[2]Comments about the current Form 1024 (as of January 1, 2005) can be found in Jody Blazek, *Tax Planning and Compliance for Tax-Exempt Organizations*, 3rd ed. (New York, John Wiley & Sons, 1999).

This book reveals the rationale behind the information requested by the IRS and adds insight to the interaction between the questions that enable a tax preparer to help prospective organizations qualify for approval. In addition to this insight, a brief discussion about statutory requirements for exemption is provided with references to the author's text with detailed explanation. The process of completing these forms is actually a healthy exercise for a new organization's creators. The gathering of the necessary information provides an excellent opportunity for strategic planning for the proposed organization. Organizers can focus on realizable goals that can be described and discard any ill-conceived or potentially nonexempt projects. All aspects of the organization's structure, mission, finances, and relationships are explored in the process of answering the questions that are required for achieving tax-exempt status. Why the organization was created and whether it evolved from a previous life must be explained. Proposed activities and grant programs are described, along with information about where the money will come from and how it will be spent. Fundraising plans are fleshed out and solicitation letters submitted. How the money will be spent, who will decide how to spend it, and who will be able to participate in its programs and receive benefits of its activities must be described. Most importantly, evidence to show that the applicant will not benefit a limited group of people (particularly those who control it) and other facts to support its qualification as a charitable organization that benefits the general public must be presented.

Successful preparation of Form 1023 involves weighing the material facts that should be submitted against their potential for generating controversy with the IRS. While the facts must be accurate, there is room for judgment in the presentation of a potentially nonexempt activity. If there is a reasonable chance that a potentially unrelated activity might be approved and the organization is prepared to agree not to undertake the activity if it is not acceptable, inclusion is warranted. The new application asks many questions about future activities that the applicant may not yet be prepared to explain. Another important aspect to consider is the possibility that the organization could be somewhat constrained to operate in the manner presented in Form 1023. The organizers must thoroughly consider their nonprofit's future before the application is submitted. Any "substantial changes" in operations are reportable annually on Forms 990 and necessitate communication with the IRS Exempt Organization Group's office in Cincinnati if the organization wishes overt approval for the changes.

Finally, many persons will view the application in the future for a number of reasons. The organization's managers will periodically review the original Form 1023 to be sure everyone understands why the IRS considers the organization to be exempt, and to see if there has been a "material change" in its operations. The application must also be available for inspection by anyone that asks to see it.[3] Copies of favorable determination letters issued by the IRS are available for 30 days after their issuance in its Washington Freedom of Information Reading Room.[4] Organizations approved for qualification under IRC §501(c)(3) that have filed 990s in the past two years are listed in IRS Publication 78 available in printed copy or on the Internet.[5]

1.1 BEFORE YOU BEGIN

Located in the front of Form 1023 is a preparation aid entitled "Form 1023 Checklist." The two-page list displays the information that is required. The IRS suggests the items be checked off as the form is prepared. The application will not be accepted and will be sent back if the checklist is not completed—box-by-box. This checklist exemplifies the significant differences between the new form and its predecessor. Note in the upper left-hand corner of Appendix B that the Form 1023 was revised in October 2004. The revision process took several years and involved a significant effort on the part of the IRS that welcomed input from the American Institute of Certified Public Accountants, the American Bar Association, and other interested organizations. The first draft was proposed in October 2002. Preparers should visit the IRS website to verify they are using the latest version and method for submitting the form. Though it may take some years to reach its goal, the IRS announced in 2003 that it plans to require that the form be filed electronically. (Some may have seen the October 2003 draft when it was posted on the IRS website and then withdrawn because people began to use it.)

The 2004 version of the form is designed to streamline the exemption application process. To do so, many questions previously asked by a reviewer after the application was submitted are now embodied in the form. Before the applicant simply described its plans in words and numbers and answered a few questions about its insiders and relationships. Now the form forces the applicant to consider this issue and a host of other technical issues. The time the IRS estimates is needed to do the recordkeeping, learn about the form, prepare it, and submit the first eleven parts of the form have increased from 67 to 104 hours. This seemingly incredible amount of time evidences the fact that the highest scrutiny that many nonprofits ever receive is when they are initially considered for recognition of tax exemption.

---

[3]Discussed in Section 1.9 of this chapter.

[4]IRS Notice 92-28,

[5]IRS Publication 78 can be viewed at http://www.irs.gov/charities&nonprofits/. Forms 990 and 990-PF for charities can be viewed at http://www.guidestar.org/.

In some respects the form is user-friendly; but it contains significant traps for the uninformed. The seven pages of instructions contained in the 1998 version have grown to 38. Given this complexity, you should keep in mind the following good, missing, and troublesome aspects of the new Form 1023 when you study it and its instructions.

(a) What's Good

- Significant increase in the probability that an application will be merit closed (i.e., approved) without further review due to extensive information that must be provided[6]
- TIP and CAUTION boxes that alert preparer to troublesome issues
- New system that displays financial data by complete years to allow for better comparison between previously distorted revenue and expense columns (see Appendix M for contrary views)
- Seven-page glossary defining terms that appear bold in the instructions
- An index of terms tied to instruction pages
- Extensive instructions, with a design format similar to Form 990, that open with a table of contents and a *What's New* section
- Clarity that the past, current, and future plans must be described
- Form 872.C replaced with a checkbox.

(b) What's Missing

- Lack of explanation about the significance of some questions
- Instructions for certain lines
- Use of the term *Disqualified Persons*
- The question about public officials
- Clear description of the Organizational and Operational Tests in Part III

(c) What's Challenging

- Addition of Part V—Information about Compensation and other Financial Arrangements containing $2\frac{1}{4}$ pages of detailed questions about planned payments to insiders

---

[6]See Section 1.5 in this chapter for an explanation of the term *merit closed*.

- For persons inexperienced with tax matters and forms, the girth of information will be daunting.
- IRS Customer Account Service staff will undoubtedly face a significant increase in phone calls to 1-877-829-5500 in response to the *Filing Assistance* suggestions (page 4 of the instructions).
- The 40-hour increase in time it takes to complete the application according to the IRS estimates.
- For most, the application will contain many more pages with extensive explanations.
- Uncertainty about how information should be provided.
- Temptation for applicants to simply say *No* to avoid having to explain.

(d) The New Part VIII

Where no instructions existed for most lines in prior versions, now Form 1023 features line-by-line explanations of the data requested. The new Part VIII, with a series of 22 questions, doubles the detailed information requested with the intention that more applications will be approved without additional information requests. The questions present a challenge, however, because the importance of the information provided is not necessarily explained in the instructions. For some questions, only the type of information requested is described. When the answer is *Yes*, an attachment is requested to explain why. Some information, particularly pertaining to transactions with and benefits for insiders, is requested in a slightly different fashion in more than one part. Most troubling for some users of the form will be that it is not always made clear whether or not *Yes* answers have a negative impact on qualification for exemption. For example, Line 14 in Part VIII asks, "Do you publish, own, or have rights in music, literature, tapes, art works, choreography, scientific discoveries or other intellectual property?" If the answer is *Yes*, the instruction asks for the attachment of agreements evidencing who owns the rights. What is not stated is the IRS's preference that the organization own the rights. The first question in Part VIII presents a serious trap for the uninformed. It is in the instruction in which one finds eventually that a *Yes* answer, stating that the organization supports or opposes candidates in political campaigns, will prevent recognition of tax-exemption as a charity. This book addresses such issues and discusses the impact of the answers line-by-line.

(e) Caution

The terms used to define organizations qualifying for exemption connote different meanings to different people. What is religious to one may be sacrilegious to another. An EO Exempt Specialist responsible for approving or denying an application construes the meaning of a proposed organization's exempt purpose within the context of his or her understanding of the rules. Chapters 2 through 10 of the companion volume to this book, *Tax Planning and Compliance for Tax-Exempt Organizations*,[7] indicate the vagaries of the rules and different standards applicable to each type of exempt activity. While the IRS specialists are knowledgeable and cooperative, they may not perceive a proposed organization in the same light as its creators. Therefore, applications must be prepared with care after reviewing the suitability test and statutory criteria for qualifying organizations.

1.2 SUITABILITY TEST

Before plunging into the time-consuming process of preparing and submitting the application, the following questions, distilled from the suitability and new organization checklists in Appendix E, should be evaluated.

- Is there a need to create a new organization rather than carrying out the project through an existing organization?
- What is the best form of organization: nonprofit corporation, trust, or unincorporated association?[8]
- Which category of exemption is appropriate to the goals and purposes of the organization: IRC §501(c)(3) or §501(c)(4)–(25)?
- Can the organizational and operational tests be met?[9]
- Might a profit-making organization be preferable? Are the creators or managers willing to forego potential profits? Will business activity be substantial?[10] Are prospects for raising venture capital better than for getting grants?
- Should more than one EO be created in view of differing purposes or funding sources? A supporting organization?[11] A lobbying branch qualified under IRC §501(c)(4)?[12] A for-profit subsidiary?[13]

---

[7]Jody Blazek, *Tax Planning and Compliance for Tax-Exempt Organizations*, 4th ed. (Hoboken, NJ: John Wiley & Sons, 1999).

[8]See ibid., Section 1.7.

[9]See ibid., Chapter 2, and Sections 2.2 and 2.3 of this book.

[10]See ibid., Section 21.3.

[11]See ibid., Section 11.3.

[12]See ibid., Section 6.1.

[13]See ibid., Section 22.3.

- Is a broadly based governing board appropriate? Should the organization be controlled by its membership?

One should also evaluate whether any of the following advantages will be useful to the proposed organization:

- Exemption from federal income tax, except on unrelated business income
- Exemption from other taxes, such as the federal unemployment tax and some state and local taxes
- Eligibility to receive tax-deductible charitable contributions for income, estate, and gift tax purposes
- Qualification for grant funding from private foundations and government entities
- Potential for other benefits such as benefiting from charitable lead or remainder trusts and tax-deferred gift annuities and postal rate privileges

1.3 STATUTORY REQUIREMENTS FOR EXEMPTION

To qualify for exemption under IRC §501(c)(3), an organization must meet two statutory tests. The characteristics and language needed to satisfy the tests are explained in detail in Chapter 2, which presents suggestions for completing each part of the form. Throughout the process of completing the form, however, preparers must keep in mind the two very basic requirements to achieve recognition as a charitable organization as follows, discussed below:

(a) Organizational Test

An organizational test requires that the organization be a corporation, community chest, fund, or foundation with specific language in its governing instrument that mandates that it be organized and operated exclusively for one or more of the following eight very specific purposes:

1. Religious
2. Charitable
3. Scientific
4. Testing for public safety
5. Literary

6. Educational

7. To foster national or international amateur sports competition (but only if no part of its activities involve the provision of athletic facilities or equipment)

8. For the prevention of cruelty to children or animals

One or more of the eight specified purposes must be named in the organization's organizing documents. An entity established "to promote community benefits" and "to develop the art of dance" does not qualify, unless its charter also stated that such activities were to be conducted for exclusively educational or charitable purposes.[14]

IRS Publication 557, *Tax-Exempt Status for Your Organization*, contains sample organizational documents and provides a comprehensive resource for issues the IRS deems important in this regard. The first page or so of the Form 1023 instructions contain an *Overview of 501(c)(3) Organizations* as well. Lastly, the instructions to Part III of the form briefly define the term *charitable* and provide examples of acceptable and unacceptable purpose, activity restraint, and dissolution clauses.

The organization's documents must contain the first two clauses below, and the tax codes requires that the entity adhere to the second two:

- All assets upon dissolutions must be distributed for charitable purposes.
- No part of its net earnings shall inure to the benefit of any private shareholder or individual.
- No substantial part of its activities shall be the carrying on of propaganda, or otherwise attempting to influence legislation (except as otherwise provided in IRC §501(c)(h)).
- The organization shall not participate in or intervene in (including publishing or distributing statements) any political campaign on behalf of (or in opposition to) any candidate for public office.

(b) Operational Test

An operational test requires that a §501(c)(3) qualifying organization actually conduct activities that accomplish and promote one of the eight specified charitable purposes. Preparers will find that Chapters 3, 4, and 5 of *Tax Planning and Compliance for Tax-Exempt Organizations* contain extensive discussions of

---

[14]Readers can find an extensive discussion of these standards with examples and citations to IRS rulings in Chapter 2, *Tax Planning and Compliance for Tax-Exempt Organizations;* see Section 2.3 of this book.

these standards with examples and citations to IRS rulings regarding the characteristics and special rules applicable to each category of qualifying Section 501(c)(3) organizations. In the instructions for line-by-line preparation of Form 1023 that follow this chapter, relevant sections from that book will be cited.

(c) Private Benefit Test

Note that the first organizational provision noted in the previous section prohibits inurement of assets to private shareholders and individuals. For purposes of enforcing this requirement to constrain financial relationships, the Internal Revenue Code identifies certain insiders as disqualified persons (DPs).[15] DPs can serve as members of the board, can be paid reasonable compensation for services they actually render, and participate in organizational activities just as any other person. They are, however, red flagged for scrutiny in all charities. The self-dealing rules applicable to private foundations prohibit most financial transactions with DPs.[16] For the purposes of this question, disqualified persons are defined to include:

- Substantial contributors (those donating $5,000 or 2% of cumulative donations entity has ever received, if more)
- Creators of trusts regardless of contribution level
- Foundation managers (officials that are empowered to make decisions)
- A member of the family of those listed above
- Controlled corporations, partnerships, trusts, or estates (over 35%)
- Another EO controlled by the EO itself or by the same persons

Questions in Part V of Form 1023 and elsewhere ask for extensive details about any activities that involve financial transactions with DPs. Using the present tense, some questions ask about financial relationships by asking "Do you" compensate, lease, or have other agreements with officials. Others ask, "Do you or will you" have such arrangements. Names, copies of leases and other agreements, and a full description of the terms for compensation and purchases or use of property must be submitted as discussed for Part V later in this book. On line 17 of the Financial Data in Part IX, actual and projected compensation of officials must be quantified.

---

[15]IRC §4946(a) and §958(f)(1). See Chapter 12, *Tax Planning and Compliance for Tax-Exempt Organizations*.

[16]IRC §4941. See Chapter 14, *Tax Planning and Compliance for Tax-Exempt Organizations*.

1.4 PROPER TIMING

(a) No Charitable Status Until Filing

Even though a newly formed organization meets all of the qualifications for exemption under IRC §501(c)(3), it is not treated as a tax-exempt organization until it properly notifies the IRS of its qualification by filing Form 1023.[17] An organization is also presumed to be a private foundation unless its properly completed Form 1023 furnishes information proving its public status. Organizations that qualify under other subsections of §501(c) are exempt without filing such notice, although the IRS will not accept Form 990 unless Form 1024 is filed to establish proof of exemption.[18] Some criticize this policy because it is not provided in the tax code. As a practical matter, however, it seems reasonable for the IRS to use its established system to ascertain when an organization can be relieved of the obligation to pay income tax.

(b) Due Date

The regulations require filing within 15 months from the end of the month of formation.[19] Since 1992, an automatic 12-month extension to this period has been provided. The 2004 instructions simply state, "If you file Form 1023 within 27 months after the end of the month in which you are legally formed, and we approve the application, the legal date of formation will be the effective date of your exempt status." The date of legal formation is entered on line 11 of Part I. Line 2 of Part VII asks if the application is being submitted more than 27 months from the month of formation. If so, Schedule E must be completed. When the 27 months have passed, the deadline may again be extended under special circumstances discussed in the comments for Schedule E. [§3.5]

(c) Effective Date of Exemption

A nonprofit's tax-exempt status is effected retroactively to its *date of formation*, if the application is filed in a timely manner and accepted by the IRS. Applications not treated as timely filed are effective only from the date of filing. A late-filing organization can request tax-exempt status as an IRC §501(c)(4) or-

---

[17]IRC §508(a).

[18]IRS Information Letter 2000-0260.

[19]Reg. §1.508-1(a)(2); Rev. Proc. 90-27, 1990-1 C.B. 514.

ganization for the period between formation and the effective §501(c)(3) exemption date; otherwise income taxes may be due on income received prior to the effective date of exemption.

To prove timely filing, it is preferable that the application be sent by certified mail, return receipt requested, or an IRS approved private delivery service. The postmark stamped on the envelope or delivery receipt transmitting the application determines the date of filing. Absent such a postmark, the date the application is stamped as received by the IRS is the receipt date.[20] If the application is simply dropped into a mailbox and is subsequently lost, the organization has no way to prove that it was sent.

(d) Incomplete Applications

A Form 1023 Checklist must be completed and submitted to demonstrate that the application contains all required information or "your application will be returned to you as incomplete." There is no mention in the instructions to explain the impact of this action on the effective date of tax-exempt status. If the resubmission date is beyond 27 months of formation, the applicant should study the regulations that take a surprisingly lenient position regarding incomplete applications.[21]

> The failure to supply, within the required time, all of the information required to complete the form, is not alone sufficient to deny exemption from the date of organization to the date such complete information is submitted by the organization. If the organization supplies the necessary additional information at the request of the Commissioner within the additional time period allowed by him (her), the original notice will be considered timely.

What constitutes a complete return is described in the procedures for filing a declaratory judgment to appeal an adverse determination. A "substantially complete" application for this purpose contains the following elements:[22]

- Signature of an authorized individual
- Employer identification number or Form SS-4[23]

---

[20]Rev. Rul. 77-114, 1977-1 C.B. 153.

[21]Reg. §1.508-1(a)(2)(ii).

[22]Rev. Proc. 90-27, 1990-1, I.R.B.514.

[23]This form can no longer be attached. The applicant must have the number before filing; see Section 2.1(d) of this book.

- Information regarding previously filed federal income tax and exempt organization information returns

- Statement of receipts and expenditures and balance sheet for the current and three preceding years (or all years of existence if less than four). A two-year proposed budget is submitted for new organizations.

- Statement of proposed activities and description of anticipated receipts and contemplated expenditures

- Conformed copy of organizing documents with proof they were approved by state authorities if applicable

- Copy of bylaws

- Correct user fee

1.5 EXPEDITIOUS HANDLING

It normally takes up to 21 days for the IRS to acknowledge that it has received an application. The time to approve a complete and unquestioned application during 2004 was about 60–75 days; such cases are said to be *merit closed*. Applications that involve requests for additional information can take up to 120 to 180 days for receipt of the approved determination letter. The timing also depends upon the IRS's workload, which is usually heavier in the fall at year-end tax-planning time, when many organizations are formed in order to facilitate deductible gifts from substantial contributors that want proof of charitable status.[24] Absent approval for special handling, submission of a complete and clearly prepared application can save considerable time in obtaining approval. When approval is needed as soon as possible, a speedy determination or expeditious handling can be requested. Reasons suggested in the instructions include:

- A grant to the applicant is pending and the failure to secure the grant may have an adverse impact on the organization's ability to continue operations.

- The purpose of the newly created organization is to provide disaster relief to victims of emergencies, such as floods and hurricanes.

- There have been undue delays in issuing a letter caused by problems with the IRS.

---

[24]IRC §170(c) defines a qualifying charity with no reference to §501(c)(3); nonetheless some require the determination letter.

A cover letter requesting special handling and describing the reason why speed is necessary should be attached. Independent documentation of the reason(s) should also be provided, such as a letter from a prospective funder stating that funds will be denied if there is a delay. The instructions maintain that the reason for processing the application ahead of others must be compelling. In the author's experience, such requests are often denied.

1.6 NATIONAL OFFICE

Some applications present questions not specifically answered by statute, regulation, IRS ruling, or court decisions. When qualification cannot be resolved by established precedent and require a legal interpretation, the application is forwarded to Washington D.C. for determination by the EO Technical Division.[25] As of October 1, 2004, the list of IRC §501(c)(3) applicant types that are reserved for EO Technical included:[26]

- Prepaid health plans (HMOs) where commercial-type insurance under IRC §510(m) is at issue
- Potentially discriminatory private school applications
- Hospitals participating in joint ventures, faculty group practice organizations, physician-hospital organizations, individual practice associations, and corporate practices of medicine
- Charter schools contracting with for-profit management service or facility providers that have substantial influence over the school
- Internet service providers, church applicants conducting activities wholly over the Internet, charitable fundraising programs through either auction or percentage fee arrangements with for-profit entities, with plans to raise funds wholly over the Internet

The IRS manual alerts examiners who review Form 1023 to identify cases that meet criteria for referral to EO Technical before they are assigned to a determination agent. It is suggested such cases may have significant regional or national impact. From time to time, the IRS also withholds determination on issues about which there is controversy or rules that are in transition. In the past, proposed activities that involved joint ventures, tax-exempt bond financing, and credit counselors were delayed in this fashion.

---

[25]Rev. Proc. 98-4, 1998-1 IRB 113.

[26]Internal Revenue Manual 7.20.1.3.

1.7 ORGANIZATIONS THAT NEED NOT FILE

Three types of organizations are specifically excused from filing Form 1023 to achieve exemption because they are automatically treated as tax-exempt—churches, modest organizations and subordinate nonprofits.[27] Despite their exception from the requirement, some of these organizations find it nonetheless desirable to file for a number of reasons. Donors may request this written IRS approval of their tax-exempt status as evidence of eligibility to receive tax-deductible donations—even though not required by IRC §170. Exempt status in some states is dependent upon federal approval. Nonprofit mailing privileges and other benefits of EOs are most readily obtained by organizations that can furnish a federal IRS determination letter.

(a) Churches

The first type of nonprofit organization excused from seeking recognition of its exempt status is a church, including its local affiliates and integrated auxiliaries,[28] and a convention or association of churches. Even though filing is not required, IRS determination may be desirable to remove uncertainty in the case of an unrecognized sect or a branch of a church established outside the United States. The IRS has developed a 14-point definition of a church which is embodied in the questions asked on Schedule A of Form 1023 [§3.1]. Churches are generally granted favorable status; for example, they need not file annual Form 990 and may receive more liberal local tax exemptions. Employment tax reporting rules for ministers are also favorable.[29]

(b) Modest Organizations

The second type of organization that does not need to file is one whose gross revenue is normally under $5,000 and which is not a private foundation. The term *normally* means that the organization received $7,500 or less in gross receipts in its first taxable year, $12,000 or less during its first two tax years combined, and $15,000 or less total gross receipts for its first three tax years combined. If an organization has gross receipts in excess of the minimal amounts above during any year after its formation, it must file Form 1023 within 90 days after the close of

---

[27]IRC §508(c)(1).

[28]Defined in Section 3.2, *Tax Planning and Compliance for Tax-Exempt Organizations*.

[29]Discussed in Section 25.4, *Tax Planning and Compliance for Tax-Exempt Organizations*.

that year. Line 2 of Schedule E allows such an organization to explain why it is not filing Form 1023 within 27 months of its formation.

(c) Subordinate Nonprofits

A third type of organization that need not file Form 1023 is the subordinate organization covered by a group exemption, for which the parent annually submits the required information, as explained in the following section.

1.8 GROUP EXEMPTIONS

To reduce overall compliance efforts on the part of each entity, the parent organization of an affiliated group of organizations centralized under its common supervision or control can obtain a *group exemption letter* recognizing tax-exempt status for itself and members of its group.[30] A central organization may be a subordinate itself, such as a state organization that has subordinate units and is itself affiliated with a national organization. Subordinate chapters, posts, or local units of a central organization, such as the American Red Cross or the National Parent-Teacher Association, need not separately seek recognition by filing separate applications; instead they can be covered under a group exemption requested by the central organization. All of the subordinate organizations in the group must qualify under the same §501(c) category of exemption, although the parent can have a different category from its subordinates. The group may not include private foundations or foreign organizations.

(a) Information Submitted

The parent organization files Form 1023 to obtain recognition of its own exemption. After being recognized, it separately applies by letter to the IRS Key District for approval of its group.[31] A letter requesting recognition of the parent's group is submitted, along with a $500 filing fee. The letter must contain the following information:

- A letter signed by a principal officer of the central organization verifying the existence of the relationship with its subordinates including a list of names, addresses, federal employer identification numbers

---

[30]Rev. Proc. 80-27, 1980-1 C.B. 677.

[31]Procedures for group exemption are outlined in IRS Publication 557.

(each subordinate must have a separate number), description of purpose, proposed activities, and financial projections. Any subordinate that already has a separate determination should be identified.

- Sample copy of the uniform governing instruments to be adopted by subordinates, which reflect general supervision and control of affiliate organizations by the parent. Subordinates need not be incorporated, but must have governing documents containing standards outlined in Section 1.3 of this chapter.

- Affirmative statement that all subordinates have given written authorization to be included in the group exemption and recognized that they are under the control of the central EO.

- Statement that all subordinates qualify for exemption under the same paragraph of IRC §501(c) (though not necessarily the same paragraph under which the central organization is exempt).

- Statement that every organization in the group agrees to have the same accounting fiscal year if it is to be included in group returns.

- For a §501(c)(3) group, two additional issues must be addressed. First, the effective date of organization of all entities must be furnished to ascertain timely filing. If a member of the group has been in existence longer than 27 months (and was not excused from seeking recognition), the group exemption may only be issued from the date of filing. Also, public charity status must be indicated, since no private foundations can be included with public charities.

- Schools must demonstrate requirements under Revenue Procedure 75-50 are met. Schools affiliated with a church must provide evidence that the provisions of Revenue Ruling 75-231 have been satisfied.

Not specifically requested, but helpful would be a proposed procedures manual containing sample financial reports to be periodically provided by the subordinates to the group holder.

New group members. Subordinates created after issuance of the IRS group determination letter report only to the central EO for recognition of exemption, not to the IRS. The new group member executes organizing documents and requests inclusion in the group. To qualify as tax-exempt under §501(c)(3) from the date of its formation, the subordinate should seek inclusion before the end of the 27th month of its formation.[32]

---

[32] As discussed in Section 1.4 of this chapter, this time period is statutorily 15 months—but now automatically extended to 27 months.

Update of affiliate information: Annually, at least 90 days before the end of the tax year, the central organization must submit information to update the master list of its subordinates with the Internal Revenue Service Center in Ogden, Utah. Three separate lists must be submitted to report the following information:

- Subordinates that have changed their names or addresses during the year
- Subordinates no longer to be included in the group exemption letter because they have ceased to exist, disaffiliated, or withdrawn their authorization to the central organization
- Subordinates to be added to the group exemption letter because they are newly organized or affiliated or they have newly authorized the central organization to include them.
- Each list must show the name, mailing address (including Postal ZIP Codes), actual address if different, and employer identification number of the affected subordinates. An annotated directory of subordinates will not be accepted for this purpose.
- If there were none of the above changes, the central organization must submit a statement to that effect.

(b) Forms 990

The parent organization must file its own separate Form 990.[33] Affiliated organizations may file a separate return for themselves or be included in a group return. The parent files a group Form 990 by combining the financial information for two or more (or all) of its subordinates. A subordinate must in writing declare, under penalty of perjury, that it authorizes its inclusion in a group return and that the information it submits for inclusion is true and complete. A list of the names, addresses, and identification numbers of included subordinates is attached to the group return.

(c) Withdrawal from Group

For a variety of reasons that usually involve human discord, a subordinate organization covered by a group exemption may wish to withdraw from the group and operate independently. To secure its ongoing and uninterrupted

---

[33]For suggestions for filing Form 990, see Jody Blazek, *IRS Form 990 Tax Preparation Guide for Nonprofits*, rev. ed. (Hoboken, NJ: John Wiley & Sons, 2004).

tax-exempt status, the withdrawing subordinate must seek its own recognition of exemption in the time frame provided for a new organization, essentially 27 months from the date of its separation.

1.9 WHERE TO SEND APPLICATION

Since 1997 all applications for recognition of tax-exempt status and letters regarding changes in the activities or organizational documents of an exempt organization are sent to the centralized processing office in Cincinnati, Ohio.[34] Applications sent by normal mail are submitted to the IRS Center, P.O. Box 192, Covington, KY 41012-0192. The IRS also accepts forms from commercial delivery services, such as Federal Express or United Parcel Service, and recognizes their dated receipts as valid for timely filing purposes.[35] The surface address for express mail or delivery companies is Internal Revenue Service, 201 West Rivercenter Blvd., Attn: Extracting, Stop 312, Covington, KY 41011.

Do not be confused by the addresses. The Kentucky address is located across the river from the Cincinnati Key District Office. Applications are first procedurally and technically screened and added to the master tracking system in Ohio. Many applications, particularly those that are *merit closed* because they contain all the necessary documents and readily qualify for recognition, are reviewed and finalized in Cincinnati. As discussed in §1.4 of this chapter, applications for certain types of activity are forwarded to the National Office in Washington D.C. for consideration. Due to staffing shortages, some applications are sent to other IRS regional offices for review.

1.10 PUBLIC INSPECTION

A copy of Form 1023 and all correspondence regarding its approval, plus the Form 990, 990-EZ, or 990-PF filed by the organization for the three most recent years, must be made available for anyone who asks to see it. The names and addresses of a public charity's contributors are not subject to public inspection and can be omitted from the copy made available to the public. Donor information, however, must be disclosed by private foundations. If the organization is submitting information regarding trade secret, patent, style of work, or apparatus that, if released, would adversely impact the organization, it can ask the IRS to allow it to withhold the data.

---

[34]IRS Announcement 97-89, 1997-36 I.R.B.1.

[35]IRS Notice 97-26, 1997-26, IRB 6.

1.10 PUBLIC INSPECTION

If the request is made in person at the organization's office, the requester must be allowed to view the documents.[36] If they are willing to pay, they must be provided copies.[37] In response to a written request, the copy must be mailed within 30 days. Between 1987 and 1997, the returns only had to be made available for inspection in the organization's offices. The specific rules for providing inspection follow:

- When providing copies, an organization may charge $1.00 for the first page and $0.15 for each subsequent page.

- Payments must be accepted in cash, money orders, personal checks, or credit cards.

- Written requests can be transmitted by mail, electronic mail, facsimile, or private delivery service, or in person and must contain the address to which the copies can be mailed.

- An organization can satisfy its public inspection requirement by making its returns available on the Internet either through its own site or that of another organization. The forms must be posted exactly as they were filed with the IRS. The Guidestar website does not qualify for this purpose.

If the organization that charges a fee for copying receives a request containing no payment, it must, within seven days of receipt of the request, notify the requester of its prepayment policy and the amount due. If the copy charge exceeds $20 and prepayment is not required, the organization must obtain the requester's consent to the charge. If the organization is the subject of a harassment campaign, it may apply to the key district office for relief. As an example, the regulations indicate the receipt of 200 requests following a national news report about the organization is not considered harassment. Receipt of 100 requests from known supporters of another organization opposed to the policies and positions the organization advocates is said to be disruptive to the organization's operations and to thereby constitute harassment. A penalty of $10 per day up to a maximum of $5,000 can be imposed for willful failure to disclose.[38]

---

[36]An organization having more than one administrative office must have a copy available at each office where three or more full-time employees work. Service-providing facilities are not counted for this purpose if management functions are not performed there. An organization that does not file its own Form 990, because it is included in a group return, must make the group return available.

[37]Taxpayer Bill of Rights 2, §1313, amending IRC §6104(e).

[38]Taxpayer Bill of Rights 2, §1313, amending IRC §6652.

CHAPTER 2

Line-by-Line Suggestions for Completing Form 1023

Form 1023 encompasses a wide range of information about how the organization intends to accomplish its mission. The application should paint a well-defined picture of the new organization, as it will operate, with both words and numbers. Some compare the Form 1023 application to a business plan. Indeed, the form asks that proposed activities be described and sources of revenue and proposed expenditures be displayed. Then, the newly revised form delves deeply into those plans by asking a long series of new questions explained below. The prospective exempt organization (EO) must evidence its qualification for tax-exemption by describing its planned activities including, for example:

- Types of programs it will conduct
- To whom they will be available (sometimes referred to as its exempt constituents)
- How charges for goods and services will be determined
- How contributions will be solicited
- How it will spend its money, including, most importantly, compensation and other payments to persons who create and manage it

The 2004 version of Form 1023 is significantly revised. On one hand, it is much more user friendly. The original seven pages of minimal instructions have grown in detail to 38 that begin with an "Overview of Section 501(c)(3) Organizations," which explains organizations that qualify, when the form is not necessary, and defines public and private charities. The form itself now contains 11 parts in 10 pages, up from the former eight pages and four parts. Many lines explain why the information is requested and essentially incorporate guidance into the form itself. This methodology will be particularly helpful for applicants unfamiliar with the details of the applicable tax code, regulations, and rulings. On the other hand, applicants need to carefully consider the depth of information to be provided in the explanations for *Yes* answers. There will be a temptation to provide more detail than necessary. In several places, a line asks a question, which is also asked on another line, and one must decide whether to repeat or refer to the other line. Too many times, the import of the response is not clear. For many applicants, plans are not fully developed and there are no written agreements to provide. The tone of the questions implies that they must be developed. When the questions involve sensitive issues, such as transactions with insiders and compensation of highly paid persons, full disclosures, with documents, should be made. For other matters noted throughout the discussion of each line, it may be suitable to simply say plans are not yet developed.

Previously, applicants were only asked to attach a copy of their organizational documents. The new Part III now asks questions that are designed to ensure those documents contain provisions to meet the statutory organizational test. This part briefly describes what is required and prompts the applicant to provide a reference for a *Yes* response to the applicable part of its own documents. In Part V, the Form 1023 asks specific questions about proposed financial transactions with the organization's insiders. If the organization expects to pay compensation or have other types of financial transactions with those that create, direct, and manage it, it must answer *Yes*. Details that prove the transactions will not give impermissible private benefits to the insiders must be provided as described below for each line.

Preparers are prompted on the top of page 1 to use the instructions and definitions of bolded terms to complete the application. The Glossary of Terms, with a brief definition, can be found on pages 30–36. These, in turn, are followed on pages 37–38 by an index to key words and topics addressed in the instructions. The author finds the expanded instructions and definitions a welcome addition and strongly suggests that preparers consult them in crafting answers for each line. Very helpful TIP boxes appear throughout the instructions. This guide will not repeat the instructions, but instead offer suggestions regarding the importance of answers not evident in the instructions. **Terms that are defined in the glossary are bolded when used in this text as a signal to double-check the IRS version of the definition.**

This chapter contains suggestions for completing each line of Form 1023. The reasons why a *Yes* or *No* answer may cause trouble are explained. Readers may find it helpful to have a blank copy of Form 1023 to follow along with the text. In addition, serving as a further guide for completing a Form 1023, readers should reference the Form 1023 filled-in for two fictitious entities— the Hometown Campaign to Clean Up America and the Active Project Fund—that are included as Appendices B and C.

2.1 PART I—IDENTIFICATION OF APPLICANT

(a) Line 1: Full Name of Organization

The name "exactly" as it appears on the organizational documents must be entered here. The determination will be issued in that name. If the organization plans to conduct its activities under some other name, the new name should be shown in parentheses. If the organization intends to change the name on its organizing documents, registering a formal change of name with state authorities prior to application is preferable. The time required to explain to donors why the determination letter has a different name—as well as the time to request a new letter—can be saved by making such a registration.

(b) Line 2: C/O Name

The name of a particular person to whose attention correspondence should be addressed is submitted here. Such a designation is unusual and should be avoided if possible. The determination letter is often applicable for a number of years and officials may change.

(c) Line 3: Mailing Address

The "complete" address to which all correspondence should be sent is requested. Many organizations submit Form 1023 before any financial, or other, activity takes place. In those instances, it is advisable to use an address that is least likely to change even though each year, when the organization files Form 990, 990-EZ, or 990-PF, it does have an opportunity to update the address. A volunteer-operated organization that expects to frequently change officers and have no permanent and/or physical location may find it prudent to obtain a post office box address.

(d) Line 4: Employer Identification Number (EIN)

For all federal tax-filing purposes, starting with Form 1023, a new nonprofit must secure and use a federal employer identification number (EIN). Form SS-4 is separately submitted by mail, phone (800-829-4933), fax (varies by state of residence), or online application (http://www.irs.gov/businesses/small/article/0,,id=98350,00.html) to request the number.[1]

The IRS Determination office does not assign EINs and there is no special category or type of identifying number issued to an EO. At this writing, the only constant is that EINs issued from online applications typically begin with 20 as the first two numbers. Form SS-4 can no longer accompany Form 1023. The application reads: "Do not submit this application until you have obtained an EIN." If the applicant is uncertain whether a number was previously issued, the instructions suggest a call to 1-877-829-5500.

(e) Line 5: Month Accounting Period Ends

The number of the month the organization's fiscal year ends is entered. For a calendar year, the number *12* is entered and for a June 30 year, *06* is entered, for example. The choice of fiscal year is influenced by several factors, including the type of ruling being sought. A definitive ruling "cannot be issued before the close of an EO's first fiscal year having at least eight months."[2] In many cases, an advance ruling is sought, so any fiscal year can be chosen to accommodate this requirement.

Another factor in choosing the fiscal year is the EO's normal programming cycle. Schools and performing arts organizations normally operate on a July 1 to June 30 or September 1 to August 31 fiscal year end. An organization funded by federal government grants often finds it convenient to match the federal year that ends September 30. A summer or fall fiscal year-end is sometimes chosen to accommodate accountants' workload.

Be sure that the accounting period reflected the fiscal year-end the applicant plans to use for annual tax reporting purposes that agrees with the organization's bylaws. An organization's fiscal year is adopted when the first Form 990 is filed and is not governed by the fiscal year reflected on Form SS-4. It is inconsequential if the ID number request reflected a different year.

---

[1]Form SS-4 itself can be obtained at http://www.irs.govforms/.
[2]See Part IX.

(f) Line 6: Primary Contact Person

The name, e-mail address, telephone and fax number of the organization person or representative to contact for additional information during normal business hours is provided. IRS representatives now commonly fax, rather than mail, inquiries. Ideally, the person listed should be familiar with the EO's activities and be an officer, director, trustee, or **authorized representative**. A good choice is someone familiar with the rules pertaining to tax-exempt organizations. Most importantly, the person should be qualified to answer any IRS telephone inquiry and to prepare written responses to questions—ideally an accountant or attorney experienced in EO matters.

(g) Line 7: Authorized Representative

This line is checked *Yes* to authorize a representative that is not an organizational official—and Form 2848, *Power of Attorney and Declaration of Representative*, is completed and attached to the application. An IRS centralized authorization file (CAF) number is not required for a person to be listed on Form 2848. If that blank if left open on the Form 2848, a CAF number will be assigned.

(h) Line 8: Other Advisors

This line requests information about persons other than officials and authorized representatives that were involved in the formation of the organization. Preparers should fill in the name, address, amount paid or promised to be paid, plus a description of the person's role. Persons to be listed are those that "help plan, manage, or advise you about the structure or activities or your organization, or about your financial or tax matters." Because there is nothing inherently wrong with the new organization engaging advisors, this line may be troubling. How much information is appropriate? What does "plan and manage" mean? Many organizations, for example, may have engaged professionals such as lawyers and accountants to develop their strategic plan, policy and procedure manual, computer network, website, or school curriculum. The instructions specifically mention a person hired to develop a program to solicit funds and one to "advise you about tax exemption." As to fundraising consultants, line 4 of Part VIII asks for similar information. Line 7 of Part VIII asks for details about outside managers. It should be suitable in most cases to provide a brief description of outside consultants with a reference to information provided elsewhere for other lines. One unacceptable situation the author believes the IRS seeks to expose with this probe is the identity of an organization created for tax avoidance reasons, such as a mail-order church.[3]

(i) Line 9: Website and E-mail

The organization's website (or address of one maintained on its behalf) and e-mail addresses are requested. Applicants can expect the IRS to peruse the site in search of activities that might jeopardize approval of tax-exempt status. There is no comprehensive IRS guidance on Internet activity, though several IRS continuing-education texts have discussed the subject.[4] The IRS position on qualification of an Internet service provider is clear. Connections offered to students, poor persons, or other members of a charitable class—at a less-than-market value basis—can constitute a charitable activity. Internet service offered to the general public or everyone in the community is not charitable.[5]

Links to other organizations, displays of sponsor acknowledgements and other revenue-producing materials will be scrutinized. The sponsorship regulations[6] contain an example that allows an organization to link to a business sponsor's site so long as the linked page does not contain an organizational endorsement of sponsor products or services. The rules that apply to evaluate activities conducted on the Internet are the same as those applied to evaluate activity conducted off the organization's website.[7] The instructions suggest the "information on your website should be consistent with the information in your Form 1023."

---

[3]See Schedule A that must be completed for a church applicant.

[4]See Section 22(j), *Tax Planning and Compliance for Tax-Exempt Organizations* and the following CPE Text articles for discussion of Internet issues: Cheryl Chasin, Susan Ruth, and Robert Harper, "Tax Exempt Organizations and World Wide Web Fundraising and Advertising on the Internet," Chapter I, 2000 CPE Text; Donna Moore and Robert Harper, "Internet Service Providers Exemption Issues," Chapter C, 1999 CPE Text; and Cheryl Chasin and Robert Harper, "Computer-Related Organizations," Chapter A, 1997 CPE Text.

[5]Priv. Ltr. Rul. 200203069.

[6]Reg. §1.513-4.

[7]Exhibit 19-10 in *Tax Planning and Compliance for Tax-Exempt Organizations* contains a checklist with which to review issues the website might present. Chapter 21 in that book addresses the unrelated business aspects of the issues.

(j) Line 10: Will Form 990 Be Required

This line allows the IRS to identify those organizations that should file annual information returns. Most applicants will check the *Yes* block. Organizations eligible to say *No* are those that are excused from filing Form 990, including modest organizations that expect annual revenue to be less than $25,000, churches and certain of their affiliates, and governmental units. All private foundations, regardless of annual revenue must file Form 990-PF.

(k) Line 11: Date Formed

This line simply asks for the date of incorporation—or formation if the organization is something other than a corporation. The date of formation is the date on which the organization comes into existence under applicable state law. For a corporation, this would be the date that the articles of incorporation are approved by the appropriate state official. For unincorporated organizations, it is the date the constitution or articles of association are adopted. This date will determine the effective date of recognition for tax-exemption and signal a need to complete *Schedule E, Organizations not Filing Form 1023 within 27 months of Formation*. Timely filing is measured from the date the organization is *formed*, or the date it becomes a legal entity.

(l) Information Not Requested

Several versions of Form 1023 have come and gone since the organization itself chose its *activity* code from a list of some 300 possibilities. If asked, most organizations would probably prefer to label themselves rather than having the IRS do so; nonetheless, the IRS now assigns an NTEE code or codes (up to three) when it considers Form 1023. This code is important because the IRS now follows a market segment approach to choose the organizations it examines each year.[8] It has identified about 40 different segments or categories of tax-exempt organizations such as churches, social clubs, low-income housing providers, or schools to name a few. To improve coverage of the sector, each year six to seven segments are examined. The NTEE code or codes are displayed for each organization listed on Guidestar.org.

---

[8]Plans are announced each year in Implementing Guidelines that set forth the EO Division's mission. These and planned initiatives and emphases can be viewed at http://www.irs.gov/charities&nonprofits/.

(m) Line 12: Foreign Organizations

On this line, the applicant answers *Yes* and discloses the name of the country in which it was formed, if it is other than (1) the United States, its territories, and possessions, (2) federally recognized Indian tribal or Alaska Native governments, or (3) the District of Columbia. A foreign organization submits Form 1023 to obtain tax-exemption for U.S. source income. A foreign entity that can qualify as a public charity[9] may also apply to facilitate its eligibility to receive grants from private foundations. The application must be completed in the English language and an English translation must accompany any documents, such as a charter, the original of which is in a foreign language. Foreign tax-exempt organizations must annually file the same Forms 990. Those who are classified as a public charity, conduct no significant U.S. activity, and have under $25,000 or gross revenue are excused. Though the income is exempt, foreign charities do not qualify as charities for purposes of the contribution deduction under section 170(c).

Canadian organizations that have received a Notification of Registration from the Canada Customs and Revenue Agency are automatically recognized as section 501(c)(3) organizations without filing Form 1023. However, they are presumed to be private charities. To obtain a determination letter of public charity status, they submit their Canadian Notification of Registration, Parts I and X and the signature line of Part XI, and Form 8833, *Treaty-Based Return Position Disclosure Under §6114*. The instructions do not suggest a user fee be attached.

A Virgin Islands organization may file Form 1023 on its behalf; or the Bureau of Internal Revenue of the U.S. Virgin Islands may complete the application itself and issue an information letter.

2.2 PART II—ORGANIZATIONAL STRUCTURE

The opening sentences to this part provide very clear guidance:

> You must be a corporation (including a limited liability company), an unincorporated association, or a trust to be tax-exempt. DO NOT file this form unless you can check *Yes* for lines 1, 2, 3, or 4.

Sole proprietorships, partnerships, or loosely affiliated groups of individuals are ineligible. It is important to note organizational documents for all four types

---

[9]See Section 2.10 of this chapter.

of organizations must contain the provisions described in the next part—a charitable purpose and a dissolution clause. The document copies must be signed, but need not be conformed or accompanied by a sworn statement by an officer or director that says they are true and correct copies. Preparers should read the instructions for specific requirements for each type of organization.

(a) Line 1: Corporation

If the applicant checks *Yes*, it was formed as a corporation, a signed copy of the articles of incorporation, showing certification of filing with the appropriate state agency, must be attached, including any amendments. If the applicant does not have a copy of its documents, the instructions allow submission of a substitute copy that may be handwritten, typed, printed, or otherwise reproduced. A declaration, signed by an official, that it is a complete and correct copy of the articles and that it contains all the powers, principles, purposes, functions, and other provisions by which you currently govern yourself must be provided.

(b) Line 2: Limited Liability Company (LLC)

It is welcome news that the IRS officially acknowledges the ability of an LLC to seek independent tax-exempt status after years of indecision on the matter. A single-member LLC that files its own application is treated as a corporation. No application need be filed for an LLC that is treated as a disregarded entity in relation to its single member. An LLC also attaches a signed copy of its articles of organization showing certification of filing with the appropriate state agency, plus a copy of any operating agreements that the LLC has entered into.

(c) Line 3: Unincorporated Association

A dated copy, containing at least two signatures, of the articles of association, constitution, or other similar organizing document, including any amendments, must be attached.

(d) Line 4: Trust

A signed-and-dated copy of the trust agreement, including any amendments, must be attached for a trust. For a testamentary trust created by a will, a copy of the relevant will provisions and a death certificate or a statement indicating the date of death is requested. The trust must state whether or not it has been funded and, if not, an explanation of how it is formed "without anything of value place in trust." A trust that provides for distributions of income or property to non-charitable interests cannot qualify.

(e) Line 5: Bylaws

If bylaws have been adopted, a "current copy showing date of adoption" is attached. Bylaws need not be signed unless they constitute the organizing document. Absent bylaws, the applicant is asked to explain how its officers, directors, or trustees are selected. When the organizational documents proscribe the method of choosing or appointing those that govern rather than the bylaws, the applicant can simply refer to the article or paragraph in the organizational documents that describes appointments or elections.

2.3 PART III—INFORMATION ABOUT THE REQUIRED PROVISIONS IN YOUR ORGANIZING DOCUMENT

The first two boxes of this part must be checked *Yes.* The tax code requires that a qualifying §501(c)(3) organization be both organized and operated for specified charitable purposes as described in Chapter 1§1 and pages 2 and 7 of the IRS instruction.[10] The organizational documents—nonprofit corporate charter or trust instrument—must contain explicit language that limits and restricts the entity's activity to one of eight specific charitable purposes listed in the tax code. Additionally, the tax code describes a qualifying charity as an entity "no part of the net earnings of which inures to the benefit of any private shareholder or individual, no substantial part of the activities of which is carrying on propoganda, or otherwise attempting to influence legislation, (except as otherwise provided in subsection (h), and which does not participate in, or intervene in (including the publishing or distributing of statements), any political campaign on behalf of (or in opposition to) any candidate for public office."

Readers will note that the questions in this part only address the purpose and dissolution clauses. The questions do not ask, as the IRS in the past routinely required, whether the organizational documents contain the additional restraining language quoted above. The regulations address the requirement

---

[10]Detailed suggestions can be found in Chapter 2 of *Tax Planning and Compliance for Tax-Exempt Organizations.*

negatively by stipulating that the organizational documents may not empower the organization to violate the code restraints.[11] They do not require the code prohibitions be literally stated in the corporate charter or trust instrument. In practice, most legal advisors knowledgeable about exempt organization do include the language as is illustrated in the Forms 1023 contained in Appendices C and D.

(a) Line 1: Purpose Clause

This line asks the applicant to check the box to confirm that the organizational documents limit its purposes to charitable purposes and, if so (must do so), to describe the location of such clause(s) in the attached documents. It is very important for an applicant to study, as the form suggests, the requirements of the *Operational* test, under *Qualification of a Section 501(c))(3) Organization* in the instructions, because the list of charitable purposes on this line is incomplete.

(b) Line 2: Dissolution Clause

To qualify as a charitable organization, the applicant's organizational documents must dedicate its assets permanently to §501(c)(3) charitable purposes. Provisions requiring that all of its remaining assets at the time of dissolution be paid over to another organization qualifying for charitable tax-exemption or a governmental unit (local, state, or federal) must be contained in the documents or required by state law. The first box of Line 2 asks if the documents contain such a dissolution clause either expressly (and if so, to describe where) or by state law. If the latter is true, the second box is also checked. An organization established in a state with statutes that automatically impose a suitable dissolution requirement say so if their documents do not contain such a provision. The IRS instructions on page 8 contain lists of states with qualifying provisions.

Additional organizational constraints are required for private foundations by IRC §508(e). In response when this requirement came into the tax law in 1969, most states have now adopted legislation that satisfies the requirement that a private foundation not violate the constraints set out in IRC §§4941-4945. There may be some confusion because the state laws outlined in Appendix B pertain only to private foundations.

---

[11]Reg. §1.50(c)(3)-1(b); and expanded discussion of this evolution in IRS policy can be found in the IRS 2004 CPE Text for Exempt Organizations entitled *Organizational Test—IRC 501(c) (3)*, by Elizabeth Ardoin

It is very important to read the specific instructions for this part, as the IRS suggests, because the question will be misleading for some. Faulty limitations on activities and/or dissolution clauses will cause the IRS to return the application and deny exemption until the faults are cured.

2.4 PART IV—NARRATIVE DESCRIPTION OF YOUR ACTIVITIES

This part fleshes out the candidate for tax exemption and paints a picture of the proposed organization. The IRS wants to know who, what, why, where, when, and how the applicant will accomplish its exempt purposes. For past, present, and planned activities, the form asks that such activities be described in detail. The IRS also wants to know how much time will be devoted to each activity and provides an open-ended opportunity to provide information. This part is, therefore, particularly challenging. It does not question; it simply asks for a description. Presenting precise and complete information is the key. Presenting unnecessary information that instigates questions not asked is not helpful. When the activity described in this part is also explained by information referred to or reported in answer to other parts, the information need not be repeated. Reference to other answers is suggested in the instructions. The IRS suggests that a paper copy of activities summarized on the organization's website that support the narrative description of activities can be attached. The instructions suggest the following information be provided:

- What is the activity?
- Who conducts the activity?
- When is the activity conducted?
- Where is the activity conducted?
- How does the activity further your exempt purposes?
- What percentage of your total time is allocated to the activity?
- How is the activity funded?

The essence of the applicant's charitable nature should be reflected in the description of activities. A complete picture of the organization must be painted with carefully crafted precision. Spare no words—but choose them carefully. Information submitted in this narrative description must be coordinated with answers to other questions as well. If, for example, the description states that monetary assistance will be provided to needy families, the IRS technician may want to know how the recipients will be chosen, and will look to Part VI, line 2 for a description of the criteria.

As another example, assume that the description states that the organization is established for literary purposes and plans to encourage emerging writers. The IRS will want to know how those writers will be chosen, how their works will be published, and who will own the copyright to the works. The description provided in this part must be coordinated with the response to Part VIII, line 10 pertaining to copyright and possibly the projected financial information in Part IX. Most importantly, the answers must indicate to the IRS how the activity furthers the exempt interests of the general public while, as a byproduct of accomplishing its purpose, it also may provide some benefits to individual writers. Retention of copyright by private individuals is thought by the IRS in some cases to provide private inurement. Payment of royalties to the writers in amounts intended not to exceed reasonable compensation may be okay, but must be carefully explained. An entity that grants awards for literary achievements should not be required to obtain copyrights.

The proposed activities to be carried out in accomplishing the exempt purposes must be described with a view to the particular standards for exemption pertaining to the organization. Chapters 2, 3, 4, or 5 of *Tax Planning and Compliance for Tax-Exempt Organizations* can be studied to review the specific rules applicable to the organization. The standards, criteria, procedures, or other means adopted or planned for choosing participants and recipients of the organization's programs must be explained in sufficient detail to indicate the activity will meet the applicable IRS standard. For example, a low-income housing project is subject to specific rules outlined in Chapter 4 and a research organization those found in Chapter 5. Special schedules are attached for churches, schools, and others as described below in the suggestions for Part VIII.

A mere restatement of the organization's exempt purposes, with a declaration that proposed activities will further such purposes, is *not* sufficient. The author prefers to answer Part IV in outline form, highlighting categories of activities as shown in the mocked-up Form 1023 contained in Appendix B. Though the question has been omitted from this version, the applicant might find it appropriate to describe the character and use of assets it owns and will acquire. This data can add facts to complete the picture of the organization in a physical sense. Hypothetical additional information follows:

- XYZ will operate from a rent-free building shared with other charities. Administrative assets, including computers, photocopiers, and office equipment, will be purchased. As funds become available, it is hoped that a vehicle for transporting neighborhood children, display cases for the food cooperative, and desks, speaker systems, and other assets to enhance the educational classes and other uses of the facilities will be obtained.

- EO is a grant-making private foundation that will receive significant funding through donations from its founders. Those funds will be used to obtain investments to produce income to meet the foundation's charitable distribution requirement and administrative assets, such as computers, telephone systems, file cabinets, and other office equipment and furniture. The foundation will operate in office space donated by its founders.

2.5 PART V—COMPENSATION AND OTHER FINANCIAL ARRANGEMENTS WITH YOUR OFFICERS, DIRECTORS, TRUSTEES, EMPLOYEES, AND INDEPENDENT CONTRACTORS

The request for information about financial transactions with the organization's officials early in the application illustrates the key criteria for approval—satisfaction of the operational test. A qualifying §501(c)(3) organization must conduct activities that promote charitable purposes rather than the private interests of its officials.[12] This part seeks information to determine if the organization will operate to provide impermissible financial benefits to its insiders. Though an IRC §501(c)(3) organization is permitted to compensate officials that provide necessary services, the pay must be reasonable and not excessive for the job performed. Exempt status will not be approved if information indicates excess benefits are paid or planned. This requirement continues throughout the life of the organization as salary information is provided each year on a Form 990. All applicants must complete line 1a of this part to list its officials. When the organization plans to compensate officials or pay more than $50,000 to employees and contractors, many answers in this part will be *Yes*. When no compensation is proposed, it is still necessary to respond to certain questions as noted below.

The Form allows leeway for reporting a person's compensation. The form title for "Compensation amount" is labeled "annual actual or estimated" and the instructions only suggest the amount must be consistent with Part IX. Undoubtedly, the amounts presented in the "Amount" column for line 1b of this part should agree with one of the columns for line 17 of Part IX. Readers will note that in the model form for the Active Project Fund presented in Appendix C the annual executive director salary reported in Part V is listed in the details for line 18 for column (b), the first full year, rather than the partial year reflected in column (a).

---

[12]Discussed in Chapters 14 and 20, *Tax Planning and Compliance for Tax-Exempt Organizations*. Penalties can be imposed on officials who receive excess benefits.

2.5 PART V—COMPENSATION AND OTHER ARRANGEMENTS

(a) Line 1a: List of Officials

A key question in evaluating an exempt organization's qualification for charitable status is the possibility of "inurement of earning" to members of the board by virtue of payment of unreasonable compensation to them. Due to the significance of this issue, it is important that the information provided evidence the reasonableness of planned compensation. Details that might serve such purpose include a full description of responsibilities (line 3), a résumé reflecting his or her education and experience, and survey statistics of salaries paid to persons with similar qualifications working for comparable organizations in the area (line 4e).

The first line of this part asks for a list of officers, directors, and trustees. Their names, titles, preferred mailing address (which can be the organization's address), and **compensation** paid or proposed to be paid, if any, must be entered. The "title" requested is internal, or the person's position in relationship to the organization—president, trustee, director, and such. It will be useful for some applicants to add a column to this list that reflects the person's outside affiliations, such as Teacher, Dean of Law School, Lawyer, Nurse, CPA, or President of ABC Company. This information will indicate whether the organization is governed by independent, outside parties that will be able to carry out the conflict of interest policy requested on line 5 of this part.

The form used to ask if persons serve on the governing body by reason of being public officials or being appointed by public officials. If so, this fact might also be described to show that the organization will be responsive to public scrutiny, particularly when the officials are designated by position, such as mayor or principal, and will rotate as their terms expire. For example, a drug prevention program might benefit from participation by the director of the local health department. On the other hand, the presence of representatives of a particular political party on the board of an organization might indicate an impermissible intention to in

The total of all compensation paid to the employed by the organization is requested. For the total should include wages, deferred compensation pension plans, health, life, and disability insurance behalf, value of use of an automobile or an auto lodging, and other fringe benefits (both taxable countable expense allowances, but not expense reimbursements. Fees paid for legal, accounting, investment, or similar service must also be reported. The amounts should be consistent with those reported on line 17 of part IX.

It is important to note again that while there is no prohibition against such payments, they will be scrutinized. A private foundation proposing to

[handwritten note: Do not have to report travel "reimbursement"]

pay compensation to its directors should carefully review the self-dealing rules and consider submission of information evidencing the amounts will be reasonable.[13] Public charity applicants compensating the persons who govern them should review the intermediate sanction rules for similar reasons.[14]

(b) Line 1b. Five Top Employees

The same information presented on line 1a must be submitted on this line for each of the five highest compensated employees, other than officials, that receive or will receive more than $50,000.

(c) Line 1c. Five Top Independent Contractors

The same information presented on line 1a must also be submitted for those persons not treated as employees that will also receive more than $50,000 for services performed or to be performed for the organization.

(d) Line 2. Relationships

The questions in this part, some with many subparts, fish for financial arrangements with persons related to organization officials that may result in impermissible benefits to those officials. Though not prohibited, except for private foundations, financial transactions between an insider, their lineal relatives and their businesses, and the organization must be entered into following the highest fiduciary standards. When the answer to one of these questions is *Yes*, an attachment describing the details, plus any written contracts or agreements, are requested. Mostly the questions are self-explanatory, but they can be traps for the unwary.

A related **family** member includes an individual's spouse, ancestors, children, grandchildren, great-grandchildren, siblings (whether whole or half-blooded), and the spouses of children. A **business relationship** can include employment or contractual arrangements or combined ownership of a business in which officials possess more than 35% ownership interest in common. Ownership for this purpose means the voting power in a corporation, profits interest in a partnership, or beneficial interest in a trust. All applicants, even those with no compensation plans reportable in this part, are apparently expected to answer lines 2a and 2b.

---

[13]See Chapter 14, *Tax Planning and Compliance for Tax-Exempt Organizations*.

[14]See Chapter 20, *Tax Planning and Compliance for Tax-Exempt Organizations*.

(e) Line 3: Job Descriptions

For all those officials, employees, and contractors named in line 1, a list showing each person's name, qualifications, average hours worked, and duties is requested. If compensation is paid to the same persons by a commonly controlled entity, the names, relationships, and compensation arrangements must be reported. Common control exists when one or more other tax-exempt or taxable organizations appoint or elect a majority of the officials of the applicant organization or a majority of the applicant organization's officials are the same as another entity. Common control is measured, as described in the last sentence above, by voting power. Again line 3a apparently should be answered even if there is no reportable compensation.

(f) Lines 4 a–d: Recommended Practices

This line asks whether the individuals that approve compensation arrangements follow the recommended practices listed below. The applicant must say whether the four practices are used in establishing compensation. A *No* answer does not necessarily mean the applicant will be denied exemption, but the adoption of the practices is a reasonable governance tool and obviously desirable from an IRS standpoint. Particularly for an organization that proposes to provide compensation potentially subject to Intermediate Sanctions,[15] the following practices are not only recommended but also establish a rebuttable presumption of reasonableness of the compensation that can protect highly compensated persons from penalties:

- Compensation is approved following a conflict of interest policy.
- Compensation arrangements are approved in advance of payment of compensation.
- Written documentation of the date and terms for approving the arrangements (minutes of meeting) are retained.
- A written record of the name of each person voting to approve or disapprove the arrangements is retained.

A two-page sample conflict of interest policy is included in the Form 1023 package. According to the IRS, "by adopting this or a similar policy, you will be

---

[15]During 2004, this amount was $90,000 and is tied to the highly compensated person number provided in IRC §414(k) for pension plan limitation purposes.

choosing to put in place procedures that will help you avoid the possibility that those in positions of authority over you may receive an inappropriate benefit."

(g) Lines 4e–g: Comparable Data

This question asks whether approved compensation is based on information about amounts paid to persons in **similarly situated** taxable or tax-exempt organizations, current compensation surveys compiled by independent firms, or actual written offers received by the prospective employee from similarly situated entities. To follow what is referred to as the "like, like, like" rule, an organization will gather data on amounts paid to persons in comparable positions at "similarly situated" organizations. A similarly situated organization is one with a comparable locale, size, purpose, and resources. The easiest source of this data is Part V or VII and Schedule A of Forms 990 filed by organizations in the applicant's geographic area. The returns are posted for anyone to see on the Internet at Guidestar.org. The *Guidestar Nonprofit Compensation Report* provides detailed information indexed by job category, gender, geography, type of nonprofit, budget size, state, and more. The Association of Small Foundations, the Society of Nonprofit Organizations, the Council on Foundations and many other associations also compile surveys of compensation information.

The applicant is asked if "you do or will record in writing both the information on which you relied to base your decision and its source?" If the answer is *No*, an explanation of how "you set compensation that is **reasonable**" must be attached. Without a doubt, all applicants should take the relatively easy steps required to be able to answer the questions on lines 4e and 4f *Yes*.

(h) Lines 5a–c: Conflict of Interest Policy

The IRS with these questions is strongly suggesting that a qualifying tax-exempt §501(c)(3) organization must adopt and follow a conflict of interest policy consistent with the sample found in Appendix A of Form 1023's instructions. If a policy has been adopted, one must explain how it has been adopted, "such as by resolution of the board." If line 5a is *No*, lines 5b and 5c must explain how the organization plans to assure that persons who have a conflict of interest will not have "influence over you in setting their own compensation" or "regarding business deals with themselves." In other words, a qualifying tax-exempt organization must adopt policies to prevent private use of its assets or benefits, referred to as *inurement*, to its insiders.[16] Depen-

---

[16]IRC §501(c)(3) and Reg. §1.501(c)(3)-1(c)(2).

dent upon the financial complexity, asset size, board composition, and proposed compensation level of officials and other employees, establishment of committees and other organizational procedures that bring checks and balances to the applicant's decision-making processes are expected by the IRS. A "note" at the end of this line says, "A conflict of interest policy is recommended though it is not required to obtain exemption." It will be interesting to learn if the IRS follows this commitment.

(i) Lines 6a–b: Nonfixed Payments

The IRS wants to scrutinize incentive compensation paid in the form of discretionary bonuses or revenue-based pay. A fixed payment is one that is either a set dollar amount or fixed through a specific formula not dependent on discretion, such as one tied to the Consumer Price Index. An organization planning to determine the pay for persons listed on lines 1a–c by the results of activities—net profits, number of patients served, funds raised, or the like—must explain the plans. The form asks:

- How the amounts will be determined
- Who is eligible for such arrangements
- Whether an overall limitation will be placed on total compensation
- How the organization does or will determine that incentive-based pay is reasonable compensation for services rendered

Incentive compensation need not necessarily result in private inurement, but such arrangements are subject to enhanced scrutiny. The following factors may evidence reasonableness of the plans:[17]

- The contingent payments serve a real and discernible business purpose of the organization itself, not the financial need of the employee. The risk of paying the higher salary due to higher revenues is self-insured by its tie to revenue or profit level.
- Compensation amount is not dependent upon curtailing expenses or skimping on services, but instead is based upon accomplishment of exempt purposes, such as serving more patients, writing more books,

---

[17]1983 CPE Text, p. 45; see also Chapter 20, *Tax Planning and Compliance for Tax-Exempt Organizations*, for a treatise with additional examples and standards for determining reasonable compensation.

or increasing test scores. A plan to pay a percentage of revenues exceeding the budgeted amount has even been sanctioned.[18]

- Actual operating results show that prices for services are comparable to those at similar organizations, and are not manipulated to increase the compensation.
- There is a ceiling or maximum amount of compensation, so as to avoid "the possibility of windfall benefit to the employee/professional based upon factors bearing no direct relationship to the level of services provided."[19]

(j) Line 7a–b: Purchases from Insiders

An organization, which plans to buy goods, services, or assets from the persons listed on line 1, must report names, terms, and other details of the transactions. The disclosure is not required for purchases in the normal course of operations of items available to the general public under similar terms and conditions, such as office supplies or printing. The details of a plan to purchase a building from an official, however, must be explained. Again, such transactions may not be prohibited (except for private foundations), but must be entered into for reasons that benefit the organization, not the official or highly compensated persons. It is preferable for the organization to be able to say it will follow its conflict-of-interest policy to assure that such transactions take place at **arm's length**. In other words, persons other than those financially involved should approve of the purchases. Equally important, a policy that requires the amount involved is no more than the **fair market value** for the item or service must apply. A fair value is the price a willing buyer will pay a willing seller in the normal market place in which the item is sold, with neither being under any compulsion to buy, sell, or transfer the property, and with both having reasonable knowledge of the relevant facts about the property.

(k) Lines 8a–f: Insider Leases, Contracts, or Loans

A detailed explanation of the terms (written or oral), parties, and amounts involved must be attached for any leases, contracts, loans, or other agreements with persons listed in line 1a–c that are planned. The information must prove the transactions will be negotiated at arm's length, will be at a price that is no

---

[18]Gen. Coun. Memo. 39674. Also see Gen. Coun. Memos. 32453, 36918, 39498, and 39670.

[19]*People of God Community v. Commissioner*, 75 T.C. 127, 132 (1980).

more than fair market, and will not result in private benefit to an insider. The concepts of reasonableness, comparability, and impartiality of approval process discussed above under lines 2–5 also apply to these types of transactions. Consider, for example, a new school that plans to loan the principal funds to relocate and purchase a home near to the school. The loan will be forgiven over the five-year term of her initial employment contract. As a part of a compensatory package, such a loan should be acceptable. However, the applicant should disclose its intention to treat the value of the forgiven interest and principal as part of her compensation. A copy of any signed documents must also be attached.

Lines 9a–f: Leases, Contracts, or Loans with an Insider's Business

The same information requested on line 8 must be submitted if the organization will rent property or equipment, borrow money from, or have other financial relationships with a business more than 35% owned by an insider, as described in line 2b.

2.6 PART VI—YOUR MEMBERS AND OTHER INDIVIDUALS AND ORGANIZATIONS THAT RECEIVE BENEFITS FROM YOU

This part analyzes the organization's participation, or membership, privileges to identify rights of a sort that would prevent recognition of exemption. To be exempt as a charitable organization under §501(c)(3), an organization must operate to benefit an indefinite class of persons, referred to as a *charitable class*, rather than a particular individual or a limited group of individuals. It may not be "organized or operated for the benefit of private interests such as designated individuals, the creator's family, or shareholders of the organization or persons controlled, directly or indirectly, by such private interests."[20] A trust established to benefit an impoverished retired minister and his wife, for example, cannot qualify. Likewise, a fund established to raise money to finance a child's medical operation, rebuild a house destroyed by fire, or provide food for a particular person does not benefit a charitable class. By contrast, a disaster aid society to benefit unnamed persons in need is charitable. An organization formed by merchants to relocate homeless persons ("throw the bums out") from a downtown area was found to serve the merchant class and promote their interests, rather than those of the homeless or the citizens.[21]

---

[20]Reg. §1.501(c)(3)-1(d)(1)(ii).
[21]*Westward Ho v. Commissioner*, T.C. Memo 1992-192.

A comparatively small group of individuals can be benefited as long as the group is not limited to identifiable individuals. The class need not necessarily be indigent, poor, or distressed. A scholarship fund for a college fraternity that provided school tuition for deserving members was ruled to be an exempt foundation.[22] On the other hand, a trust formed to aid destitute or disabled members of a particular college class does benefit a limited class. The "general law of charity recognizes that a narrowly defined class of beneficiaries will not cause a charitable trust to fail unless the trust's purposes are so personal, private or selfish as to lack the element of public usefulness."[23]

Limitations on eligible service recipients can cause denial of exemption. How the charitable class of beneficiaries is selected, if there is a limitation, must be explained. For example, schools must adopt a nondiscrimination policy and comply with requirements outlined in the Schedule B attachment. A hospital might be denied exemption unless its provides free care to indigents or can otherwise prove its charitable nature with answers to questions in Schedule C.[24] An artists' cooperative that exhibited only work of its members has been found to serve its members, not the general public. Such an applicant was found not to qualify, despite the educational nature of the art.[25]

The questions in this part can be troublesome because the term *member* has different meanings. For governance purposes, a membership organization is one that grants voting control to its member(s) pursuant to the governing documents. Some nonprofit organizations designate financial supporters as members without delegating any control to them. For purposes of this question, a member can be thought of as one that pays dues or a similarly designated fee, shares the common goal for which the organization was created, and actively participates in its activities, whether or not he or she has voting rights. When members are contributors that receive rights with *de minimus* monetary value such as free admission, there is no problem. A membership fee structure that only allows members to participate in exempt activities suggests a non-charitable, or private, characteristic. Membership open only to a narrow group, such as those living in a particular subdivision or on a specific street, can be troublesome. An art appreciation society whose membership is limited to persons who own works of a particular living artist might or might not qualify as benefiting a charitable class dependent on its plans to conduct educational programs for the public.[26]

---

[22]Rev. Rul. 56-403, 1956-2 C.B. 307.

[23]Gen. Coun.Memo. 39876 (July 29, 1992)

[24]Discussed in Section 4.6, *Tax Planning and Compliance for Tax-Exempt Organizations*.

[25]Rev. Rul. 71-395, 1971-2 C.B. 228.

[26]Defined in Section 2.2, *Tax Planning and Compliance for Tax-Exempt Organizations*.

Line 1b can be a trap for the unwary when it asks whether the applicant provides its benefits to another organization. Conceptually a charitable organization must limit its benefits to charitable purposes and the organization to which it limits its benefits must similarly serve a charitable purpose. Certainly an applicant that limits its benefits to a qualifying §501(c)(3) organization can safely answer this question *Yes*. A supporting organization dedicated to one or more particular charities can simply refer this question to Schedule D that it must complete with details of its qualification under §509(a)(3). Similarly, an organization established to conduct fundraising for another charity(ies) could refer to information it provides in answer to lines 13 or 15 of Part VIII.

Educational arms are often established by civic associations qualified under §501(c)(4) and business leagues qualified under §501(c)(6). For those charitable applicants, the detailed information furnished for Part IX should be sufficient as a response to a *Yes* answer here. So long as the applicant's activities are limited to one of the eight listed charitable purposes and procedures are established to maintain a separation between the organizations with different categories of exemption, this answer can safely be *Yes*. The details of transactions anticipated to occur between the applicant and other non-§501(c)(3) nonprofit organization(s) can be revealed and will be carefully scrutinized. Questions about such relationships are asked each year on Form 990 to assure that the charitable §501(c)(3) is not operated to benefit a §501(c)(4) or other non-(c)(3) nonprofit organization.

(a) Lines 1a–b: Description of Goods and Services Provided

This line asks the applicant to describe goods, services, or funds provided to individuals (1a) or organizations (1b) in carrying out the exempt purposes. For most organizations with such plans, the response to this question can be coordinated with the description of activities in Part IV. For example, the typical grant-making private foundation can simply say it plans to make grant payments to qualifying public charities.

(b) Line 2: Limitations on Participants

When line 2 asks whether the organization's benefits are limited to a particular individual or group of specific individuals, the answer should most often be *No*. The answer, however, might be *Yes* when benefits are limited to members that constitute a charitable class, such as a church congregation or a cultural society operating a museum. In such a case, an explanation of requirements for membership and the dues structure should be explained. When different levels of membership exist, privileges each level receives should be explained. Membership discounts, reduced prices, or free admission are acceptable so long as nonmembers have access to the activities. It is acceptable for nonmembers to be required to pay some fee. In member-privilege situations, estimates of member and nonmember participation might be useful to reflect the organization's public nature. For example, a research organization may limit use of its laboratories to members, but have a policy of publishing results and conducting public seminars. The instructions ask for a sample membership application. A member solicitation or flyer should be provided if the organization has no formal membership application form. This response can be coordinated with line 4 of Part VIII that requests information about fundraising activities or the Schedules suggested above for applicants that benefit other organizations.

(c) Line 3: Related Parties

Lastly, when line 3 asks if there is a family or business relationship between any individuals who receive goods, services, or funds through the organization's programs, the organizational officials, and highly compensated persons, the best answer is *No.* For a *Yes* answer, the eligibility of such persons must be explained. When the programs are open to all, the participation of such persons should be acceptable. The fact that the principal's child can attend the school, the minister's wife can attend services, or the director's father can visit the museum is okay. Eligibility for scholarships, however, may be problematic. A similar question is asked in Schedule H in line 7 of Section I when it asks, "what measures are taken to ensure unbiased selections?"

What This Line Does Not Ask. The questions posed in this part have other aspects not necessarily apparent. The primary concern is the issue of whether the organization operates to benefit a limited group of persons rather than a charitable class of individuals. Gone from this version of the form is the question that asked whether recipients of goods and services from the organization are required to pay for them and. if so, how charges were determined. A copy of a current fee schedule was requested then. Services do not have to be provided for free to be charitable, but the concepts of private inurement and charitable class must be kept in mind in setting such policies. There is no prohibition against some amount of built-in cost recoupment, as the prices of private college tuition and hospital stays exemplify. An applicant that plans to provide services of a type also provided by commercial companies—management consulting, job placement, or credit counseling[27]—should in this part

---

[27]Watch for new developments as the IRS, in 2004, started to examine these organizations.

or Part IX describe how charges will be calculated. This information will allow the IRS specialist to evaluate the possibility of unrelated business activity.[28] Suggestions of comments about charges for services follow:

- Classes, workshops, and educational materials will be priced according to their direct cost; overhead expenses will be covered by donations.
- Charges for hospital services will be determined in accordance with the guidelines for Medicare/Medicaid reimbursements and the currently prevailing rate for comparable services in the community. Charges will be waived for persons who prove that they are unable to pay.
- Charges for legal services will be determined on a sliding scale according to the client's family income level. See attached client engagement letter and fee arrangement for details.

Secondly, certain membership benefits are treated as consideration for goods and services provided by the organization. The value of such benefits must be disclosed to members[29] and may reduce the contribution portion of members' dues and impact the public support test calculated in Part X. Maybe the most important unspoken issue, for which there is no question in this part and only a line on the financial data, is whether the goods and services are unrelated to the organization's exempt purpose. It is critical that the nature of, and reason for providing, goods and services be made clear in this part and Part IV.

2.7 PART VII—YOUR HISTORY

(a) Line 1: Successor Organization

This line simply asks whether the applicant is a **successor** to another organization and says answer *Yes* if:

- You have taken (or will take) over substantially all of the assets or activities of another organization
- Been converted or merged from another organization
- Installed the same officers, directors, or trustees as another organization that no longer exists and that had purpose(s) similar to your purpose(s)

---

[28]See Chapter 21, *Tax Planning and Compliance for Tax-Exempt Organizations.*

[29]These rules are the subject of Chapter 24, *Tax Planning and Compliance for Tax-Exempt Organizations,* and deserve careful attention once the organization solicits funding.

When the answer to line 1 is *Yes*, detailed information must be furnished on separate Schedule G to evidence that charitable, rather than private interests, are served by the transaction. Though there are no instructions for this question or Schedule G, the questions asked in Schedule G delve into relationships, assumption of debt, and other impermissible terms of a conversion/combination. The TIP here says the predecessor organization may be or may have been an exempt or nonexempt organization, or in other words, a new nonprofit organization can be established as a successor to a for-profit entity.

(b) Line 2: Late Filing

It is desirable that the answer to this question be *No;* the application was filed in a timely fashion within, rather than after, 27 months of its formation. According to the tax code, a charitable §501(c)(3) organization is not treated as a tax-exempt organization until it notifies the IRS by filing Form 1023.[30] Timely filing is measured from the date the organization is formed, or the date it becomes a legal entity.[31] The date of formation is the date on which the organization comes into existence under applicable state law. For a corporation, this normally will be the date the articles of incorporation are approved by the appropriate state official. For unincorporated organizations, it is the date the trust instrument, constitution, or articles of association are adopted. When the Form 1023 is timely filed, recognition of exemption retroactively applies to the date of creation.

Applications filed late, as a general rule, are effective only as of the date the application is postmarked. The limited circumstances for automatic extension of the 27-month rule are explained in Schedule E.

The consequence of late filing is primarily a potential obligation to pay Federal income and various state taxes on the taxable income received during the pre-recognition period. A late filer that fails to receive retroactive approval may be classified as a (c)(4) organization for the period between formation and filing and avoid income tax. Voluntary donations are not treated as taxable income if they qualify as gifts under IRC §103. Many donors, and particularly private foundation grantors, require IRS recognition before they will provide funding to a new organization. Technically, however, the deductibility of charitable contributions under IRC §170 depends on proper organizational structure not on recognition as an IRC §501(c)(3) organization.

---

[30]See discussion in Section 1.2 of this book.
[31]Rev. Proc. 90-27, 1990-1, CB. 514.

2.8 PART VIII—YOUR SPECIFIC ACTIVITIES

This part emphasizes the issues, in addition to private inurement to insiders explored in Part V, that can jeopardize tax-exempt status. The questions in this part present challenges. Again for *Yes* answers an explanation is requested to explain why. For many lines, the requested information repeats or is a slightly different version of information provided in other parts of the form that may suitably be cross-referenced. The instructions for this part are inconsistent—sometimes provided, sometimes not—what instructions there are should be studied when an answer is *Yes*. The instructions do not necessarily explain the reason why (or whether) a *Yes* answer may have a negative impact on qualification for exemption. The issues to consider for some programs, such as joint ventures and foreign organizations, are complicated with years of case law and IRS rulings and new developments that may influence qualification. Preparers should be alert for policy changes. The IRS website can be searched by subject to find any new publications or announcements.[32] (A thorough discussion of such subjects can also be found in *Tax Planning and Compliance for Tax-Exempt Organizations* cited in the footnotes that follow.)

(a) Line 1: Electioneering

The answer on this line must always be answered *No*! The question asked is, "Do you support or oppose candidates in political campaigns in any way?" The instructions begin by saying, "You participate in a political campaign if you promote or oppose the candidacy of an individual for public office. Your explanation should include representative copies of your political literature, brochures, pamphlets, etc. Candidate debates and nonpartisan voter education are permitted." It is regrettable that it is not until the second sentence of the Tip does it say an entity that supports or opposes candidates for election cannot qualify as a §501(c)(3) organization.

An applicant can have absolutely no plans to participate in influencing the election of candidates for public office and its organizational documents must prohibit such involvement. Overt endorsement of, or opposition to, a candidate for public office is prohibited. A charity, however, can encourage the public to vote, can educate voters, and discuss issues of public policy that are the subject of debate during an election period so long as the programs are nonpartisan. A new entity that proposes to conduct voter education can qualify, but must carefully study the IRS rulings and articles that provide examples of the fine line

---

[32]View at http://www.irs.gov/charities&nonprofits/.

between permissible education of voters and promotion of a candidate.[33] Think tanks, such as the Brookings Institute and the Heritage Foundation, are good examples of qualifying educational organizations that focus on public affairs.

(b) Line 2: Lobbying

Line 2a asks if the applicant attempts to **influence legislation**. A private foundation must answer this question *No*. For other §501(c)(3) organizations, a *Yes* answer is okay. Public charities may spend a limited amount on attempts to influence legislation. Permissible lobbying may be *direct* meaning contacts, or communications, with members of a legislative body to advocate the adoption or rejection of legislation. An organization may also conduct *indirect*, referred to as grassroots, lobbying efforts to convince the general public to contact legislators to propose, oppose, or support legislative action.

For applicants that answer *Yes* to line 2a, an explanation of *how* lobbying will be conducted is requested. The instructions ask that the percentage of total time and total funds to be spent on legislative activities be provided, along with representative copies of "your legislative literature, brochures, and pamphlets." Though not requested, it is helpful for the budget projections submitted for Part IX to quantify expected lobbying expenditures and cross-reference that information to this part. The October 2003 version of the instructions asked for slightly different information that may provide a clearer picture of proposed lobbying efforts as follows:

- Amount of time to be expended by organization representatives (both paid and unpaid) on behalf of the organization in connection within lobbying efforts
- Description of issues involved and method proposed for carrying out lobbying activities
- Any written materials published or disseminated to the public or to government officials

Applicants are reminded that they are prohibited from engaging in a **substantial** amount of lobbying and that what is substantial depends on the facts and circumstances of their proposed activities. What is not said is that efforts of board members and volunteers, donated professional services and use

---

[33]See Chapter 23, *Tax Planning and Compliance for Tax-Exempt Organizations*, which explains Rev. Ruls. 86-95, 1986-2 C.B. 73, Rev. Rul. 80-282, 1980-2 C.B. 15. The IRS CPE, for several years, contained an article titled "Election Year Blues."

of facilities, and other factors not numerically measured for tax purposes may be taken into account in the substantial part test. The vagueness of this test prompts many advisors to recommend that those organizations, which plan to lobby, elect to apply IRC §501(h) as explained below.

Providing the requested information in answer to this question is particularly difficult for an organization that has vague plans to conduct some amount of lobbying activity in the future. Even if it has not yet developed its plans, a *Yes* answer requires an explanation. Such an organization might keep in mind the fact that the IRS Form 990 each year will ask whether it has conducted any activities not previously reported. Absent concrete plans, an applicant can choose to answer this line *No* and submit information on its annual report later as its plans develop.

Line 2b asks whether the applicant has made or is making an election to have its legislative activity measured pursuant to §501(h).[34] The amount of permissible lobbying by a public charity, other than a church, can be measured by two very different tests: the *expenditure*, or 501(h) test or the *no substantial part* test (described above). Under IRC §501(h), specific dollar limits apply. To evaluate impact of the different limitations for direct versus grassroots lobbying, an applicant should fill in page 5 of Form 990, Schedule A (2004 version). Additionally, the definition of lobbying for this test is very specific. Educational materials that discuss the pros and cons of a legislative proposal, without telling the reader to contact a legislator, is not lobbying when §501(h) applies. Dependent on other facts, such a communiqué could be treated as lobbying under the substantial part test.

If the applicant is so electing, Form 5768 *(Election/Revocation of Election by an Eligible Section 501(c)(3) Organization to Make Expenditures to Influence Legislation)*[35] is attached. If the form was previously filed, a copy is requested. Churches and private foundations are not allowed to make this election. The form itself actually has no financial information, although line 1a of this part requests it.

(c) Line 3: Bingo or Gaming Activities

Applicants that plan to conduct gaming activities—bingo, keno, pull-tabs, raffles, split-the-pot, and other games of chance—must provide details about their plans. The how, where, when, and who, including how worker

---

[34]Issues to consider in making the decision are outlined in Chapter 23, *Tax Planning and Compliance for Tax-Exempt Organizations*.

[35]Reproduced in Appendix I.

compensation will be calculated is requested. A projection of revenues and expenses is not specifically requested, but submission of a financial projection for the revenues and expenses for gaming either here or in Part IX is appropriate. Revenues should be reported gross, not net, of commissions or fees. The IRS concern with these activities is three-fold:

- Are unreasonable amounts allocated to commercial interests operating the game?
- Are employment tax rules observed?
- Should any of the income be treated as unrelated business income?

Net profits from bingo games that are not conducted in violation of any state or local law are not taxable.[36] Bingo is defined as "a game of chance played with cards that are generally printed with five rows of five squares each on which participants place markers to form a preselected pattern to win." Other games of chance, including, but not limited to, keno, dice, cards, and lotteries, are not bingo and may create unrelated business income[37] despite classification by the state gambling authorities. During 1990, the IRS aggressively examined nonprofits and assessed tax on any bingo variations not strictly meeting the code and regulation definitions.[38] Applicants with such plans should study IRS Publication 3079, *Gaming Publication for Tax-Exempt Organizations*. The possibility that raffles of donated goods might be conducted in connection with fundraising events in the future may not need to be reported.

(d) Line 4: Fundraising

Efforts to raise funds through appeals for financial support that represent donations, or gifts, are surveyed on this line. This question does not pertain to charges or fees for goods and services that are functionally related activities explained in Part VI. Nor does it apply to production of investment income or revenues earned in certain unrelated business activities. Those few applicants with no fundraising plans, such as private foundations, can simply say *No*. Lack of plans to seek donated funds, however, can be a negative fact for those organizations that provide businesslike services, such as credit counseling or

---

[36]IRC §513(f) says wagers must be placed, winners determined, and prizes distributed in presence of all person placing wagers.

[37]Reg. §1.513-5; *South End Italian Club, Inc. v. Commissioner*, 87 T.C. 168 (1986).

[38]*Julius M. Isreal Lodge of B'nai B'rith No.2113 v. Commissioner*, 78AFTR 2d _96-5482 (5th Cir.), aff'g. TCM 1995-439; see also *Women of the Motion Picture Industry, et al. v. Commissioner*, T.C. Memo. 1997-518.

business consulting. Supplementing earned income from services provided with donated funds can evidence the charitable nature of the organization.

If the applicant says, "Yes, we plan to solicit donated money," one or more of the 10 types of solicitation methods must be checked. The 10th box allows for "other" fundraising programs. There are several common types of fundraising efforts not listed in the boxes, for example, gala balls, sponsorships, fun runs, spaghetti suppers, donations solicited for a resale shop, low-cost article distribution, and premiums from group insurance or credit cards sold to supporters. IRS specialists will be alert to the fact the some of these "other" programs are actually unrelated activities subject to special rules and exceptions. Funds raised in such efforts may constitute earned, rather than donated, income because the payors receive something in return for their money. Because such activities are not normally conducted in a businesslike fashion, that is, operated by volunteers or conducted irregularly for a brief period of time, they are not treated as taxable income and the net income is excluded from normal income tax.[39] In an inconspicuous place under the left-hand list of boxes, there is a request to explain each fundraising program. Though not specifically requested for this line, the projected contribution portion of fundraising programs can be disclosed by giving some detail for line 1 of Part IX, on which "Gifts, grants, and contributions received" are reflected.

It is possible, but not necessarily desirable, to state that the fundraising program has not yet been developed. If the projected sources of support consist primarily of grants from other exempt organizations, a lack of plans will probably not pose problems. If fundraising events and exempt function revenues are to be the primary sources of support, the IRS expects detailed information. At a minimum, the organizers should submit mock-ups of letters it will be using to request funding from private foundations, governmental entities, and individuals. A membership organization should attach its member application form.

Line 4b: Fundraising Contracts

This line asks whether any individuals or companies will be engaged to conduct the applicant's fundraising efforts. The level of detailed information to provide for a *Yes* answer on this line depends primarily on the manner in which such a person or company's compensation will be calculated. The significant issues to address include:

---

[39]IRC §§512 and 513. Unrelated business income tax issues are discussed in Chapter 21, *Tax Planning and Compliance for Tax-Exempt Organizations*.

- Facts indicating the terms of the compensation agreement(s) will not result in private inurement to fundraisers through payments of unreasonable salaries or fees based upon a high percentage of the contributions collected.

- Proof that the *commensurate test* will be satisfied. This test examines the net profit received by the organization from its fundraising programs. If promoter fees and other expenses are high in relation to proceeds, the organization itself may be deemed to operate to benefit the fundraisers rather than the required charitable constituency.[40]

The line requests a description of the fundraising activities, including all revenue and expenses for the same periods reported in Part IX. The descriptions of fundraising programs in answer to boxes checked in line 4a should be coordinated with the information with this line. Since Part IX presents all sources of revenue and expenses for the organization, the report will be unique to this part and should contain some details.

The line also asks, "who conducts" the activities and for a copy of any contracts or agreements with such persons. Assume, for example, the organization plans to establish a development department with salaried employees. If the job descriptions suggested for Part IX, lines 17 and 18 are provided, the response can refer to that information. If the person(s) to conduct fundraising is highly paid, the details in Part V can be referenced. If the person(s) is to receive incentive compensation based on the result of the fundraising, the concepts discussed in Part V, line 6 should be carefully considered. Certainly if the persons to be compensated are officials or their related parties, the information should also be coordinated with information in Part V, line 6.

(e) Line 4c: Fundraising for Another Organization

When the applicant does or plans to conduct fundraising on behalf of another organization, the issue the IRS seeks to examine is whether the recipient organization will devote the funds to a charitable purpose. Fundraising for another §501(c)(3) organization or a governmental unit should cause few problems. It may not be acceptable, however, for the §501(c)(3) applicant to raise money to support a labor union or business league. When the answer is *Yes*, a description of the plans and copies of all contracts and agreements are requested. No financial details, however, are asked for. If the information is also supplied in response to Part IV (narrative description of your activities),

---

[40]See Section 2.2, *Tax Planning and Compliance for Tax-Exempt Organizations.*

Part VIII, line 15 (relationships with other organizations), or Schedule D (a supporting organization), this part can be referenced to that part.

(f) Line 4d: Location of Fundraising Activity

The states and local jurisdictions, including an Indian reservation, in which fundraising is and will be conducted is requested. The line asks for the name of each location in which you will conduct fundraising for your own organization, for another organization, or in which another organization fundraises for you. This location information should have no impact from a Federal tax-exemption standpoint. Because the application is open to public inspection and filed in some states, the author presumes this information will enable states to regulate fundraisers by identifying organizations that should file solicitation registrations.

(g) Line 4e: Donor-Advised Fund

An organization that does or will offer a donor-advised fund program must attach a description of the program. All the line asks for is a description of the degree of control donors have in directing their contributions and authority regarding investments. The issues for donor advised funds have complications not implied by the simplicity of this request for information. It is regrettable that there are no instructions.[41]

The applicant must show that the organization, rather than the donors to advised funds, has absolute discretion and control over the funds, both as it regards regranting and investments. Such funds are created generally by persons that wish to avoid the complexity and expense of creating an individual private foundation. The author understands that the IRS, particularly for those funds created by financial institutions, such as Fidelity Investments, requires that the fund agree, to achieve approval, that it will each and every year distribute overall at least 5% of the value of its assets. This rule is referred to as the minimum distribution requirement imposed on private foundations.[42] Therefore, if the answer to this line is *Yes*, the applicant should, in advance of making an application, develop and attach a sample agreement that it plans to enter into with its donors. Such documents should specify the organization's control over the funds and the rights, if any, of the donors to the

---

[41]See Section 11.3, *Tax Planning and Compliance for Tax-Exempt Organizations*, which discusses community foundations.

[42]IRC §4942.

fund. Many cities have existing community foundations that maintain donor-advised funds. Organizers of such funds can find useful information about policies and procedures of established donor-advised funds on the Internet.

(h) Line 5: Affiliation with a Governmental Unit

An organization that is created by, controlled by, or closely related to a governmental unit must answer *Yes*. Governmental units include a state, a possession of the United States, or any political subdivision of a state or possession, the United States itself, and the District of Columbia. Importantly the instructions point out that a governmental unit does not itself qualify for tax-exemption. The reason lies in the concept of separation of states and the Federal government. A governmental unit is an entity that can exercise certain sovereign powers, such as the power to tax, police powers to enforce the law, and to exercise eminent domain.

What this question does not ask is whether the applicant plans to perform services that lessen, or relieve, the burdens of government. Such an entity may or may not be created or controlled by a governmental unit. This can be a complicated question for such organizations and deserves further study to provide appropriate information.[43] Mostly, the applicant must evidence the governmental unit "objectively manifests" its expectation that the organization will benefit it, for example, by maintaining a volunteer fire department or operating the mass transit system. The degree of cooperation and involvement of the governmental unit whose burdens are being relieved must be explained.

An applicant who answers *Yes* is asked to simply explain its affiliation with a governmental unit. The instructions expand this request by suggesting that the details of any financial reports or audits required and any powers or authority given to you by the governmental unit be described. If there is a written agreement regarding the affiliation, it should be attached even though it is not requested.

(i) Line 6a–b: Economic Development

This line is checked *Yes* if the organization was formed to combat community deterioration by assisting businesses located in a particular geographic area in which the economy is depressed or deteriorating. The instructions list the

---

[43]Rev. Proc. 95-48, 1995-47 I.R.B. 13 defines a governmental unit. A host of rulings, cited in Section 4.3, *Tax Planning and Compliance for Tax-Exempt Organizations*, have considered what constitutes "relieving the burdens:"

type of activities they conduct to include grants, loans, provision of information and expertise, and creation of industrial parks. Economic development programs may also seek to eliminate prejudice and discrimination or lessen the burdens of government.

The key to qualification for such an organization is the area of focus for development must be one that has been declared blighted or economically depressed by a government finding. One organization failed to qualify when it was designed to increase patronage for existing stores in such an area.[44] A project located in a non-blighted area might be classified as a community welfare organization qualified under §501(c)(4) or a business league defined in §501(c)(6). Again, most of the detailed information suitable to explain the organization's programs will also be provided in the Narrative Description of Your Activities, Part IV, and can be referenced, rather than being repeated. Line 6b specifically asks for a full explanation of who benefits from the programs.

(j) Line 7a–c: Developers and Managers

This line delves deeper into the same issues addressed in Part V, lines 8 and 9. Line 7a asks, "Do or will persons other than your employees develop your facilities? If yes, describe the facility, the role of the developer, and any business or family relationship(s) between the developer and your officers, directors, or trustees." Line 7b asks the same question in regard to managers of facilities and programs. **Develop** for this purpose means the planning, financing, construction or provision of similar services involved in the acquisition of land and buildings. **Manage** means to direct or administer. If written agreements with a developer or manager exist, they should be attached. There is nothing inherently wrong with the applicant using an outside professional or company to accomplish its programs. The issue is whether the financial terms of their engagement provide more than a reasonable return for the skills they bring to the project and the risks they accept. If a management company is hired to operate a hospital cafeteria, for example, the hospital should report, if possible, that the share of revenues it will receive is equivalent to customary fees in the food industry.

Line 7c seeks information about any relationships between the prospective developer or manager and organizational officials and asks they be identified, relationships explained, proof that agreements were entered into at arm's length be provided, and a copy of any contracts or agreements be attached. The types of questions the IRS specialist asks him or herself in evaluating any contracts include the following:

---

[44]Rev. Rul. 77-111, 1977-1 C.B. 144.

- Do management arrangements in any way take unfair advantage of the charity?
- Is the fee reasonable for services to be rendered?
- How does it compare to prevailing rates charged other businesses or to the overall budget?
- Is the fee related to performance (e.g., a percentage of profits or other arrangement reflecting a business transaction)?
- Are contracts entered into with related parties (refer back to Part V, lines 8 or 9)?

(k) Line 8: Joint Ventures

If the organization has or will conduct an exempt activity or activities within a joint venture or limited liability company as a partner with for-profit individuals or companies, a very thorough explanation should be provided. The fact that the IRS defines the term *joint venture* as a "legal agreement in which the persons jointly undertake a transaction for mutual profit" should signal a preparer to proceed with care and consult with a lawyer or accountant knowledgeable about the subject. A nonprofit organization seeking recognition as a tax-exempt organization cannot promote for-profit interests. Conceptually, it has been IRS policy that such partnerships must be controlled by the §501(c)(3) and the agreements must specify devotion to tax-exempt purposes in conducting the activities.[45] In 2004, a ruling on the tax consequences for a university that formed a limited liability corporation (LLC) with a company that specialized in video training programs illustrates the issue. The arrangement was found not to jeopardize the organization's exempt status since the activities conducted through the LLC were not a substantial part of the university's activities. The video was used in summer seminars for elementary school teachers and was considered substantially related to the university's exempt purposes.[46]

(l) Line 9a–d: Childcare Organization

A childcare organization may be eligible to qualify for tax-exemption as either a childcare organization under §501(k) or as a school. A childcare entity is one

---

[45]Rev. Rul. 98-15, 1998-12 IRB 6 as discussed in Section 4.6, *Tax Planning and Compliance for Tax-Exempt Organizations*, which outlines the characteristics of a charitable venture versus a commercial venture.

[46]Rev. Rul. 04-51, 2004-22 IRB 974.

that provides care for children away from their homes to enable their parents or caregivers to work or seek work to be gainfully employed (line 9b). To qualify, substantially all (at least 85%) of the care must be provided to enable persons to work (line 9c) and the facility must be open to the general public. A facility operated exclusively for a particular employer (line 9d) cannot qualify as charitable.[47] To determine if the organization should seek to qualify itself as a school, see line 19 and study the questions in Schedule B.

(m) Line 10: Intellectual Property

If the organization does or will publish, own, or have the rights in music, literature, tapes, artworks, choreography, scientific discoveries, or other intellectual property, the answer here is *Yes*. If so, the applicant must explain all aspects of the ownership:

- Who owns or will own any copyrights, patents or trademarks
- Whether fees are or will be charged
- How the fees are determined
- How any items are or will be produced, distributed, and marketed

As a general rule, the IRS usually expects that a tax-exempt organization will retain ownership of intellectual property. The circumstances under which ownership will be shared, such as a partial royalty interest granted to the scientist developing a new drug, must be carefully described and any contracts or agreements provided. The issue is primarily whether the organization, in permitting individuals or outside companies to own or share in ownership of the property, will allow impermissible private benefit to occur. Will the organization's resources be used to provide excess economic benefits to such persons? The concepts described for reasonable compensation in Part V, lines 4–9 should be studied in preparing the response to this question.

A parallel issue with such property is whether the use and economic exploitation of the property will constitute an unrelated business. If a symphony orchestra plans to record and sell tapes of its performances, the educational purposes for the program should be explained. The factors that distinguish its publishing program from that of commercial record companies can be described.[48] The standards for development and dissemination of the

---

[47]See Section 5.1(c), *Tax Planning and Compliance for Tax-Exempt Organizations*.

[48]See Section 21.13, *Tax Planning and Compliance for Tax-Exempt Organizations*.

research and resulting patents should be studied by a proposed scientific research organization. Research that serves the public interest is certainly a charitable activity, but the IRS may wish to place constraints on potential commercialization of the results.[49]

(n) Line 11: Noncash Donations

When an organization plans to solicit gifts of property that have no easily ascertainable value, the IRS is concerned that the organization develop policies and procedures for accurately valuing and acknowledging the donation of such properties. The fact that there is no instruction for this line belies the potential for trouble with this question. This question raises several issues, dependent on the type of property involved, as follows:

- How are the gifts valued? Are appraisals required?
- Is the property used in the charitable program (given to needy persons) or are they sold?
- Is the property maintained as an income-producing investment asset?
- If the property is disposed of, is a dealer involved, and if so, what portion of the sales price goes to the charity?
- Is there an agreement that limits the charity's use or resale of the property?

Plans to seek gifts of encumbered land, conservation easements, art works, patents, copyrights, or certain other types of personal or real property must be explained. If closely held corporate stock is to be given and a buy/sell or redemption agreement is planned, the agreement should be attached. Real estate gifts can be described by attaching the deed of gift, if possible, and a report on the purpose for which the property will be used (for example, an office building to be held as an investment property or used for administrative offices). If the property is subject to debt, proof that its fair market value exceeds the debt to which it is subject must be furnished. An independent appraisal may be requested. Repayment terms and any other obligations the charity is assuming, or taking the property subject to, must also be reported. Documents creating an income interest in property might be attached, and must evidence the donative intent and benefit to be received by the charity. Types of instruments that might be attached include a trust instrument creat-

---

[49]See Section 5.3, *Tax Planning and Compliance for Tax-Exempt Organizations.*

ing a life estate or a royalty interest assignment. A proposed automobile, boat, plane, and other vehicle donation program will be carefully scrutinized. The IRS has been concerned for some years that such gifts are often overvalued. They find too often dealers handling the donation program retain the majority of the sales proceeds. Congress has passed and is considering further limitations on the contribution deduction for gifts of used cars, intellectual property, and conservation easements.

(o) Line 12: Foreign Activities

An applicant planning to operate in a foreign country must name the countries and regions, the nature of the program(s), and the fashion in which the activity will advance its exempt purpose. The tax code places no constraints on the geographic location of charitable programs and the detailed description of programs in Narrative Description of Activities, Part IV, may be sufficient to provide the information requested for this line. What is not asked that should be described is what procedures the organization will implement to assure its support does not aid persons identified by the government as terrorists in violation of the U.S. Patriot Act. Executive Order 13224 bans humanitarian aid to Specially Designated Nationals and Blocked Persons. The U.S. Treasury Department has issued voluntary guidelines an organization conducting programs in foreign countries should consider adopting.[50] The websites of The Council on Foundations (http://www.cof.org/), Independent Sector (http://www.independentsector.org/), and Grantmakers Without Borders (http://www.gwob.net/) contain lists of designated persons and organizations and other information to assist the applicant to devise compliance plans in this regard.

(p) Lines 13a–g: Grant and Loan Programs

Extensive details are requested for an organization that does or will make grants, loans, or other distributions to other organizations. The questions imply the applicant must have sufficient plans—application forms, grant proposals, criteria for selection, selection committee (can be those that govern the organization), evaluation systems including follow-up grantee reports—in place to assure the funds are devoted by the recipients to charitable purposes.

---

[50]"Anti-Terrorist Financing Guidelines: Voluntary Best Practices for U.S. Based Charities" were published on November 7, 2002.

Grantee contracts and loan documents are requested, along with a description of the records that will be retained regarding each grant. A supporting organization that will make grants to organizations stipulated in its charter can refer this question to Schedule D.

This line will, however, be troublesome for an applicant that has not activated its grant program. Many may be unable, as line 13d requests, to "identify each recipient organization and any relationship between you and the recipient organization." It should be acceptable for a private foundation that plans to make grants to unrelated public charities, not yet identified, to simply say so. Similarly for lines 13c and f, the applicant may not have developed grant documents and should be able to say so. An applicant might make a statement of its intention to only grant funds in furtherance of its exempt purposes in response to line 13g. In the author's experience, this information has not been requested of grant-making organizations in the past. There is no specific provision in the code or regulations that requires written requests or follow-up reports other than expenditure responsibility reports of a private foundation. Conceivably, determining that the grantee is listed in IRS Publication 78 as a qualified §501(c)(3) is sufficient proof of the charitable nature of its activities. Certainly for a loan or program-related investment program, a description of anticipated terms for repayment, security, and the like will be expected by the IRS, even if the documents have not been developed. At a minimum, the applicant should design and attach a sample grant award letter that requires it funds be used exclusively for charitable purposes. A private foundation's (PF) letter might also require that the grantee be a public charity and that it agree not to spend its funds on lobbying or other activities prohibited for a PF.[51] It remains to be seen how the IRS will respond to an organization that says it does not plan to develop paperwork and will make grants to other charitable organizations of its choice.

(q) Line 14: Grants to Foreign Organizations

Plans to make grants to foreign organizations raise two important issues. It is imperative that the applicant describe procedures it will adopt to assure that the money will be devoted to charitable purposes and not be used to advance terrorists as described above in line 12. Line 14b requests the names of organizations and the country in which they are located. When specific grantees have not yet been identified, follow the suggestions for line 13.

---

[51]See Chapter 17, *Tax Planning and Compliance for Tax-Exempt Organizations*, for the Taxable Expenditures rules that constrain PF spending and sample letters.

2.8 PART VIII—YOUR SPECIFIC ACTIVITIES

The answers to questions in lines 14 c–f must be *Yes*. For line 14c–d, the applicant must evidence it will not serve to circumvent the income tax rule that disallows a donation deduction for a gift to a foreign organization. Only gifts to domestic organizations, those created or organized in the United States, are deductible for U.S. tax purposes.[52] This limitation, plus the fact that U.S. tax-exempt organizations are permitted to conduct activities anywhere in the world, prompted creation of domestic *Friends of* organizations to raise U.S. support for foreign charities. So long as the U.S. charity has control and discretion over the ultimate spending of the money, funds raised to regrant to a foreign organization do qualify as charitable contributions for individuals.

Questions in line 14e–f ask for a description of preliminary and follow-up steps the organization will take to assure its grants will be used for charitable purposes. In responding, the applicant should consider the following standards suggested by the IRS:[53]

- The U.S. organization's charter, bylaws, or other governing instruments do not restrict activities to domestic programs; there is no constraint on support for foreign organizations (and in silence allows it).

- Solicitation for and acknowledgment of donations from and to U.S. and foreign individuals and businesses refer to support for the domestic organization's programs. (A sample solicitation can be attached.)

- The making of grants to the foreign organization is within the exclusive power of the domestic organization's board of directors. The power is evidenced by overt board approval prior to payment of such grants. Funding is either authorized as part of the annual budget for such programs or specifically approved at board, executive, or staff meetings.

- The U.S. charity obtains a written grant proposal or proposals from the foreign organization(s) that it funds. The proposal is subject to same approval systems applied to domestic programs. Authorizing officials are provided sufficient detail to allow them to satisfy themselves that the grant serves the domestic charity's purposes. Brochures and other materials describing the domestic organization's programs contain a description of information to be submitted with grant requests and terms under which grants are awarded.

- Grant recipients submit annual reports to show that the grant funds were expended for the purpose for which they were approved by the

---

[52]IRC §170(c). In addition, a corporation is only permitted an income tax deduction for gifts to be used within the United States of any of its possessions exclusively for charitable purposes.

[53]Rev. Rul. 66-79, 1966-1 C.B. 48.

board. Reports should contain copies of exhibition catalogs, photographs of installations, and other actual evidence of the program.[54] For a private foundation, this report may be contractually agreed to ahead of time in the expenditure responsibility agreement.[55]

- Grant payment accompanied by an award letter reiterating the terms of the agreement and outlining documentation requirements grantees must complete.

(r) Line 15: Close Connections

This is again a line that asks for information without explaining the import of the possible answers and also asks for information provided on other lines. Connections do not necessarily impede recognition of tax-exemption as a charity. A close connection occurs according to the instructions when one of the following situations exists.

- *You control the organization or it controls you through common officials, or through authority to approve budgets or expenditures.* Common control is not necessarily a negative situation. This response can refer to the other lines shown in parentheses where information describes relationships. To qualify as a supporting organization, the supported organization(s) must possess some control or representation and authority as to budgets and expenditures (Schedule D). A separate charity formed to conduct fundraising (Part VIII, line 4d) or to hold the investment assets of another charity may possess elements of common control.

- *You and the organization were created at approximately the same time and by the same persons.* Concurrent formation of a charity to conduct educational activities, a business league to advance the profession, and a political organization to electioneer is the example provided in the instructions. A charity that plans to operate in different states might form separate entities in each state. A performing arts organization and a for-profit subsidiary to commercially exploit its intellectual property (Part VIII, line 10) might be created at the same time. These are positive examples that evidence an intention to separate charitable and noncharitable activities. Another example might be a joint ven-

---

[54]Rev. Rul. 75-65, 1975-1 C.B. 79.

[55]A sample agreement is illustrated in Section 17.6, *Tax Planning and Compliance for Tax-Exempt Organizations.*

ture (Part VIII, line 8). Someone might create two private foundations named after each of his or her parents.

- *You and the organization operate in a coordinated manner with respect to facilities, programs, employees, or other activities.* The sharing of resources between one charity and another should be trouble-free. A sharing arrangement between a charity and noncharitable organization or individual must protect the charitable resources (Part V, lines 8–10).

- *Persons who exercise substantial influence over you also exercise substantial influence over the other organization and (1) you either conduct activities in common or (2) have a financial relationship.* Substantial influence occurs in the instructions when a voting member of the charity's board is also a voting member of the board of a business league with which the charity has a joint project or loan. Another example would be the creator of a charity that owns the building the charity rents to conduct a program (Part V, line 9).

(s) Lines 16–22: Special Types of Organizations

The last seven lines of Part VIII identify organizations subject to special rules as follows:

- Line 16: Cooperative hospital service organization—§501(e)
- Line 17: Cooperative service organization of operating educational organizations—§501(f)
- Line 18: Charitable risk pool—§501(n)
- Line 19: School—§170(b)(1)(A)(ii) [Schedule B]
- Line 20: Hospital and Medical Care—§170(b)(1)(A)(iii) [Schedule C]
- Line 21: Low Income, Elderly, or Handicapped Housing [Schedule F]
- Line 22: Scholarships [Schedule H]

For each of the above organization types, applicants may find it insufficient to simply study the instructions. Some may find it useful to engage a professional familiar with the tax rules applicable to the specific organization. The requirements are relatively stringent, particularly so for healthcare entities, and subject to evolving IRS policies. The last four lines prompt the completion of detailed schedules noted in Chapter 3. Interestingly, there is no line asking if the organization will qualify as a church and, therefore, should complete Schedule A, presumably because churches are not required to file Form 1023. One that does submit the application is commonly not associated with an established religion and must meet the 14-point test outlined in the schedule to achieve recognition as a church. Once so classified, a church is excused from annual filings of Form 990.

2.9 PART IX—FINANCIAL DATA

This part of Form 1023 remains mostly unchanged since the 1990 version and, as the title implies, presents the prospective tax-exempt organization's financial information. The display in which the information is reported in this part differs from financial statements presented in accordance with generally accepted accounting principles (GAAP) and IRS Forms 990 and 8734 (calculation of the public support test). The finances presented in this part are a key piece of information that should be, whether it is past, present, or planned, consistent with other information presented in the application. Applicants requesting public charity status under one of the public support tests list in Part X are reminded to show contributions from the public and receipts from providing exempt functions. The IRS does not say so in the new instructions, but it has previously acknowledged the organization's actual financial results may vary from its projected amounts. Form 990 each year asks a tax-exempt organization to describe any new activities or other changes in its operations.

(a) Section A: Statement of Revenue and Expenses

This section is required for all organizations, both newly formed ones presenting projected or proposed financial data, and those having actual financial history. If the information is prepared on a method of accounting other than cash, an explanation is requested. Although the instructions for this part do not request details for many of the revenue and expense categories, the author's experience, as noted previously, indicates furnishing details with the application avoids requests for them later. In preparing this part, one must be conscious that the successful application paints a picture of the organization in the reviewer's mind.

The information must be coordinated with responses to other parts of the application that ask for financial information [shown in brackets in this paragraph]. A display of details for line 1 "gifts and contributions" by expected types of donors—individuals, businesses, governments, and grants from private foundations and public charities—can aid in reflecting a potential public charity's qualification [Parts VIII-3 and X]. Detailed pricing schedules for services, program fees, and books and other items to be sold should be provided that, when combined with circulation and attendance numbers, reflect projected gross revenue on line 9 [Part V]. For lines 17 and 18, personnel listings with salary for each position and brief job descriptions can reflect the reasonableness of proposed salaries [Part V and VIII]. For lines 14 and 22, the fees proposed for professionals such as fundraisers, physicians, management companies, or architects, for example, are the kind of details that the IRS routinely requests if they are not furnished [Part VIII-3, 4, 7, 8]. Particularly as it regards compensation for personal services, the more information provided in this part, the more complete the application will be and the higher the chances for a merit close (approval without any follow-up questions).

An organization that has been in existence less than one year is instructed to include a projected financial statement for the current tax year, plus projected activity for the next two years. For an organization in existence for more than one, but less than four, years, actual financial results for each completed year, plus a projection for the current year is provided. The IRS requests information for up to four years. For example, an organization filing on May 15, which was chartered on January 1, 2005 and chooses a fiscal year ending in June (compared in parenthesis to an entity that has completed prior fiscal years) submits the following periods of information:

- Column (a). A projection for the current tax year ending June 30, 2005, combining any actual financial activity (January to May) with projection for the month of June. If instead the organization has chosen a calendar year, the five months of actual activity would be combined with a projection of expected activity for June through December. (An organization with prior fiscal years would similarly report the combined actual and expected activity for the current fiscal year ending in 2005.)

- Column (b). An organization without a prior fiscal year inputs the 12-month financials expected for July 1–June 30, 2006. (An organization with prior activity presents its immediately preceding year ending in 2004.)

- Column (c). A 12-month projection of expected financial activity expected in its third year ending on June 30, 2007, is reported. (The organization with prior activity inputs financials for its year ending in 2003.)

- Column (d). This column will be blank for the new organization. (Financial activity for 2002 would be input for an organization in existence for three full prior years.)

A summary of the order of years suggested above follows:

- New entity that has not completed a full fiscal year: 2005, 2006, 2007
- New entity that has completed only one full year: 2005, 2004, 2006
- Existing entity with two or three full years: 2005, 2004, 2003, 2002

It seems logical to the author for an existing entity to present the information in descending and, conversely, for a new entity to present ascending years, but comments are welcome. Previously this part asked the organization, for column (a), to input its financial activity for whatever number of months in its current fiscal year it had completed within at least 60 days of the date of the application. The new system of reporting complete fiscal years in each column, with column (a) combining actual and projected, provides a better comparative view of the financials. (See Appendix M for a different view of the presentation.) Whether to present a first fiscal year that included actual and projected amounts was not clear in the past. The IRS has reasonably corrected the confusion that previously existed.

The arrangement of the lines for reporting the financial information is different from Forms 990 and 990-PF, but the contents are basically the same. Suggestions for choosing the lines on which to input financial information and details to supply follow.[56]

(i) Line 1: Gifts, Grants and Contributions Received. Income reported on Part I, line 1 of Forms 990, 990-PF, and 990-EZ is displayed on this line. Voluntary contributions and grants from individuals, businesses, grants from other charitable organizations, indirect public support from United Way or similar type organizations, donation portion of fundraising event proceeds, and certain government grants are included on this line. Donations are those amounts paid by supporters without any expectation of receiving benefits or services in return. Donations are said to stem from disinterested and detached generosity.[57]

No detailed listing of contributors is requested for this line. For an organization seeking a definitive ruling of its public status based upon sources of support, sufficient details of contributor revenue are submitted in Part X, line 6b, to allow the IRS to calculate its qualification.

Voluntary submission of the expected types of donors is also advisable for other organizations, particularly one that expects to receive extensive fee-for-service revenues. The receipt of donative support can evidence the charitable nature of service-providing project.[58] The following table shows the suggested detail that will help the IRS understand the contribution sources.

---

[56]Chapter 2, *IRS Form 990: Tax Preparation Guide for Nonprofits*, can also be consulted if there is any question about choice of lines.

[57]See Chapter 24, *Tax Planning and Compliance for Tax-Exempt Organizations*.

[58]Reg. §1.170A-9(e)(ii) says a service providing entity receiving an insignificant amount of donations cannot qualify as a public charity under §170(b)(1)(A)(vi).

	Year 1	Year 2	Year 3
Board members (4–20 persons)	$ 200,000	$ 200,000	$ 40,000
Memberships ($20–$250 @)	30,000	50,000	100,000
Private Foundations ($25,000 @)	0	50,000	200,000
Business Sponsorships	0	100,000	200,000
Total Contributions and Grants	$ 230,000	$ 400,000	$ 540,000

Organizations that plan to seek government grants should carefully read the instructions to assist in distinguishing those grants that represent contributions rather than gross receipts for performing services reportable on line 9. The distinction is somewhat vague and the GAAP rules differ from this tax concept. The general rule is payments a governmental unit makes to enable the organization to provide services to the general public are contributions.[59] Unusual grants are reported separately on line 12.

(ii) Line 2: Membership Fees Received. The Form 1023 instructions say amounts received from members to provide support to the organization go here. The 990 instructions direct membership fees that constitute donations instead be reported as donations and the author agrees. Charges for member services (such as admissions, merchandise, or use of facilities) are included on line 4 or 9, not here. Line 3 of Forms 990 and 990-EZ contains the same revenue. The issues discussed under Part VI should be considered and coordinated with this line where the details can reflect the number of members and the estimated membership fee per person. For most applicants, this line may be zero.

(iii) Line 3: Gross Investment Income. Dividends, interest, payments on security loans, rents, and royalties are the common forms of investment income that are reported on this line. Interest received for program-related investments, such as student loans, is reported on line 8. Rents received from residents of a low-income housing project also go on line 8. This amount combines that reported on lines 4–7 on Form 990, lines 3–5 on Form 990-PF, and line 4 of Form 990-EZ. Capital gains and losses from investment, or capital, assets are reported on line 11.

(iv) Line 4: Net Unrelated Business Income. Income from unrelated businesses that are regularly carried on in a businesslike manner and reportable as taxable on Form 990-T are included on line 4. The sale of advertising for an

---

[59]Regs. §1.170A-9(e)(8) and 1.509(a)-3(m). See Section 11.5, *Tax Planning and Compliance for Tax-Exempt Organizations*, for more discussion on this topic.

organization's publication or its website and rental income from an indebted building are examples of unrelated income reportable on this line. Certain unrelated income may be excluded from tax for several reasons. A revenue raising activity that is conducted intermittently (irregularly) or by volunteers is not taxed. Sales of donated goods or operation of a café, housing unit, parking lot, or other services for the convenience of the organization's members are also not treated as businesslike, not taxed, and not entered on this line. Excluded unrelated income is included on line 8. The many exclusions and modifications provided in the tax code make this a complicated subject.[60] The important issue for exemption purposes is that too high an amount of unrelated business income on this line in relation to overall revenue indicates the primary purpose of the organization is not necessarily charitable.

(v) Line 5: Taxes Levied for Your Benefit. Amounts collected by local tax authorities from the general public and either paid to, or spent on behalf of, the organization are to be reported here. Schools and human service organizations receive this type of revenue, which is commonly reportable on line 1 of Forms 990 unless the amounts are paid in return for services the organization renders.

(vi) Line 6: Value of Services or Facilities Furnished by a Governmental Unit without Charge. Facilities and services donated to the EO from a governmental unit are reported on this line and counted for public support purposes. In contrast, the value of donated and use of facilities given by individuals or businesses are not reported here or as revenue for Form 990 purposes.

(vii) Line 7: Any Revenue Not Otherwise Listed Above or in Lines 9–12 Below. In the author's experience, an amount is rarely reported on this line. If any amount is reported, it must be described in an attachment.

(viii) Line 9: Gross Receipts from Admissions, Merchandise Sold or Services Performed, or Furnishing of Facilities in any Activity That Is Related to Your Exempt Purposes. This line asks for gross receipts (meaning without reduction for related costs) paid to the organization by participants in charitable, educational, or other exempt activities. Student tuition, hospital charges, publication sales, and laboratory fees are good examples.

This line also includes revenue from fundraising events and projects, raffles, bingo games, thrift shops, and other revenue-producing activities that

---

[60]See Chapter 21, *Tax Planning and Compliance for Tax-Exempt Organizations*, for an extensive presentation of this complicated type of income.

are not reported on line 4 as unrelated business income (because of an exclusion or modification) or on line 1 (the donation portion of event tickets). This line used to ask for revenue that was "not an unrelated business within the meaning of section 513." Although an explanation is not required, the application is more understandable if the details of this revenue are submitted and coordinated with the answer to Part VII, line 1 and Part VIII, line 4. For example, the description for exempt function revenue for a school might say:

	Year 1	Year 2	Year 3
Student tuition	0	$ 200,000	$ 600,000
Sale of textbooks	5,000	10,000	40,000
Student activity fees	5,000	20,000	50,000
Laboratory usage fees	0	10,000	30,000
Total Exempt Function Revenue	$ 10,000	$ 240,000	$ 720,000

(ix) Line 11: Gain or Loss on Sale of Capital Assets. Property an organization holds as an investment and property used in performing exempt functions are its capital assets. A description of each asset sold, the name of the person to whom it was sold, and the amount received is to be reported in detail for capital transactions that have occurred or are expected to occur. When such a sale involves an organizational insider, the attachment for this line should be coordinated with Part V, line 7. Evidence that such sales transaction transpired at fair market value, or a price beneficial to the organization, should be explained in Part V. For difficult to value property such as real estate or art, the attachment of an appraisal evidencing value might preclude its later request from the IRS examiner. For security sales through a brokerage company, the name of the purchaser is not required. Sales of objects held for resale in both an exempt function and fundraising context are reported on line 9.

(x) Line 12: Unusual Grants. Grants that are unusual, unexpected, and received from an unrelated party may be reported on this line rather than line 1. Identifying such grants can be important for an organization that is seeking classification as a public charity based on its sources of revenue. This segregation allows such grants to be excluded from both the numerator and denominator of the public support test calculations. Detailed information about such grants is requested on line 7 of Part X.

(xi) Line 13: Total Revenue. A careful applicant uses this line to calculate the ratio of its projected expenses to expected revenues. There are no specific limitations, but enhanced scrutiny might occur if fundraising expenses shown on line 14, disbursements to benefit members on line 16, or compensation of officials on line 17 are high in relation to total revenue. High fundraising expenses might be needed for a new organization, but careful disclosure of the reasonableness and coordination with the response in Part VIII, line 8 would be prudent. Conversely a high percentage of contribution expense on line 15 in comparison to revenue would be a positive fact.

The next group of lines presents the organization's actual and proposed expenses. An organization that expects to pay expenses in connection with its investments, such as investment management fees or expenses for a rental building, must consider where to include them. For two reasons, inclusion on line 23 seems preferable. Their inclusion on lines 18–22 could distort operational expenses. For financial statement purposes, such expenses are normally netted against revenue.

(xii) Line 14: Fundraising Expenses. Its appearance as the first expense item shows the IRS's concern for this subject. During 2004, the IRS Exempt Organization Compliance Unit in Ogden, Utah, sent letters to organizations reporting donations and little, if any, fundraising costs. The message was "do not net such expenses against the revenue." Similarly, for this line the "total expenses incurred in soliciting contributions, gifts, grants, etc." are reported, such as:

- Commissions and fees paid to fundraising professionals that conduct solicitation programs on behalf of the organization
- Salary and all associated costs of personnel that conduct fundraising
- Cost of printing and mailing solicitations
- Facility and other costs of development department
- Direct cost of food
- Prizes
- Green fees
- T-shirts, and other premiums and benefits provided to participants in events

The instructions indicate that other types of expenses that have a portion allocated to fundraising should be reported in an itemized fashion. It is advisable, even though it is not requested, that a detailed description of the amount of each category of fundraising expenses be provided, particularly if the amount on this line is 10–15% of total expenses.

Forms 990 do not reflect this item as an amalgamated expense total. On Form 990, page 1, the direct costs associated with fundraising events and inventory sales are deducted against the gross revenue to arrive at total revenue on page 1 and other fundraising expenses are displayed in a separate column on page 2. The responses to lines 3 and 4 of Part VIII should be coordinated with this line and line 9 above.

(xiii) Line 15: Contributions, Gifts, Grants and Similar Amounts Paid. An itemized list showing the name of each recipient, a brief description of the purposes or conditions of the grant and the amount paid is requested. If the organization is new and has made no actual payments, the annual amount expected to be paid is shown with an explanation that qualifying charitable recipients have not yet been chosen. The attachment for this line should be coordinated with descriptions of grant-making procedures in Part VIII, line 13 and 14. If scholarship grants are planned, the attachment can refer to information presented on Schedule H. Pursuant to the Family Educational Rights and Privacy Act, the names of students may be omitted by certain educational institutions.

The following example is suitable for a new organization. An existing organization that has made grant payments is asked to provide a list of grantees.

	Year 1	Year 2	Year 3
College Scholarships	0	$ 100,000	$ 300,000
Grants-in-aid to needy individuals	0	100,000	200,000
Total Grants Projected ·	$ 0	$ 200,000	$ 500,000

(xiv) Line 16: Disbursements to or for the Benefit of Members. An attachment is requested showing the name of each recipient, brief description of the purposes or conditions of payment, and the amount paid. This category of expense is potentially a "red flag" area as discussed under Part VI. Member benefits must serve a charitable purpose, such as a newsletter published for educational purposes.

(xv) Line 17: Compensation of Officers, Directors and Trustees. The instructions for this line, somewhat innocently, only ask for the total amount of compensation paid to officials. Applicants must keep the operational and organizational tests in mind—neither the assets nor income of the organization may be used to provide private benefit to officials.[61] This information should be coordinated with Part V, where all the details of each board member's annual compensation, title, address, and duties are described.

---

[61]See discussion in Sections 1.3 and 2.5 of this book.

(xvi) Line 18: Other Salaries and Wages. All other compensation paid to persons treated as employees is reported on this line. Amounts paid to consultants, accountants, lawyers, and other independent contractors are reported on line 22, except for that paid to fundraising consultants reported on line 14. Again, private benefit can be an issue. It is advisable to include a detailed listing of positions with a brief job description, compensation to be paid and expected hours worked (or to be) per week.

(xvii) Line 19: Interest Expense. Total interest expense should be supplied for this line—except that included in occupancy expense because it is paid on a mortgage on the building that the program and administrative staff uses, which must be reported on line 20 instead. When the applicants plans to secure financing for purchase of equipment or buildings, details of the lending terms are requested for line 14 of the balance sheet.[62]

It would be unusual, but not impermissible, for a new entity to borrow money for its initial working capital. If interest is paid on a loan from a disqualified person not permitted for a PF, an explanation of the manner in which the loan serves the organization's exempt purposes is imperative. The IRS's concern is that such loans do not provide private benefits. For this reason, details of loans are also furnished as an attachment to the balance sheet and explained in Part V, line 8. The organization should provide a copy of the loan agreement to avoid a later request from the IRS.

(xviii) Line 20: Occupancy (Rent, Utilities, Etc.). The total cost of the physical space occupied by the organization for offices and exempt function activities is to be presented, including rent, mortgage interest, taxes, utilities, maintenance, and other costs of the facilities. Expenses pertaining to investment rental properties should be reported on line 23.

(xix) Line 21: Depreciation and Depletion. Assets that have a useful life exceeding one year are capitalized and carried on the balance sheet on line 7 and/or 8. A portion of the cost is written off each year. The cumulative write off reduces the asset balance and is called accumulated depreciation. Say the organization plans to spend $20,000 on computers it expects will be useful for 4 years. Each year an expense of $5,000 would be recorded. After two years, the net cost on the balance sheet would be $10,000. The annual expense is called depreciation (buildings and equipment) or depletion (minerals, patents, and other intangible properties) and is reported on this line. No attachment is requested for this line, however, the detailed list of assets re-

---

[62]See Section 2.9(b) in this chapter.

quested for line 7–8 of the Balance Sheet can contain a column reflecting the useful lives assigned and corresponding depreciation expense.

(xx) Line 22: Professional Fees. Fees charged by accountants, lawyers, building managers, or other nonemployee service providers (independent contractors) are presented on this line. Professionals who assist with fundraising plans, but do not solicit contributions, are reported on this line rather than 14. If the amount is more than 5% of the total expense, details should be attached.

(xxi) Line 23: Any Expense not Otherwise Classified Such as Program Services. An itemized list of all other "significant" expenses not listed on some other line is requested to support the total on this line. The instructions suggest that a single total may be reported if the amount is not substantial. In the interest of avoiding questions that may delay the application process, detail is recommended unless the amount is under five percent of the total and is truly miscellaneous. Page 2 of Form II, Statement of Functional Expenses, on Form 990 may be used as a guide to the suitable types of expense categories. As noted above, expenses associated with investment properties may be presented on this line to avoid distortion of operational expenses.

(xxii) Line 24: Total Expenses. Expense totals are shown for each year without an overall total. Reported expenses in column (a) for a most applicants include both actual and projected amounts on this version. No "net income" appears and amounts on this page will not necessarily agree with the net asset total reported on the balance sheet.

(b) Section B: Balance Sheet

An organization that has completed a full year presents a balance sheet as of its most recent year-end. A new organization presents the most current information available. A new organization with no financial activity prior to the date of filing can say so. See Appendix C, page 10 of model 1023. The instructions for this part do not mention accounting methods. It is suitable, however, for this information to follow the cash or accrual method used to keep the organization's financial records and also used to complete section A. Assets of an unrelated business activity are not mentioned in the instructions. They should not be segregated, but instead are combined with investment assets as is customary for financial reporting purposes. Unlike Section A of this part, the organization does not make projections for this section. Often a new organization has no assets and may simply say so. Except for lines 1, 2, 3, 9, 13 and 17, an itemized list of assets reported on each line is requested.

(i) Line 1: Cash. All cash assets, including checking, petty cash, savings, money market, certificates of deposits, and U.S. Treasury obligations due in less than one year are included on this line.

(ii) Line 2: Accounts Receivable. Amounts due to be paid to the organization that arose from the sale of goods or performance of services (related and unrelated) are presented here. For example, a university might report tuition receivable, amounts due on a grant paid on a reimbursement basis, accounts receivable for its literary press, football season-ticket-holder balances, and insurance reimbursements due to the health center. Charitable gifts receivable under a pledge system would be reported on line 10.

(iii) Line 3: Inventories. Materials, supplies, and goods purchased or manufactured and held for sale or use in some future period are considered inventory. The university's bookstore, science lab, football team, and property management office might all have inventory. Although items that produce both related and unrelated income are combined for this line, the proceeds of selling them are reportable either on line 4 or 9 of the Statement of Revenue and Expense in Section A of this part.

(iv) Lines 4, 5, and 7: Investments. Organizations owning bonds, notes receivable, stocks, buildings, land, mineral interests, or any other investment assets report them on these lines. Details are requested for all assets, other than government bonds, and in the case of stocks, both the book and fair market value of each holding must be reported. The instructions ask for specifics and should be followed by organizations reporting investments.

(v) Line 6: Loans. In a straightforward manner, the instructions ask for details about each loan—the borrower's name, purpose of the loan, repayment terms, interest rate, and the original amount of the loan. What it does not ask is if the lender is a related party—a fact that is to be fully disclosed in Part V, lines 8 and 9. It is vital that information evidencing why the loan serves the organization's exempt purpose, rather than the private interests of the official and his or her businesses, be provided. This line might refer to Part V responses rather than details being repeated here.

(vi) Line 8: Buildings and Equipment. Real and tangible personal property not held for investment, but used instead for exempt purposes, is reported here. A detailed list of the assets sorted by asset type should be attached, along with the depreciation information to coordinate with line 21 of the Expense Statement in section A of this part.

(vii) Line 9: Land. Land held for exempt purposes, not for investment, is presented here. Land purchased for exempt use in the future is included if it is not income producing; otherwise, it would be shown as an investment on line 7.

(viii) Line 10, Other Assets. All assets not reported on other lines go here. The instructions suggest intangible properties, such as patents, as an example. The cash surrender value of a life insurance policy donated to the organization, prepaid expenses, a rental deposit, and an art collection are other examples. The Form 990 instructions say program-related investments are other assets.

(ix) Line 12: Accounts Payable. Amounts due to be paid to suppliers and others, such as salaries, accrued payroll taxes, and interest accrued on notes payable are reported here. An entity keeping its records on a cash basis does not reflect accounts payable on its balance sheet.

(x) Line 13: Grants Payable. Commitments for grants and contributions to other organizations and individuals due to be paid in the future and booked for accrual accounting purposes are reportable on this line. Coordinate this data with line 13 of Part VIII.

(xi) Line 14: Mortgages and Notes Payable. Details including the lender, terms for repayment and interest, purpose of the loan, and the original amount, are called for. This line should be coordinated with line 19 on the Expense Statement and possibly lines 7–8 of Part V if the loan is due to an organizational official.

(xii) Line 17: Fund Balance or Net Assets. A single total for all of the organization's net assets is reported on this line. If the organization uses fund accounting, all funds are combined. Likewise, an organization that designated its net assets as "capital stock," "paid-in capital," and "retained earnings" combines all net assets. This balance sheet may be frustrating for accountants because the fund balances do not tie to the Statement of Income and Expenses in section A of this part.

(xiii) Line 19: Substantial Changes in Assets or Liabilities. The last line of this part is a question that asks for an explanation if there have been any significant changes since the balance sheet date. For a new organization that has not completed a full year, this answer should be *No* because it is instructed to use the most current information possible. An entity that has completed a full year some months before it makes application may find this situation exists. Say a school was created in May 2003, adopts a June 30 fiscal year, devoted the first year to planning, and commenced classes in the fall of 2004. The balance sheet it is instructed to attach would be dated June 30, 2004. If the amount of revenue reported in Column (a) significantly exceeds expenses (for a full fiscal year ending 2005 that combines actual with projected amounts), it might deserve an explanation.

2.10 PART X—PUBLIC CHARITY STATUS

The significance of "public charity" status for organizations tax-exempt under IRC §501(c)(3) is multifaceted, and is of utmost importance to both private and public exempt organizations. Knowing the meaning of the four parts of IRC §509 is the key to understanding public charities. All §501(c)(3) organizations, other than those listed in §509 are private foundations. The four categories of public charities are:

1. §509(a)(1). Organizations that engage in inherently public activity and those that receive revenues from the general public

2. §509(a)(2). Organizations whose revenue stems primarily from charges for exempt function services

3. §509(a)(3). Organizations that support another public charity

4. §509(a)(4). Organizations that test for public safety

As the IRS introduction to this part says, "public charity status is more favorable." Private foundations (PF) must comply with operational constraints of IRC §§4940-4945.[63] The allowable contribution deductions for gifts to private foundations are less than those afforded for public charities.[64] A PF must pay a 1–2% excise tax annually on its investment income. A PF cannot buy or sell property, nor enter into financial transactions (called *self-dealing*) with its directors, officers, contributors, or their family members, under most circumstances. A PF's annual spending for grants to other organizations and charitable projects must meet a "minimum distribution" requirement. A public charity has no specific spending requirement, other than those imposed by its funders. Holding more than 20% of a business enterprise, including shares owned by board members and contributors, is prohibited for PFs, as are jeopardizing investments. No such limits are placed on public charities by the tax code, although

---

[63]See Chapters 12–17, *Tax Planning and Compliance for Tax-Exempt Organizations*, for an in-depth consideration of these rules.

[64]See Chapters 12 and 24, *Tax Planning and Compliance for Tax-Exempt Organizations*.

fiduciary responsibility standards apply. It is therefore very useful for a charitable organization, when possible, to obtain and maintain public status.

(a) Line 1: Private Foundation

Line 1a is checked *Yes* by an applicant that expects to receive most of its revenues from a few donors and investment income so that it will not qualify as a public charity. Line 1b asks whether the prospective private charity's organizational documents require its adherence to special constraints placed on private charities by the tax code. For PFs in all states except Arizona and New Mexico, this answer is *Yes* because all other states (see list in Appendix B of Form 1023) impose statutory provisions that satisfy this requirement. Some lawyers place the overt language in their PF clients' charters even though it is unnecessary. A PF that expects it may at some point in the future convert its classification to that of a public charity should omit the constraining language.

(b) Line 2–4: Private Operating Foundations

The tax code creates a special type of foundation that is essentially a cross between a private foundation and a public organization. A private operating foundation (POF) is a charity that does its own thing, or, in the language of the statute, "actively conducts activities constituting the purpose or function for which it is organized and operated."[65] A POF sponsors and manages its own charitable projects, although it can also make grants to other organizations over and above its requirements. An example is an endowed institution operating a museum, library, or other charitable pursuit not included in the list of organizations that qualify as public charities because their income comes primarily from investment income. A POF must meet two annual distribution requirements: one based on its income levels and another on its assets or sources of its revenues. It must spend the requisite amount in support of its own projects and satisfy an asset or endowment test. Importantly, for its funders, donations to a private operating foundation are afforded the higher deductibility limits allowed for gifts to public charities.

    An applicant is asked on line 2 if it is a POF. If this answer is *Yes*, one of the next two lines apply. A *Yes* on line 3 indicates the prospective POF has been in existence for one or more years and is submitting financial information

---

[65]IRC §4942(j)(3); Reg. §53.4942(b)-1(b). See Section 15.5, *Tax Planning and Compliance for Tax-Exempt Organizations* and IRS Publication 578.

to evidence its qualification. A new POF answers *Yes* on line 4 to express its intention to qualify even though it has had no activity. Then it submits either (1) an affidavit or opinion of an attorney, CPA, or accounting firm with expertise in tax matters that contains sufficient facts to likely satisfaction of the tests; or (2) its own statement describing proposed operating (and financial information) that indicate it can qualify as a POF. This version of Form 1023 omits a schedule for this purpose; see Appendix C for the suggested format included in the model application for a POF.

(c) Line 5a–i: Public Charities

A wide variety of organizations qualify as public charities under IRC §509(a)(1). The (a)(1) category includes all those organizations tax-exempt under IRC §501(c)(3) that are described in IRC §170(b)(1)(A)(i)–(vi), which lists organizations eligible to receive deductible charitable contributions. The definition is complicated and rather unwieldy because it includes six distinctly different types of exempt entities.[66] Because of the code's design, the categories are labeled with numerical letters.

The first five categories of §509(a)(1) include those organizations that perform what is called *inherently public activity*. The first three achieve public status because of the nature of their activities without regard to sources of funds with which they pay their bills—even if they are privately supported. The fourth and fifth are closely connected with governmental support and activities. Last, but certainly not least, because it includes a wide variety of charities, are those organizations that balance their budgets with the revenue from many sources. They must receive at least $33\frac{1}{3}\%$[67] of their annual revenues from supporters, such as the United Way, American Red Cross, governmental grants, or individual and business donors that provide no more than 2% of their support. They must meet a mathematically measured and contribution-based formula and can be referred to as *donative* public charities.[68] If facts and circumstances concerning the organizations board, public involvement, and fundraising efforts indicate it is a broad-based charity, an organization may request public status under §509(a)(1) with as little as 10% public support.[69]

---

[66]The Tax Court characterized the regulations under this section as "almost frighteningly complex and difficult" in *Friends of the Society of Servants of God v. Commissioner*, 75 T.C. 209, 213 (1980)

[67]Reg. §1.170A-9(e)(3); can be as little as 10% if a facts and circumstances test applies.

[68]A consideration of the rules that pertain to both donative public charities and service provider entities is important to understanding public charities. A comparison of the differences between the categories can be found in Section 11.5, *Tax Planning and Compliance for Tax-Exempt Organizations*.

[69]Reg. §1.170A-9(e)(3); see Chapter 5.2 in this book.

Lastly, service-providing organizations receiving fees from the provision of goods and services may qualify under §509(a)(2).

One of nine boxes must be checked by organizations claiming to qualify for public charity status. Organizations qualify as public for one of three reasons. Types (a)–(c) are public by virtue of the activities they conduct. They may claim a definitive ruling from their inception, as long as they evidence their primary activity will be to operate as a church, school, or hospital. Types (d) and (f) are public because they exclusively benefit another type of public entity. Types (g),(h) and (i) may qualify as public based upon their revenue sources.

(i) Line 5a. Churches complete Schedule A and must meet a strict 14-point test.[70]

(ii) Line 5b. Schools must complete Schedule B.[71]

(iii) Line 5c. Hospitals and medical research groups must complete Schedule C.[72] A cooperative hospital service organization under §501(e) also checks this box but does not file Schedule C.

(iv) Line 5d. Supporting organizations check this blank and complete Schedule D.[73]

(v) Line 5e. Entities testing for public safety, not qualified to receive deductible contributions.[74]

(vi) Line 5f. A supporting organization benefiting a college or university that is a governmental unit (this type must also be publicly supported but does not seek an advance ruling).

(vii) Line 5g. Publicly supported organizations qualifying because their support comes from a broad segment of the public must meet the mechanical tests illustrated in Appendix D of this book.

(viii) Line 5h. Service-providing organizations must satisfy the tests shown in Appendix E of this book.

---

[70]Outlined in 3§2, *Tax Planning and Compliance for Tax-Exempt Organizations*.

[71]Outlined in 5§1, *Tax Planning and Compliance for Tax-Exempt Organizations*.

[72]See Section 4.6, *Tax Planning and Compliance for Tax-Exempt Organizations*.

[73]See Section 11.6, *Tax Planning and Compliance for Tax-Exempt Organizations*.

[74]See Section 11.7, *Tax Planning and Compliance for Tax-Exempt Organizations*.

(ix) Line 5i. Entities that are not sure which category they qualify under check this blank to request the IRS decide the correct status.

(d) Line 6a. Request for Advance Ruling

A newly created organization with limited operational history may receive an advance ruling that it will be treated as a qualifying public charity during its first five years of existence. An organization requests an advance ruling by checking the box on Line 6a. A separate form, Form 872A, has now been eliminated. By signing the application with this box checked, the organization agrees to extend the statute of limitations for payment of the PF excise tax on investment income earned during the advance ruling period, if public status is not achieved.

A report of support sources is submitted on Form 8734 five years later, within 90 days after the period ends, to allow the IRS to make a final determination of public charity status.[75] Failure to file can result in reclassification as a private foundation. Placing a tickler on a reliable person's or firm's calendar is very important. Donors may rely upon the public status determination until the IRS publishes a notice of revocation, unless the donors are in a position to cause, or be aware of, the organization's failure to qualify.

(e) Line 6b: Definitive Ruling

As the name connotes, a *definitive ruling* is essentially an immediate determination of qualification for public status. Those organizations listed on lines 5a–f, classified as public entities by virtue of their activity, normally receive a definitive ruling. A line 5g or line 5h charity that has completed its first tax year of at least eight months may also receive a definitive ruling if it has had sufficient financial activity to allow the IRS to make that determination. A more than one-year old organization that has not yet received sufficient public support can request an advance ruling. See Chapter 5 for more discussion of an advance versus a definitive ruling and factors to consider that are not presented in the IRS instructions.

---

[75]Because the support test calculation is submitted each year in Schedule A of Form 990, elimination of Form 8734 has also been strongly suggested. See Section 5.3 of this book for issues about reporting back to the IRS.

(i) Line 6b(i): Under Two Percent Donors. In calculating the §170(b)(1) (A)(vi) test, donations of no more than 2% of the includible support (line 8 in Part IX) are counted as public donations. Donations from governmental units and certain other public charities are fully included. Unusual grants (line 12 of Part IX) are excluded from the calculation. A list of the >2% donors is requested; if there are none, the box for this line is checked.

(ii) Line 6b(ii), Nonpublic Support. In calculating the §509(a)(2) test, donations and exemption function revenues (lines 1, 2, and 9 of Part IX) received from disqualified persons[76] are not counted [item 6b(ii)(a)]. A list of donations from such persons is requested. Amounts received from purchasers of exempt functions services and goods (line 9 of Part IX) that exceed 1% of total fees are also not counted as public support [line 6b(ii)(b)]. A list of the names and amounts received from both (a) and (b) categories must be attached.[77]

(f) Line 7: Unusual Grants

Substantial contributions and bequests from disinterested persons that due to their size adversely affect classification as a public charity may possibly be excluded from the support tests. The instructions ask for an explanation of the grant, and list only three attributes of an unusual grant:

- Unusual
- Unexpected
- Received from an unrelated party

The regulations contain six other factors that might also be added to the description:

- The gift is a liquid asset, such as cash or marketable securities, rather than difficult to dispose of and not pertinent to the organization's exempt activities.
- There are no materials restrictions on the use of the gift.
- The gift is added to an endowment fund or pays for a capital item (not used for normal operations).
- An active, and successful, fundraising program exists.

---

[76]Defined in Section 1.1 of this book.

[77]See Section 11. of *Tax Planning and Compliance for Tax-Exempt Organizations,* and Appendices D and E for examples of public support calculations.

- A representative and broadly based governing body controls the organization.

- Prior to the receipt of the unusual grant, the organization qualified as publicly supported.

Not all factors must be present. An applicant claiming it has or will receive unusual grants that should be excluded from the public support test calculation is asked to attach a list of names, dates, amounts, and an explanation of how the gifts qualify as *unusual* applying the criteria listed above.

2.11 PART XI—USER FEE INFORMATION

This part reminds applicants that Form 1023 will be not be processed until a user fee is paid. The normal fee is $500. If the average annual gross receipts (total amount shown on line 10 of Part IX) have not or will not exceed $10,000 over a four-year period, the fee is reduced to $150. The check or money order in payment of the fee must be made payable to the U.S. Treasury. A caution that fees could be changed refers applicants to http://www.irs.gov/ or (877) 829-5500 to check the current fee. Since it has not changed for many years, this caution signals a potential increase to the author. The fee can be paid with a bank check without delaying the process. Previously applications submitted with a check were held until the check cleared the bank so that submission of a cashier's check was previously recommended to speed the process.

CHAPTER 3

The Schedules

The new version of Form 1023 continues the practice of providing a separate set of questions to solicit additional information from churches, schools, hospitals, supporting organizations, housing for elderly and low-income persons, and scholarship programs—and the qualification standards for such applicants are unique. Omitted from this version are separate schedules for a private operating foundation and a childcare organization. The schedule that had been titled Successor to for-Profit Organization has been retitled in the new Form 1023: Successors to Other Organizations. Page 6 in the previous version of Form 1023, titled Technical Requirements, has become Schedule E for Late Filers (27 months beyond formation).

The following types of organizations must answer specific questions to enable IRS specialists to satisfy themselves that the organization can qualify for such a category of §501(c)(3) exemption.

- Schedule A: Churches
- Schedule B: Schools, College and Universities
- Schedule C: Hospitals and Medical Research Organizations
- Schedule D: IRC §509(a)(3) Supporting Organizations
- Schedule E. Organizations not Filing Form 1023 within 27 Months of Formation.
- Schedule F: Homes for the Elderly or Handicapped and Low Income Housing

- Schedule G. Successors to Other Organizations
- Schedule H: Organizations Providing Scholarship Benefits, Student Aid, etc., to Individuals
- The Schedules can be found in Exhibit G.

3.1 SCHEDULE A—CHURCHES

To preserve the separation of church and state, churches are granted automatic exemption and actually need not file Form 1023. Nonetheless, groups not formed as a part of the established Judeo-Christian religions may need to file the form. Proof that the IRS considers the organization a church may be necessary to obtain local and state exemptions and other privileges of tax-exemption.

This schedule's 17 questions are designed to ascertain whether the applicant church meets the IRS's 14-part test displayed below. Questions on lines 8d, 15, and 16 probe for private benefit to the church's creators in order to uncover churches that have been created as a tax scam.

(a) What is a Church?

The special tax privileges afforded to a church include:

- No annual filing of Form 990 is required, and a significant degree of abuse must be present for the IRS to seek to examine a church.
- Parsonage allowances are exempt from income tax, and ministers have other special employment tax rules.[1]
- A church qualifies under §509(a)(1) and §170(b)(1)(a)(i) as a public charity without regard to its sources of support.

The challenge for a nontraditional religious group seeking recognition as a church begins with the fact that there is no definition of church in the tax code or regulations under §501(c)(3). The brief definition found in the regulations on contributions and unrelated business income reads as follows:

The term *church* includes a religious order or organization if such entity (1) is an integral part of a church, and (2) is engaged in carrying out the functions of a church.

---

[1]See Chapter 25, *Tax Planning and Compliance for Tax-Exempt Organizations.*

What constitutes proper church conduct is to be determined by the tenets and practices of a particular religious body constituting a church. The functions of a church include only two activities according to the regulations:[2]

- Ministration of sacerdotal functions (communion, marriages, and so on)
- Conduct of religious worship

The decision in an early case noted that Congress left the definition of church to the "common usage of the word."[3] A religious order, organized under the auspices of the Roman Catholic Church to train members to teach in Catholic schools, was found not to be a church. Similarly an organization formed by missionaries affiliated with different Christian churches was not a church.[4] The court declared that the Congress used *church* more in the sense of a denomination or sect than in a generic or universal sense, though to be considered a church, organizational hierarchy or buildings were not required, yet a congregational component is necessary. A judge said, "A man may, of course, pray alone, but in such a case, though his house may be a castle, it is not a church. Similarly, an organization engaged in an evangelical activity exclusively through the mails would not be a church."

(b) 14-Part Test

The IRS provides a list of characteristics that a church must possess to gain church status. The criteria are not exclusive; any other facts and circumstances that may bear on the organization's claim for church status may be considered.[5] The instructions to Schedule A say that "although it is not necessary that each of the criteria be met, a congregation or other religious membership group is generally essential. A church includes mosques, temples, synagogues, and other forms of religious organizations." The attributes listed in the 14-part test are:[6]

1. Distinct legal existence
2. Recognized form of worship and creed (written version requested)

---

[2]Reg. §1.170-2(b)(2) and §1.511-2(a)(3)(ii).

[3]*De La Salle Institute v. U.S.*, 195 F. Supp. 891 (N.D. Cal. 1961.

[4]*Chapman v. Commissioner*, 48 T.C. 358 (1967).

[5]2003 EO CPE Text, *Public Charity or Private Foundation Status*, by Virginia G. Richardson and John Francis Reilly.

[6]Exempt Organizations Handbook (IRM 7751) §321.3.

3. Definite and distinct ecclesiastical government

4. Distinct religious history

5. Formal code of doctrine and discipline

6. Membership not associated with any other church or denomination (provide number)

7. Organization of ordained ministers

8. Ordained ministers selected after completing prescribed courses of study

9. Literature of its own (writings that inform beliefs of church)

10. Places of worship

11. Regular congregation (persons who regularly attend and take part in services)

12. Regular religious services (report days and times)

13. Sunday schools for religious instruction for youths

14. Schools for preparation of its ministers

Determinations are not made simply on the basis of the number of characteristics the organization possesses. Given the variety of religious practices, a determination of what constitutes a church is inherently unquantifiable. The 1981 IRS CPE text cited items 5, 7, 11, 12, and 13 as the most significant attributes.

> At a minimum, a church includes a body of believers or communicants that assembles regularly in order to worship. Unless the organization is reasonably available to the public in its conduct of worship, its educational instruction, and its promulgation of doctrine, it cannot fulfill this associational role.[7]

The first case to apply the 14-point test concluded, at a minimum, an organization failed the test because it did not have a body of believers that assembled regularly in order to worship.[8] A religious publishing organization without membership also failed.[9] An organization founded to spread "God's

---

[7] 1981 EO CPE Text at 44.

[8] *American Guidance Foundation, Inc. v. U.S.*, 490 F. Supp. 304 (D.D.C. 1980). Lack of membership, or a congregation, also caused failure of the test in several cases; *see Church of the Visible Intelligence That Governs the Universe v. U.S.*, 14 Ct. Cl. 55 (1983), *Universal Bible Church, Inc. v. Commissioner*, T.C.M. 1986-170, *Church of Eternal Life and Liberty, Inc. v. Commissioner*, 86 T.C. 916 (1986).

[9] *First Church of Theo v. Commissioner*, T.C.M. 1989-16.

love and hope throughout the world" also did not qualify as a church.[10] It conducted bimonthly programs with prayers and gospel music in an amphitheater. It built a small chapel for unsupervised meditational activities and individual prayer; but it did not conduct religious services in the chapel. Although the society argued that the test discriminated against new, rural, and poor religious organizations, the court agreed that the IRS's standard for qualification as a church was appropriate. The failure to meet three particular criteria influenced the court:

- The society did not have a regular congregation and its attendees did not consider it their church.

- It did not ordain ministers but held services conducted by guest ministers.

- It did not conduct school for religious instruction of the young.

A television ministry known as the Foundation for Human Understanding had its status as a church challenged by the IRS because about one-half of its budget went to pay for broadcasts to its 30,000 regular listeners. Its estimated total audience was 2 million persons. There was no question that television broadcasts alone do not qualify an organization as a church. This entity, however, conducted regular services at two locations for 50 to 350 persons under the guidance of an ordained minister. Religious instruction was provided and it had a "distinct, although short, religious history." Therefore, the court felt it possessed most of the criteria to some degree, the critical factors were satisfied, and church classification was permitted.[11] The court also noted the diversity of religious beliefs and First Amendment rights must be respected in identifying a church.[12]

A group forming a church may face IRS reluctance to approve such status before it has written liturgy, regular services, a congregation, and sufficient proof that it will meet the 14-part test. Nevertheless, a TIP in the instructions states: "You may request classification as a church at a later date after you establish a congregation or other religious membership group." Such a group, therefore, can either delay application (within the 27-month deadline) or apply to qualify as a religious organization with an advance ruling with plans to submit information once church activity commences.

---

[10]*Spiritual Outreach Society v. Commissioner*, 91-1 USTC 50, 111 (8th Cir. 1991).

[11]*Foundation for Human Understanding v. Commissioner*, 88 T.C. 1341 (1987).

[12]For more information see IRS Publication 1828, *Tax Guide for Churches and Religious Organizations*, that is available on their website, http://www.irs.gov/pub/irs-pdf/p1828.pdf. This 28-page publication surveys the applicable tax rules in an understandable, thorough, and helpful fashion.

3.2 SCHEDULE B—SCHOOLS, COLLEGES, AND UNIVERSITIES

Schools, like churches and hospitals, occupy a privileged category of §501(c)(3) organizations that are classified as public charities because of the activity they conduct rather than the sources of their revenue. This schedule is complex and addresses three issues:

- Does the applicant plan activities that meet the definition of a school (line 1 of Section I)?

- Will the school follow a racially nondiscriminatory policy (lines 4–6 of Section I and lines 1–6 and 8 of Section II)?

- Will the financial transactions result in private benefits to insiders (line 2 of Section I and line 7 of Section II)?

(a) Meaning of Term *School*

The definition of educational organizations that qualify for classification as a school is very specific and embodies what can be thought of as the three *regulars*. The first question in Schedule B asks if the applicant requesting status as a school is a formally organized entity and possesses the following attributes:[13]

- Regular faculty of qualified teachers and curriculum

- Regularly enrolled body of students

- Regular place where the educational activities are carried on

The second question of Section I asks if the presentation of formal instruction is the primary function of the school. The term includes primary, secondary, preparatory, and high schools, and colleges and universities. Schools publicly supported by federal, state, and local governments qualify for this category by definition, and in most cases also qualify as governmental units.[14] A school possessing this duality might seek recognition of §501(c)(3) qualification to facilitate fundraising. When the state school has tax-exempt status, however, it is subject to the organizational and operations tests. Advisors for a school can test its qualification for this category by studying the IRS

---

[13]Reg. §1.170A-9(b)(1).

[14]Reg. §1.170A-9(b). See discussion in Section 10.2, *Tax Planning and Compliance for Tax-Exempt Organizations*.

examination guidelines for colleges and universities developed for use by its specialists.[15] Factors considered by the IRS to determine that a school can continue to qualify can also be used as a reference for organizations seeking recognition as a school. The IRS addressed the special issues involved in the qualification of Charter schools in its year 2000 training materials.[16]

Early childhood education centers have qualified.[17] Boards of education that employ all the teachers in a school system and that supervise all the schools in a district have qualified.[18]

For an organization that conducts both regular school activity and non-school activities, the latter must be merely incidental. A university can operate a museum or a theatre and remain a school. A museum's art school, however, does not make the museum a school.[19]

(b) Proof for Regular Tests

All four elements must be present to achieve recognition as a school: regular faculty, students, curriculum, and facility. The instructions ask for proof of qualification by requesting the following:

- List of curriculum including required courses of study, dates, and times courses are offered
- Evidence that the applicant has a regular faculty of qualified teachers includes certification by the appropriate state authority or successful completion of required training
- Records of regular attendance of members of the student body
- Evidence of a place where the exclusively educational activities occur—either a lease or a deed to the property
- Signed agreement, if any, with state or local government under which the applicant operates and receives funding

The word *curriculum* was loosely construed in a ruling that permitted an elementary school to qualify despite the fact that it had no formal course

---

[15]EO Examination Guidelines Handbook 7(10)69.

[16]2000 EO CPE Text, Chapter J.

[17]*Michigan Early Childhood Center, Inc. v. Commissioner*, 37 T.C.M. 808 (1978); *San Francisco Infant School, Inc. v. Commissioner*, 69 T.C. 957 (1978); Rev. Rul. 70-533, 1970-2 C.B. 112.

[18]*Estate of Ethel P. Green v. Commissioner*, 82 T.C. 843 (1984).

[19]Rev. Rul. 76-167, 1976-1 C.B. 329.

program and espoused an open learning concept.[20] However, leisure learning classes, in the eyes of the IRS, do not present a sufficiently formal course of instruction to qualify as a school. Lectures and short courses on a variety of general subjects not leading to a degree or accreditation do not constitute a curriculum.[21] Also, invited authorities and personalities recognized in the field are not considered to be members of a regular faculty.[22] The duration of the courses is not necessarily a barrier. An outdoor survival school, whose classes lasted only 26 days but were conducted with regular teachers, students, and course study, was classified as a school despite the fact that part of the facilities it used were wide open spaces.[23] A home school providing private tutoring is not a school for this purpose.[24] Likewise, a correspondence school was not approved under this section because it lacked a physical site where classes were conducted.[25]

(b) Race Discrimination

Schools must adopt and practice, in good faith, policies prohibiting racial discrimination. A statement that it has a racially nondiscriminatory policy must be included in its charter, bylaws, or other governing instrument or be effective by resolution of its governing body. The tone, beginning with the question on line 4 of Section I, reflects the well-established policy that a school cannot qualify for tax-exemption if it does practice racial discrimination. School brochures, catalogs, and other printed matter that are used to inform prospective students of the school's programs must contain a policy statement as it relates to admission applications, scholarships, and program participation. The statistical information reflecting the racial composition of the student body requested in Section II, lines 5 and 6, must be continually maintained by a school to evidence the existence of its nondiscrimination policy. A prospective school is asked to provide an estimate of the racial mix of its student body.

Schools must complete a special page of Form 990, Schedule A, to inform the IRS that it continues to meet this requirement each year. The nondiscrimination policy must be made known, or publicized, to all segments of the gen-

---

[20]Rev. Rul. 72-430, 1972-2 C.B. 105.

[21]Rev. Rul. 62-23, 1962-1 C.B. 200.

[22]Rev. Rul. 78-82, 1978-1 C.B. 70.

[23]Rev. Rul. 73-434, 1973-2 C.B. 71.

[24]Rev. Rul. 76-384, 1976-2 C.B. 57.

[25]Rev. Rul. 75-492, 1975-2 C.B. 80

eral community served by the school. A school that, in fact, has currently en-rolled students of racial minority groups in meaningful numbers may be ex-cused from the media publicity requirement. Form 5578 is due to be filed by schools that are not required to file Form 990, primarily including church schools that qualify as an integrated auxiliary of a church.[26] Some denomina-tions file this form on behalf of their schools.

A private school that adopted a nondiscrimination policy in connection with seeking application for recognition of its exemption as an educational or-ganization was denied exemption when the subsequent information revealed that it, in fact, did discriminate—it failed the good faith test.[27] The school was established concurrently with court-ordered desegregation plans and no African-American student had ever been admitted. The facts of this case imply the circumstances that the IRS asks about in Section II, line 7b.

In 1980, a district court issued an injunction presuming any private school formed in Mississippi at the time of court-ordered public school inte-gration was created with a racially discriminatory purpose and could not qualify for tax exemption. A published exemption letter indicates how a Mis-sissippi school, which lost its exemption under the injunction, regained ex-empt status subject to the following conditions:[28]

- The school adopts a nondiscriminatory admission policy.
- It takes positive steps to recruit black students.
- It provides the IRS, for a period of three years, information concerning the racial composition of its student body, faculty, and students re-ceiving financial aid.

3.3 SCHEDULE C—HOSPITALS AND MEDICAL RESEARCH ORGANIZATIONS

The promotion of health as a charitable pursuit is conspicuously absent from the tax code and regulations, which contain no guidance on the requirements to be classified as pursuing this very important charitable purpose. The crite-ria for exemption, illustrated by the questions in Schedule C, distinguish char-itable entities from privately owned businesses that provide identical health

---

[26]See Blazek, *IRS Form 990 Tax Preparation Guide for NonProfits*.

[27]*Calhoun Academy v. Commissioner*, 94 T.C. 17 (1990).

[28]Exemption letter dated April 7, 1993 to Rebul Academy, Inc., citing *Green v. Connelly*, 330 F. Supp. 1150 (D.D.C. 1971), aff'd sub nom. *Coit v. Green*, 404 U.S. 997 (1971).

services. The fact that for-profit and nonprofit healthcare providers operate in a somewhat indistinguishable fashion complicates this category of exemption. A qualifying hospital or medical research organization must be able to prove it will operate to benefit a charitable class rather than the healthcare professional that create and operate it. The instruction TIPS highlight the two issues of primary concern to the IRS: (1) admission policies that allow treatment of those that cannot pay and (2) a board that is representative of the community served. The issues primarily involve private inurement:

- Who benefits from the healthcare entity's operations: the sick or the private doctors and investors who are in control?
- What recruitment incentives are provided to physicians?

The rules are constantly evolving; any organization seeking qualification under this category must carefully study the instructions, the latest developments, and/or seek the assistance of an experienced professional.[29] Additionally answers to these questions should be coordinated with those provided in Part V and VIII.

A hospital does not qualify as a charitable organization merely because it promotes health. Over the years, there have been controversies between the IRS, courts, healthcare organizations, and the doctors who staff them seeking to find a suitable definition for a healthcare entity that qualifies as a charitable one. In 1974, a court had to remind the IRS that promotion of health is a charitable purpose listed under the law of charitable trusts.[30] The instructions say a hospital provides medical care and medical education and research, including treatment of a physical or mental disability or condition on an inpatient or outpatient basis. Therefore, a rehabilitation institute, community mental health facility, or drug treatment center can be a hospital. A home for children or the aged, a hospice, blood bank, or convalescent home is not a hospital.

The guidance on this subject is complex. After first arguing a charity hospital had to provide care to the indigent, the IRS compromised with a community benefit standard.[31] A healthcare organization is expected to satisfy most of the following factors to be considered as charitable:

---

[29]The IRS now publishes articles in its Continuing Professional Education Technical Instruction Program on their Internet site, rather than in book form, once a year. In recent years, there has annually been an extensive article on healthcare exemption issues. The 2004 CPE series includes *Health Care Provider Reference Guide* by Janet E. Gitterman and Marvin Friedlander.

[30]*Eastern Kentucky Welfare Rights Organization v. Simon*, 506 F.2d 1278, 1287 (D.C. Cir. 1974).

[31]Rev. Rul. 69-545, 1969-2 C.B. 117.

- Control by a community-based board with no financial interests in the hospital
- Open medical staff with privileges available to all qualified physicians
- Emergency room open to all, unless this duplicates services otherwise provided in the community
- Provision of public health programs and extensive research and medical training
- No unreasonable accumulation of surplus funds
- Limited funds invested in for-profit subsidiaries
- High level of receivables from uncollected billings

The IRS states, "Operating a full-time emergency room open to all regardless of a person's ability to pay is strong evidence that a hospital is operating to benefit the community."[32] In *Geisinger Health Plan*, the court said a hospital must "do more than design a subsidized dues program for the indigent." The facts indicated a minuscule amount of services were provided to indigents.[33] Again, in the more recent *Redlands Surgical Services* case, the tax court thought one of the indicators of community benefit is whether the organization provides free care to indigents.[34] The objective of the community benefit standard is to ensure that adequate health care services are actually delivered to those in the community who need them.[35]

3.4 SCHEDULE D—IRC §509(A)(3) SUPPORTING ORGANIZATIONS

Charitable organizations that are sufficiently responsive to and controlled or supervised by or in connection with one or more public charities are classified as public charities, even if they are privately funded. Essentially, *supporting organizations* (SO) dedicate all of their assets to one or more public charities that need not necessarily control them—although a supporting organization cannot be controlled by disqualified persons.[36] This schedule seeks information to prove that the requisite control and relationship exists between the newly created

---

[32]Rev. Rul. 83-157, 1983-2 C.B. 94; Field Service Advice 200110030.

[33]*Geisinger Health Plan v. Commissioner*, 985 F.2d 1210, 1216 (3rd Cir. 1993).

[34]*Redlands Surgical Services v. Commissioner*, 113 T.C. No. 3, *aff'd* 242 F.3d 904 (9th Cir. 2003).

[35]Rev. Rul. 83-157, 1983-2 C.B. 94, *The Wiley Nonprofit Series* includes Thomas K. Hyatt and Bruce R. Hopkins, *The Law of Tax-Exempt Healthcare Organizations*, 2nd ed. (New York: John Wiley & Sons, 2001); see also 4§6, *Tax Planning and Compliance for Tax-Exempt Organizations*.

[36]See Section 1.3 in this book for its discussion of disqualified persons and private inurement; see Section 11.6, *Tax Planning and Compliance for Tax-Exempt Organizations*.

organization and the public charity it is organized to support. Beneficiary organization(s) must be specified, but can be changed under certain conditions. This flexibility makes SOs popular with benefactors who want neither to create a private foundation nor to make an outright gift to an established charity. The rules are not entirely logical and the regulations are quite detailed and extensive. The questions answered on Schedule D are instructive. An SO must meet three unique organizational and operational tests as follows:

- It must be organized to, and at all times thereafter, operate exclusively for the benefit of, to perform the functions of, or to carry out the purposes of one or more specified public charities (purpose test).

- It must be operated, supervised, or controlled by or in connection with one or more public charities (organizational test).

- It cannot be controlled, directly or indirectly, by one or more disqualified persons.[37]

The IRS rather reluctantly issues public charity status to SOs.[38] Applicants seeking recognition as a Test 3-type of SO must verify whether a Senate Finance Committee proposal to eliminate the "operated in connection with" test has been enacted. Test 3 embodies the *responsiveness* and *integral part* tests explored on lines 4, 5, and 6. The rules for qualification as a supporting organization are complex and the distinctions sometimes unclear, as indicated by the Code designations. Again the author suggests that an applicant seeking this classification of public charity seek the assistance of a qualified professional.

3.5 SCHEDULE E—ORGANIZATIONS NOT FILING FORM 1023 WITHIN 27 MONTHS OF FORMATION

The statute says an application for recognition of exemption is due to be filed 15 months after the end of the month the organization is formed.[39] Tax exemption is recognized effective as of the date on which the organization is *formed*, or the date that it becomes a legal entity,[40] if the Form 1023 is timely filed. Since 1992, an automatic 12-month extension is available simply by

---

[37]IRC §509(a)(3)(A).

[38]2001 IRS CPE Text, Chapter G, "Control and Power: Issues Involving Supporting Organizations, Donor Advised Funds, and Disqualified Person Financial Institutions."

[39]IRC §508. See discussion in Section 1.4 of this book.

[40]Rev. Proc. 90-27, 1990-1, CB. 514.

checking a box (Part I, line 11) and filing within 27 months of the organization's formation. A *reasonable action and good faith standard* applies to allow the extension. This schedule begins with the questions on lines 1–4 asking if the organization was not previously required to seek exemption because it was a church, organization with gross receipts less than $5,000 annually, a subordinate in a group exemption, or created before October 9, 1969. Line 5 must be carefully considered if the prior answers were *No*.

The important issue in this part is whether §501(c)(3) recognition will be effective from the date of formation, rather than the filing date, because the application is treated as timely filed. Note applications should always be sent by certified mail, return receipt requested, or a designated commercial delivery service to obtain proof of the filing date. When the 27 months have passed, the deadline can be extended if the interests of the government are not prejudiced by the extension. Voluntary filing within any period of time before the IRS discovers the failure is presumed to evidence good faith.[41] If the IRS discovers that the application is late,[42] retroactive recognition may still be permitted. A *Yes* answer to line 5 requests such an extension. The IRS asks that the applicant to prove it acted reasonably and in good faith by submitting the following information:

- "You filed Form 1023 before we discovered your failure to file."
- "You failed to file because of intervening events beyond your control." That is, illness of responsible party or loss of records due to a natural disaster.
- "You exercised reasonable diligence but you were unaware of the filing requirements." The complexity of your filing and experience in these matters is taken into consideration.
- "You reasonably relied on written advice from us."
- "You reasonably relied on the advice of a qualified tax professional who failed to file or advise you to file Form 1023."

The efforts made by the applicant to determine filing requirements should be described. The names and occupation or titles of the persons contacted, the approximate dates, and the substance of the information obtained can be provided to explain how and when the organization learned, or failed to learn, about the requirements.

---

[41]Rev. Proc. 92-85, 1992-2, C.B. 490; also see IRS Publication 557, *Tax-Exempt Status for Your Organization*.

[42]Because, for example, Forms 1099 are filed to report interest income paid to a nonprofit that files no Form 1120 or 990. Filing Form SS-4 to obtain an identification number for a new nonprofit organization does not register a requirement to file Form 990 or 1120 in the IRS systems. Federal income tax filing requirements are based instead on the receipt of income.

Line 6a asks whether the applicant is eligible to receive a definitive ruling and refers back to line 6 of Part X. An organization that expects its future financial activity to differ significantly from its past answers *Yes* to line 6b and provides a projection on line 7. This information should be coordinated with Pat IX where the actual financial activity to date is reported.

Lastly, line 8 is checked *Yes* by an applicant that is filing 27 months beyond the date of formation and not eligible for an extension of filing time. A late-filing organization can request tax-exempt status as a §501 (c)(4) organization for the period between formation and the effective §501(c)(3) exemption date to avoid income tax on income received prior to the effective date of exemption. What is not avoided is the fact that voluntary contributions received by a §501(c)(4) organization prior to the filing date may not be eligible to be treated as charitable donations.

3.6 SCHEDULE F—HOMES FOR THE ELDERLY OR HANDICAPPED AND LOW-INCOME HOUSING

Homes for the elderly or handicapped are eligible for tax exemption as charitable organizations only if they meet the special needs of the elderly or handicapped. Their special needs must be met with residential facilities designed to meet their physical, social, recreation, healthcare, and transportation needs. Section I of this schedule requests a description of the type of housing provided—apartment complex, condominium, cooperative, or private residences—and the nature of the facility—assisted living, continuing care, nursing home, or low income facility. A detailed description of the type of housing, copies of application forms, description of methodology for making the public aware of the facility, and a sample residency or ownership contract or agreement are requested on lines 1–5. Lines 6, 7, and 9 ask about relationships with builders, managers, or promoters of the facility that might result in private inurement. The form reminds applicants to "make sure the answer is consistent with the information provided in Part VIII, lines 7 and 8." The information must evidence a dedication of assets to serve the elderly or handicapped rather than the organization's officials and their businesses.

(a) Charitable Policies

The lines of Section II, Schedule F, address the following specific policies that a home must maintain to qualify as charitable. These lines also ask that a copy of any printed materials informing the public about the policies be attached:[43]

- Have a commitment to maintain in the residence any person who becomes unable to pay his or her regular charges, or do all that is possible to make other suitable arrangements for their care (line 3)
- Provide its services at the lowest feasible cost, taking the facts and circumstances of the home into account (for example, cost of facility or wages in the area)
- Charge fees affordable by a significant segment of the elderly population so as to evidence benefit to the community in which it is located (line 2c)
- Adopt policies to protect itself financially and enable it to meet its obligation not to expel aged residents who become unable to pay

A home may require its applicants to make a deposit upon admission of an amount of assets calculated to secure their care.[44] A home might also permit residents to establish trusts, the income of which is payable to the home during the resident's life. Income from trusts is exempt function income to the home because it is paying the fees.[45] Charitable status can be allowed for a senior citizen home that allows full-paying elderly to keep their assets, subject to a requirement that such assets could be used, if necessary, to supplement income to meet the monthly charges.[46]

(b) Services Provided

Line 1 of Section II asks who qualifies for the housing and how they are selected. Line 2 seeks details about entrance and maintenance fees to satisfy the tests outlined above. On line 3, the applicant describes arrangements the organization has or will have with welfare agencies, sponsoring organization, or others to assist residents who become unable to afford to remain in the facility. Lines 4 and 5 ask how healthcare, physical, emotional, and other needs of the residents are provided.

---

[43]Rev. Rul. 79-18, 1979-1 C.B. 152.

[44]Priv. Ltr. Rul. 9225041.

[45]Rev. Rul. 81-61, 1981-1 C.B. 355.

[46]Priv. Ltr. Rul. 9307027.

(c) Low Income Housing

Section III surveys qualification as a charitable low income housing provider, a subject on which the instructions are silent. Acquisition and maintenance of low-income housing units has long been considered a charitable activity because it accomplishes several purposes: relieving the suffering of the poor, eliminating discrimination, relieving the burdens of government, combating community deterioration, and promoting social welfare.[47] The IRS adopted a baseline, or minimum level of low-income residents, of 75% in 1993 when factors indicating whether the housing project serves a charitable class were added to the Internal Revenue Manual.[48] The standards were effective prospectively enabling existing units to continue to be tax-exempt as operated. The standards were again revised in 1995, and in 1996, the safe harbor proposals were finalized in a revenue procedure.[49] It behooves applicants to show they conform to the following safe harbor rules, particularly when the more lenient facts and circumstances might apply.[50]

- At least 75% of the units are occupied by residents who qualify as low-income individuals.

- Either 20% of the residents renting units must qualify as very low income, or 40% of the units must be occupied by residents whose income does not exceed 120% of the area's very low-income limit.

- Up to 25% of the units may be rented at market rates to persons whose income exceeds the low-income limit.

A project not meeting the safe harbor percentages can still seek to qualify for exemption by demonstrating qualification through facts and circumstances, such as combating community deterioration, lessening the burdens of government, and eliminating discrimination and prejudice. The facts and circumstances that can be considered include:

---

[47]Rev. Rul. 70-585, 1970-2 C.B. 115.

[48]See also Priv. Ltr. Rul. 9311034 for application of the guidelines to a charity formed by a commercial real estate company for the purposes of buying low-income housing from the Resolution Trust Company; *Housing Pioneers, Inc. v. Commissioner*, T.C. Memo. 1993-120, aff'd (9th Cir. June 20, 1995); and Tech. Adv. Memos. 200218037 and 200151045.

[49]Rev. Proc. 96-32, 1996-20 I.R.B. 1.

[50]IRS Announcement 95-37, 1995-20 I.R.B. 18. See the 1996 IRS EO CPE Text, Topic B, *Recent Developments in Housing Regarding Qualification Standards and Partnership Issues,* by Lynn Kawecki and Marvin Friendlander and 2003 IRS EO CPE Text, *Housing Partnership Agreements*, by Mary Jo Salina and Robert Fonterose.

- A substantially greater percentage of residents than required by the safe harbor with incomes up to 120% of the area's very low-income limit
- Limited degree of deviation from the safe harbor percentages
- Limitation of rents to ensure that they are affordable to low-income and very low-income residents
- Participation in a government housing program designed to provide affordable housing
- Operation through a community-based board of directors, particularly if the selection process demonstrates that community groups have input into the organization's operations
- The provision of additional social services affordable to poor residents
- Relationship with an existing §501(c)(3) organization active in low-income housing for at least five years, if the existing organization demonstrates control
- Acceptance of residents who, when considered individually, have unusual burdens such as extremely high medical costs that cause them to be in a condition similar to persons within the qualifying income limits, in spite of their higher incomes
- Participation in a home ownership program designed to provide home ownership opportunities for families that cannot otherwise afford to purchase safe and decent housing
- Existence of affordability covenants or property restrictions (line 3b)

3.7 SCHEDULE G—SUCCESSORS TO OTHER ORGANIZATIONS

There are many aspects of a conversion from a for-profit to a not-for-profit entity that can be troublesome, particularly when the potential tax-exempt organization is inheriting obligations that exceed the assets it receives. Line 1 of this schedule asks such an applicant to "explain why you took over the activities or assets of a for-profit organization or converted from for-profit to non-profit status." Lines 3–5 pertain to all applicants completing this form and ask for all the facts: names and federal identification numbers of organizations and parties, ongoing relationships that will occur, and details as to assets and obligations transferred. For all applicants, line 6 asks for a description of assets transferred, whether by sale or gift, with details of how the value of each asset was determined, an explanation of any restrictions placed on use or sale of the assets, and a copy of agreements of sale or transfer.

(a) Nonprofit to Nonprofit Succession

Line 2 asks for an explanation of the relationship to the other organization that resulted in its creation when the applicant is a successor to, or creation of, a nonprofit organization. A reportable succession occurs when the new organization has taken over 25% or more of the fair market value of another organization. Line 2e asks a similar question, "Explain why you took over the activities or assets of another organization." Line 2b asks for the predecessor's tax status.

When both the successor and predecessor are §501(c)(3) organizations, recognition of the new entity is customarily trouble-free. A good example of such a situation is the creation of a supporting organization to receive and hold investment assets of an existing §501(c)(3) public charity. A museum might create a separate educational organization to conducts its museum school. On the other hand, when a §501(c)(6) business league or §501(c)(4) civic association establishes a charitable arm to conduct its educational programs, the applicant should provide evidence of the procedures it will follow to maintain separation of the two entities with different tax-exemption categories. The IRS focus is to assure the new organization performs a charitable function and operate separately from its non-charitable affiliate.

Situations in which the applicant itself or its predecessor previously applied or failed to receive approval for or lost tax-exemption are the subject of lines 2c and 2d. When the answers are *Yes*, an explanation of "how the application was resolved" or "corrections made to re-establish exemption" are requested. Copies of the IRS denial or revocation letters can be provided with a careful explanation of the facts that led to denial or loss of exemption and steps that have or will be taken to remedy the situation. A common example is an organization that voluntarily decided not to take steps requested by the IRS for approval of its original application.[51]

(b) For-profit to Nonprofit Conversions

A nonprofit organization created to receive the assets and operations of a for-profit entity has the burden of proving that the transfer creates no unacceptable benefits to the owners of the for-profit entity. The issue is whether the owners of the for-profit predecessor reap any gain from the takeover. Private benefit may be indicated by the terms of the deal, the price being paid for the

---

[51]See Section 4.4 of this book for a discussion of situations that create disputed applications.

predecessor's assets, liabilities being assumed, proposed excessive rental for privately owned facilities or equipment, and other benefits to insiders or controlling individuals. Lines 5–9 of this schedule fish for such factors.[52]

Line 5 asks if the applicant has a "working relationship" with persons listed in line 4—the governing officials of the predecessor. In either case (non-profit to nonprofit or for-profit to nonprofit), a "working relationship" must result in fair and reasonable financial transactions that do not provide unreasonable compensation, fees, or purchase prices to private persons. This information should be coordinated and may simply be referenced if full disclosure of agreements with business-owners are disclosed in Part V.

Lines 6 and 7 pertain to the property and associated liabilities transferred by gifts or sale of assets to successor charitable organization. The answer to these lines should be coordinated to evidence that the new charity is receiving assets in excess of any liabilities it is assuming or agreeing to pay to acquire the assets. Starting with attachment of any written contracts or agreements, the applicant must attach a detailed report in response to *Yes* answers to these questions. The value of the assets should be demonstrated with appraisals and other evidence of value of properties received. The amount and terms of any liabilities transferred with an explanation of how the debt was determined and to whom it is due is requested on line 7. There must be no indication that the new charity is ending up in a negative financial position as a result of the transaction. This information must be coordinated with the responses provided in Part V regarding transactions with insiders.

Ongoing relationships between the for-profit and new charitable non-profit in the form of leases of property to or from the for-profit, must be explained for *Yes* answers to lines 8 and 9. Again the issue of excessive financial benefits to private persons is at issue. Information, including comparable rental rates or competitive bids might be provided to evidence the fairness of the proposed arrangements and must be coordinated or referred to Part V.

3.8 SCHEDULE H—ORGANIZATIONS PROVIDING SCHOLARSHIPS, FELLOWSHIPS, EDUCATIONAL LOANS, OR OTHER EDUCATIONAL GRANTS, AND THE LIKE TO INDIVIDUALS

A charitable organization that provides scholarships, grants, loans, and other distributions for educational purposes complete this schedule. The responses to the questions must evidence the following:

---

[52]See Section 20.7, *Tax Planning and Compliance for Tax-Exempt Organizations,* for further discussion of the issues involved in such a conversion.

- Awards are made on a nondiscriminatory fashion in terms of racial preference.
- Awards are based on need and/or merit.
- Awards are paid to a charitable class in terms of being available to an open-ended group, rather than to preselected individuals.

All applicants must complete lines 1–7 of this part to describe plans to award educational grants. The purpose is to establish that individual grants will be made in an objective and nondiscriminatory manner without favoritism to certain individuals, particularly not to family members of founders, directors, trustees, or other interested parties.

(a) Evidence of Charitable Class

The responses to questions on this schedule must reflect plans to award educational grants to members of a charitable class. The lines of this schedule are mostly clear as to the information sought and the import. A significant amount of detail is requested:

- How grantees are selected
- How grants will be awarded
- How much will be granted
- How awards will be renewed
- How the grants will serve charitable purposes

The instructions ask for additional information not noted for certain lines that pose the following issues:

- *Line 1c.* Describe any other loan institutions involved in your program. A relationship with a for-profit lender must be carefully described to prove the program does not contain terms that provide benefit to the for-profit entity.
- *Line 1d.* Explain whether you publicize your program to the general public or to another group of possible recipients, such as those in a specific geographic area. Will newspaper advertisements be placed; will school district and community groups be notified? As discussed in responses to Part VI, lack of public announcements could evidence the grant program will not benefit a sufficiently broad group of persons to constitute a charitable class.

- *Line 2*. Do you keep case histories of grant recipients? This answer should be *Yes*. "Adequate records and case histories showing the name and address of each recipient pursuant to Revenue Ruling 56-304" is requested.

(b) Private Foundations

Private foundations are not allowed to make educational grants to individuals until their plan for awarding such grants is approved by the IRS. Line 1 of Section II of this schedule[53] requests information to request such approval for two types of awards:

- *§4945(g)(1)*. Grants to an individual as a scholarship or fellowship for study at an educational institution
- *§4945(g)(3)*. Grants or loans to individuals for travel, study or other similar purpose to enhance a particular skill of the grantor or to produce a specific product

The answers to questions on lines 2 and 3 of Section II must be *Yes*. These are requests for an agreement on the part of the PF to adhere to the rules imposed on educational awards paid by IRC §4945(g). The question on line 4 pertains only to what is referred to as *company scholarship plans*. A foundation created by a for-profit company that awards scholarships to the company employees and/or their children must meet very specific mathematical tests. The plan cannot operate to benefit company executives and highly-paid persons. Nor can the plan represent a compensatory arrangement. Applicants may wish to seek professional assistance as it regards measuring qualification of a plan to award grants to private company personnel and their children.[54]

---

[53]Public charity applicants respond *N/A* to line 1 of Section II.
[54]See Section 17.5(e), *Tax Planning and Compliance for Tax-Exempt Organizations*.

CHAPTER 4

Getting a Positive Determination

Once Form 1023 is completed with adequate information to allow the IRS to evaluate qualification, the next requirement is patience. In the past, it normally required 60 to 120 days to receive a determination letter. If the reviewer questions any of the facts or circumstances or denies the organization's eligibility for exemption, some methods of responding are more effective than others.

4.1 APPLICATION PROCESSING SYSTEM

An IRS notice of receipt, Notice 3367 (see Appendix K), may be expected to arrive within 21 days from the date the IRS receives the application. A document locator number is assigned. Subsequent inquiries about the application should be referenced with the case number. Failure to receive such a notice means that something is amiss and the IRS Exempt Organization Group office in Cincinnati should be contacted at (877) 829-5500. This is particularly important if timely filing is an issue. At this point, however, the case has not been assigned to a particular technical specialist.

In 2004, it took from 60 to 75 days to approve a complete and unquestioned application—such cases are said to be *merit closed*. Applications that involve requests from the Exempt Organization Group office in Cincinnati for additional information took up to 120 days for receipt of the approved determination letter. (In spring 2005, it was taking 120 to 180 days.) The timing also depends upon the IRS's workload, which is usually heavier in the fall, at year-end tax planning time, when many organizations are formed in order to receive deductible gifts from substantial contributors that want proof of charitable status. A delay also occurs when applications are sent to other IRS offices because the Cincinnati workload is too high. With the new form, these time frames may change.

4.2 BEST CASE SCENARIO

In the best-case scenario, the application is approved without questions, or **merit closed**, and a Determination Letter (Appendix G) is received within a month or two. This letter may be the single most important piece of paper that an exempt organization possesses. It is often the document furnished to state and local authorities to obtain their recognition of tax exemption. Without it, contributions from some sources, such as private foundations, are impossible.

4.3 WHEN QUESTIONS ARE ASKED

IRS exempt organization specialists may seek additional information. Non-substantive amendments can often be made during this time and do not alter the effective date of the application in most cases.[1] For example, the agent might recommend one of the following tactics:

- Amend the charter's dissolution or purpose clause to specifically name IRC §501(c)(3) in order to restrict distributions and activities to §501(c)(3) purposes. In some states, the standard nonprofit charter acceptable to the state does not contain this restriction distinction, which is necessary to meet the federal requirements.[2]

- Change the public status category from §509(a)(2) to §509(a)(1) or vice versa. The IRS policy is to grant §509(a)(1) status in all cases when the organization qualifies for both types of public charity status.[3]

- Change level of planned lobbying activity and propose classification as a §501(c)(4) rather than a §501 (c)(3) organization.[4]

---

[1]Rev. Proc. 90-27, 1990-1 C.B. 514; IRS Pub. 557 (revised July 2001), p. 4.

[2]The organizational test is discussed in Section 1.3 of this book and Section 2.3, *Tax Planning and Compliance for Tax-Exempt Organizations*.

[3]See Sections 2.10 and 5.6 of this book.

[4]See Section 2.8(b) of this book.

- Revise proposed compensation to or other financial transactions with insiders.[5]

What if the IRS reviewer suggests the applicant is not eligible for exemption under §501(c)(3)? It is extremely important to request the "basis in law" for suggestions made by the IRS reviewer. It is useful to realize the published revenue rulings used as precedents in making IRS determinations are sometimes not relevant to a contemporary situation. A reviewer's personal bias and experiences may also play a part in his or her opinion. For example, if it is suggested the organization should have independent outsiders (not staff) on the board, ask for a citation to IRS procedures or policy, particularly if officials are not compensated. Question why an artist's press must satisfy the requirements found in a revenue ruling pertaining to a spiritual publishing company. Why does a discussion group have to meet the qualifications for a school? Why can't the organization question the policy of the president sending troops to fight in a foreign land, as long as the materials presented are unbiased?

Consider seeking the assistance of a knowledgeable professional if the exempt organization is unwilling to make a change or is skeptical about the need for the change. If funds are not available to hire a professional, a volunteer may be found through a public service agency. While most IRS exempt organization reviewers are well trained, helpful, and cooperative, the organization seeking exemption must remember that the rules are broad and vague. The specialists apply published revenue rulings to judge a newly established organization, even though it is unique and distinguishable. In these cases, the applicant may find knowledgeable advisers particularly useful.

If the examiner suggests a negative answer, the applicant should submit a brief, or rebuttal, indicating the reasons and citing authority for the position that the organization does qualify for tax-exemption. Before an adverse determination is issued, the case will be reviewed. The brief can make it easier for the reviewer's superior to overturn the recommendation for denial. The policies followed by the examiners are contained in IRS Manual 7751: *Exempt Organizations Handbook*, Manual 7752: *Private Foundations Handbook*, and the annual *Exempt Organizations Continuing Professional Educational Technical Instruction Program*.

Occasionally, the determination specialist at the Exempt Organization Group in Cincinnati is unable to consider an application and will refer it to the National Office for determination. Such a referral is made automatically for any type of organization whose exempt status is pending in litigation or is

---

[5]See Section 2.5 of this book.

under consideration within the IRS. In the past, hospital reorganizations, publications with advertising, mail-order churches, and other controversial exemptions have been sent to Washington.[6]

4.4 DISPUTED CASES

When the IRS specialist cannot make a favorable determination, there are a number of steps an organization can take. The choice of alternatives is guided primarily by the strength of the case. If the organization clearly qualifies for exemption, but the examining agent apparently misunderstands the facts and circumstances, an appeal may be indicated.

(a) Appeal

Allow the examiner to issue an adverse report denying exemption and follow the appeal procedure. A protest of the determination may be filed within 30 days from the date of the adverse letter. Request a conference in the Appeals Office. See IRS Publication 557, page 5, for more information, and seek competent counsel. Proper appeal procedures must be followed in order to be later able to file the appeal in court.

(b) Amend

If the reasons for denial are curable and negotiations remain amicable, the EO can request (or the IRS may offer) the opportunity to amend the application, altering planned projects or fundraising activities to eliminate the ones not considered appropriate for a tax-exempt organization. Usually, the EO examiner gives the organization 60 to 90 days to reform itself and essentially resubmit the application. When the EO has already commenced operations and the changes are substantive, the exemption may be granted only prospectively, from the effective date of the changes in operations.

(c) Withdraw

An application can be withdrawn at any time before issuance or denial of a determination letter. The effects of withdrawing an application are outlined

---

[6]See Section 1.6 of this book.

by the IRS under three different scenarios. As a rule, the withdrawal cancels previous notice, the time period prior to withdrawal is lost, and a resubmitted application is treated as a new filing, so that exemption will be effective prospectively from the date of resubmission. The IRS considered the following possibilities:

- *Scenario 1.* Form 1023, seeking §501(c)(3) status, is filed 10 months after the organization is created, but is withdrawn. Two years later it is operating, the application is resubmitted, asserting that the organization had operated as exempt from "day one" and, therefore, that exemption may be allowed from the original date of filing.
- *Scenario 2.* Same facts as Scenario 1, except upon withdrawal, the organization requests classification as a §501(c)(4) from date of formation through date of resubmission.
- *Scenario 3.* A subordinate member of a group exemption withdraws from the group and, within fifteen months of withdrawal, submits an independent application.

In the first scenario, under the old rules, exemption was effective only from the date of resubmission. Due to the automatic extension policy,[7] a resubmission within 27 months of the organization's creation can be granted retroactively. The second example now applies for organizations resubmitting 27 months or more beyond date of organization. In the third scenario, exemption is effective from the original inclusion in a group continuing on with new timely filing when such notice was required (can be 27 months).[8]

Withdrawal may be appropriate when an EO has failed to file income tax or other returns that were required of it as a nonexempt organization. Upon withdrawal, it has not been customary for notification to be made to the Internal Revenue Service Center. Upon denial, however, the Center is notified. Procedurally, it is desirable to voluntarily file delinquent returns and to request relief from any penalties for failure to file, rather than wait to be notified of the need to file. A principal officer or representative with a power of attorney must make a written withdrawal request. No information submitted to the IRS will be returned, but such information can be used by the IRS in any subsequent examination of the organization's returns or requests.

---

[7]Discussed in Section 3.5 of this book.

[8]See Section 1.8 of this book.

4.5 DECLARATORY JUDGMENT

When all administrative remedies have been exhausted in negotiating a positive determination of exempt status and the IRS persists in denying exemption, a declaratory judgment may be requested. See IRS Publication 556 for appeals to the courts. It is important to remember that the correct steps must be taken first—and court *is the last resort*.

CHAPTER 5

Advance versus Definitive Rulings

In response to a Form 1023 application, the IRS determines whether the organizational and operational plans entitle it to be classified as an exempt organization. A determination is also made as to whether the organization is a public charity or, instead, a private foundation based on information submitted in Part X of Form 1023. Public status is based either upon the organization's sources of support and revenue or upon its activities. Churches, schools, hospitals, and other types of charities listed in lines 5a–f of Part X qualify as public due to the nature of their activities without regard to their support sources. Such applicants receive what is called a *definitive ruling*. Organizations listed in lines 5g–I of Part X, which seek qualification as a public charity based on the nature of their financial support, must indicate if they qualify for and are requesting a definitive ruling of public status by checking the box on line 6b. Box 6a is checked instead by an organization requesting an advance ruling. The categories of public charities are discussed in Section 2.10 of this book. The calculations are illustrated in Appendices D and E.[1]

---

[1]Chapter 11 of *Tax Planning and Compliance for Tax-Exempt Organizations* presents detailed descriptions of the various categories of public charities, explains the types of revenues qualifying as public support, compares the categories, and illustrates the tests.

5.1 DEFINITIVE RULING

A definitive, or final, determination as to public status for a charitable organization listed in §170(b)(1)(A)(i)–(v) and §509(a)(3)—a church, school, hospital, governmental unit, or supporting organization—can be made before the organization has any financial activity based upon the nature of its activity. Those organizations classified as public charities for reasons of their sources of support can only be issued a final determination after they have completed a tax year of at least eight months.

The choice of fiscal year is therefore important for an EO seeking advance or immediate determination of public status based upon sources of support. For example, an entity incorporated in June, which adopts a year ending December 31, cannot seek a definitive ruling if it files before its next succeeding year-end. It would have to choose a year ending between December and April to receive a definitive ruling. The EO can subsequently change its tax year if it is useful for financial reporting and programming standpoint.[2]

Second, to achieve approval for a definitive ruling, the EO's sources of support and revenue and activities must be clearly and unquestionably suitable for public status. If the ratios are too close or if fundraising plans are insufficient, the IRS may prefer to make a tentative, or advance, ruling described below.

A final determination is only effective so long as the organization's sources of support continue to provide it with the requisite one-third public support ratio. A continuing four-year moving average of support is calculated annually throughout the organization's life when it files Form 990 as noted in Section 5.5 of this chapter, Change of Status and Failures to Qualify. There is essentially a two-year time lag between the year that the ratio is deficient and the year the organization becomes classified as a private charity. Public support status for the current year is based upon the preceding year's ratio. Except for a contributor or grantor that has reason to know their support will cause loss of public status, donors are entitled to rely upon the IRS determination of public charity status until notice of the change is published in the *Internal Revenue Bulletin* as discussed in Chapter 6 of this book.

5.2 ADVANCE RULING

An advance ruling is a determination that proposed activities and structure qualify for classification as a charitable entity; but it is tentative as it regards

---

[2]See the rules for changing a tax year in Section 18.3(d), *Tax Planning and Compliance for Tax-Exempt Organizations*.

public versus private foundation status. An advance ruling is effective for the exempt organization's first five tax years.[3] For all purposes, the exempt organization is considered a public charity during the advance period. Contributors who were not in a position to know that the EO would not qualify for public status are entitled to calculate their income tax deductions based on public status. Eligibility for advance determination is indicated when one of two very different factors exist:

- First tax year is less than eight months.
- Contributions and activities during the startup phase contain insufficient public revenues.

The information furnished to the IRS by a newly created organization must indicate that the organization can reasonably be expected to meet the public support tests. The pertinent facts and circumstances that might be taken into account by the IRS include:[4]

- *Composition of governing body.* Is the board made up of persons representing a broad segment of the community in which the charity is organized? Does it include persons having specialized knowledge relevant to the EO's activities? Is the entity a membership organization anticipating a broad base of individual members? A small board made up of major donors indicates private status.

- *Initial funding.* Will the EO's initial funding come from a few contributors or from many? Are the anticipated projects the type that will attract a broad base of support, or are they attractive only to a few contributors? Initial funding from only a few contributors must be offset with anticipated public appeal.

- *Fundraising plans.* Are concrete solicitation programs implemented or anticipated to reach a broad group of contributors? Are there firm funding commitments from, or working relationships established with, civic, religious, charitable, or similar community groups?

- *Government or public grants.* Will part of the revenue be received from governmental agencies or public charities in support of its community services, such as slum clearance and employment opportunity programs?

---

[3]Reg. §1.509(a)(3)(d) provides for a two-year advance period because it was adopted prior to passage of the Deficit Reduction Act of 1984 by which Congress extended the period to five years.
[4]Reg. §1.509(a)3(d)(3).

- *Membership dues.* Will the EO enroll a substantial number of persons in a community, area, profession, or field of special interest as contributing members?

- *Exempt function revenues.* Does the EO plan to conduct exempt activities for which it will charge, such as theater performances, job counseling, or educational classes?

5.3 REPORTING BACK TO THE IRS

It is important to emphasize the temporary nature of an advance determination, because failure to report at the end of the advance period results in reclassification as a private foundation. An organization holding advance recognition as a public charity must report back to the IRS's Tax Exempt and Government Entities (TE/GE) Division in Cincinnati at the end of its first five years of operation. Under current rules, the organization is to report within 90 days of an advance determination's ending date. Since this step is critical to ongoing public status, this filing deadline should be verified and noted on a responsible person's calendar. Once the advance-ruling period has ended, funders, particularly private foundations, may be unwilling to make grants to the organization until it has received verification of the new determination of its public status. It is therefore extremely important that Form 8734 (see Appendix F) be filed as soon as possible after the advance-ruling period ends. The form is due 90 days from the end of the fiscal year, so that many organizations must file Form 8734 with unaudited numbers. Even though the financial data is subject to later review by the accountants, it is usually desirable to submit the preliminary numbers. At this time only revenue information is submitted to show whether the requisite base of public support to receive a final determination of its non-PF status. If the amount of contributions or exempt function revenues is sufficient, the IRS issues a definitive, or permanent, ruling. As noted below, however, such status can be changed if the organization fails to subsequently retain its public support levels.

The General Accounting Office (GAO), in a 1990 report entitled *Tax Administration: IRS Can Improve Its Process of Recognizing Tax-Exempt Organizations*, suggested that the IRS expand its advance-ruling follow-ups to include consideration of activities. The GAO report criticizes the IRS for making no effort to look at the manner in which the charities use their support, and recommends that the advance-ruling process be expanded to include a review of activities. The GAO observed that "the expenditures data as well as revenue data could provide IRS insight into whether the organization is fulfilling its exempt purpose and whether there are other potential issues, such as private inurement or unreported unrelated business income." To date, this recommendation has not been enacted by the IRS. During Senate Finance Committee hearings on tax-exempt organizations in the summer of 2004, it was suggested all tax-exempt organizations be evaluated every five years.

5.4 FAILURE TO MEET SUPPORT TESTS AT END
OF ADVANCE-RULING PERIOD

If the exempt organization fails to meet the public support test and is reclassified as a private foundation after its advance period, it must pay the §4940 excise tax on investment income, plus interest, for income earned during the advance-ruling period. Even if the EO receives sufficient public support, failure to report back to Cincinnati can cause the organization to be reclassified as a private foundation unless relief is allowed for reasonable causes.

5.5 FAILURE TO SUBSEQUENTLY MEET SUPPORT TEST

An organization classified as a public charity might also fail the support test in a year beyond the initial advance-ruling period due to changes in its support. Importantly, the loss of public charity status is not immediate; if the financial tally submitted with the organization's 2004 return (reflects support for the years 2000—2003) was less than the requisite one-third, public status continues through the year 2005. If a material change in the organization's sources of support not caused by an unusual grant occurs, a five-year testing period may apply.[5] Until a change of status is announced in the Internal Revenue Bulletin, contributors are entitled to rely upon the latest IRS letter as described in Chapter 6.

A charitable organization classified as a public charity for reasons of its revenue sources should monitor its ongoing qualification with projections of future support. Fundraising targets should be set with a view both to the annual spending needs of the organization and also to meeting the $33\frac{1}{3}$ percent test. Because the test is based on a four-year moving average, the results can vary significantly from year to year. Say, for example, a new organization was successful in soliciting donations for an endowment fund from a significant number of supporters in its first year of existence. Or for a different but similar situation, assume a new organization was created to receive the assets of a nonprofit hospital (meeting the §170(b)(1)(A)(vi) tests) that sold its healthcare operations to another entity. The funds are to be invested to raise

---

[5]Reg. §§1.170A-9(e)(4) and 1.509(a)3(c)(1)(ii).

funds to support public health programs. In both cases, the support in its first year of existence results in a very high public support level of 80 percent. The donations in the first year affect (and improve) the ratio for four years. It is in the fifth year, when they are not counted, that the ratio could fall to below 33⅓ percent (when most of the funding comes from investment income).

An organization that expects its support level may fall below 33⅓ percent can take a number of steps. First, the accounting classification of its revenues and the category of public support should be evaluated to be sure that they are correct. It is often the case that an organization can qualify as both a §509(a)(1) and a §509(a)(2) organization. For that reason, the calculations should be made under both categories. Accounting standards treat some government grants as fee-for-service revenue that under tax standards can be treated as donations.[6] Next, past donations can be reviewed to determine if any major grants can be excluded from the calculation because they possess most of the eight criteria for an "unusual grant."[7] For §509(a)(1) classification purposes only, the organization would also review its satisfaction of the nine criteria for meeting the "facts and circumstances" test.[8] Both of these tests involve some amount of subjective judgment as to qualification. The organization must show that, despite its receipt of large donations from a few sources, the organization is responsive to and designed to benefit a broad public constituency and is not controlled by private individuals.

5.6 CHANGES OF PUBLIC CHARITY STATUS

Sometimes the sources of a public charity's support change, causing it to fail to qualify under one category or another. When the change indicated is reclassification from §509 (a)(1) to §509 (a)(2) or vice versa, the organization has a choice to make. At a minimum, the correct category should be checked on its Form 990, Schedule A, and appropriate financial information completed on that page to evidence the correct category. Submission of information on the annual return has not solicited a response from the IRS in the past. As a result the organization finds itself with a determination letter that indicates a public charity category different than its Form 990—a situation unacceptable to some private foundation funders. To notify the IRS of the change and request a new determination letter, the organization must choose to seek overt IRS approval by sending the information to the IRS TE/GE Division in Cincinnati, Ohio.

---

[6]Discussed in Section 11.5(c), *Tax Planning and Compliance for Tax-Exempt Organizations*.

[7]See discussion for Part X in Section 2.10 and elsewhere in Chapter 2 of this book.

[8]Reg. §.170A-9(e)(3).

CHAPTER 6

Reliance on Determination Letter

After a positive determination letter is issued, the exempt organization can rely upon the IRS's approval of its exempt status as long as there are no substantial changes in its purposes, operations, or character. Absent such changes, the IRS only revokes exemption due to changes in the law or other good causes. Therefore, it is very important that Form 1023 accurately portrays the proposed operations and that changes be reported annually on a Form 990. Now that the filing deadline is essentially 27 months from the date an EO is established, it may sometimes be useful to delay filing until adequate plans are developed to file an accurate application—if collection of revenues from donors and other exemptions can await the delay.

Contributors, however, cannot necessarily rely upon the IRS's original determination of overall exempt status and qualification for public charity status dated sometimes in the past. A critical question for givers and grant makers to publicly supported §501(c)(3)s, particularly private foundations, is whether an organization's status is the same as originally stated in its determination letter.

6.1 CHECKING CURRENT STATUS

Current status can be requested by calling the IRS Exempt Organization Group office in Cincinnati at (877) 829-5500. The number is often busy. If the call involves an organization with an expired advance ruling period, the

Customer Service representative will provide no information about current status until Form 8734 has been approved. The issues a private foundation faces in this situation are discussed in Appendix L of this book, *Compliance Monitoring,* by Jeffrey D. Haskell, Senior Vice President, Foundation Source. Alternatively, two different IRS publications—Publication 78 and *Internal Revenue Bulletin*—are available on the Internet and can be searched.[1]

The first place to check on the status of a §501(c)(3) organization is the IRS master list of exempt organizations, Publication 78, *Cumulative List of Organizations Described in IRC §170(c) of the Internal Revenue Code of 1986.* This publication lists most of the currently qualifying §501(c)(3) organizations and indicates their public or private status. The list is issued annually with semi-annual updates and includes organizations qualifying according to the IRS master file.

Searching Publication 78 on the IRS website is not always easy. Because the database contains over 300,000 names, searching for an organization with a commonly used word in its name, such as *institute* or *charitable*, can result in a large number of responses, particularly if it is located in a major city. For a successful search, it is, therefore, important to use the unique portion of an organization's name and sometimes to omit the location. Some organizations make a search impossible when they function under a different name than that listed on their IRS file. There seem to be somewhat random reasons why organizations are listed. Often, modest organizations that do not file Forms 990 are not included. Although not always the case, name and address corrections reported on Forms 990 are not necessarily entered into the master database.

The second place to check is the *Internal Revenue Bulletin.* Revocation of exemption and removal from the list is reported to the general public in this weekly bulletin in a "deletions list." Until the IRS communicates a deletion, contributors are entitled to rely upon Publication 78 unless the contributor was responsible for or aware of the EO's loss of such status.[2] When the IRS failed to publish notice in the Bulletin when it revoked a school's exemption, the Tax Court ruled that mere omission of the school's name from Publication 78 was sufficient notice.[3]

Alternatively, one can search the web site of http//www.guidestar.org. This site registers updates from the IRS weekly and may, therefore, be more current than Publication 78. The site displays Forms 990 and 990-PF and for a

---

[1] To check Publication 78 and *Internal Revenue Bulletin*, visit http://www.irs.gov/charities/.

[2] Reg. §§1.170A-9(e)(4) and 1.509(a)-3(c)(1)(iii); Rev. Proc. 82-39, 1982-17.

[3] *Estate of Sally Clapton*, 93 T.C. 25 (1989).

fee, a function now called "Charity Check" can be accessed to verify the public charity status of a grant applicant.

It is important to remember that the reliance cushion is different for insiders or donors who are in a position to be aware of organizational changes. For them, the change in status can be effective retroactively to the time the change occurred. A private foundation making a grant to another organization whose revocation has not been announced can rely upon the determination letter, unless the public charity is controlled by the PF.[4]

6.2 NAMES MISSING FROM PUBLICATION 78

Absence from the list does not necessarily mean that the entity has lost its exempt status. In the past, the IRS excluded organizations that had not filed annual Form 990 for two years. This policy omits a significant group of charities, including churches and their affiliates, state colleges and universities, subordinates under a group exemption, and those not technically required to file Forms 990 because their annual gross revenue is under $25,000. The United States Catholic Conference and some state universities, among others, have specifically sought group exemptions, despite the fact that filing is not required, to assure their inclusion in Publication 78.

Individuals and organizations must complete a thorough investigation of a proposed grant recipient's tax status and cannot rely totally upon inclusion in or exclusion from Publication 78. The IRS has reinforced its policy that omission from Publication 78 is sufficient notice of loss of exemption. If the omission of nonfilers from the list continues, obtaining proof of exempt status for those organizations will be burdensome. Form 990-EZ can be filed annually by organizations with gross revenue under $25,000 to avoid this problem; only the top portion of the first page is completed for such entities.

6.3 CONTACT THE IRS

A call to the IRS Exempt Organization Group in Cincinnati, Ohio at (877) 829-5500 may yield an answer. This number reaches a customer service representative that has the ability to look up an organization on the master list. Knowing the federal identification number of the organization makes the

---

[4]Rev. Proc. 89-23, 1989-1 C.B. 844.

process easy. Name searches don't always yield the right answer due to the alphabetizing method or some change in the name since recognition.

An organization that cannot locate its determination letter or has one evidencing an expired advance-ruling period can also call to request verification of its continued exempt status and a new letter stating their qualification.[5]

---

[5]See Chapter 18, *Tax Planning and Compliance for Tax-Exempt Organizations*, for more information regarding communication with the IRS, when to report back to the IRS, and the consequences to donors and tax filing status of an organization that loses its exemption.

CHAPTER 7

State Tax Exemptions

Many states—as well as local government entities—allow exemption from some or all of their income, franchise, licensing fees, property, sales, or other taxes for religious, charitable, and educational organizations and other Section 501(c) organizations. The process for obtaining such exemptions varies with each state and locality. Each new tax-exempt organization should obtain current information and forms directly from the appropriate state or local authorities.

In Texas, for example, the state filing schedule starts when a nonprofit charter is filed with the Secretary of State. There is no filing or registration for trusts or unincorporated associations. A status report is next filed with the Comptroller of Public Accounts, indicating which category of federal exemption is being sought. No formal application process is required for exemption. State charitable exemption is automatically granted when the exempt organization furnishes a copy of its federal exemption to the comptroller's office. An organization may furnish a copy of its completed Form 1023 and a letter requesting state exemption, if it desires state recognition prior to receiving the federal approval. The effective date of Texas sales and franchise tax exemption is generally the date of qualification for §501(c)(3) exemption. If the federal exemption process is delayed over a year, a franchise tax return is due to be filed and potentially a tax must be paid. An organization with less than $150,000 of annual revenue is exempt from the franchise tax. Any tax paid is refundable once the exemption is approved.

As a contrast, California has its own application for exemption—Form 3500—that is required to be filed with the Franchise Tax Board (FTB). This form is filed at the same time as the Form 1023 is filed with the IRS. The instructions for Form 3500 indicate that the FTB *may* require proof of federal exemption before it makes a ruling on state exemption. Approval of Form 3500 grants exemption from sales and franchise tax.

In New York, Form CT-247 must be filed to request exemption from franchise and sales tax. To be considered tax-exempt, the corporation must be a not-for-profit corporation, must not have stock, net earnings must not benefit any disqualified person, and it must be federally exempt under IRC §501(c)(3). Both New York and California maintain that unrelated business income is not covered under this exemption and separate forms must be filed to report and pay tax on those revenues.

Two significant cases have considered eligibility for exemption from local sales taxes. The Supreme Court decided in *Jimmy Swaggart Ministries v. Board of Equalization of California* that a sales tax could be imposed upon the sale of religious articles if it is equally imposed on other nonprofit organizations.[1] The argument, focused primarily upon the First Amendment, is protection of the free exercise of religion. In *Texas Monthly, Inc. v. Bullock*, the Supreme Court held that state sales tax exemption for religious publications violates the establishment clause of the First Amendment when religious organizations are the only beneficiaries of the exemption.[2] Most states automatically grant exemption from sales tax when federal exemption has been granted. (Consult Appendix J of this book for state-by-state sales tax exemption and annual filing information.) It is important to remember that exemptions from sales tax usually are related to an organization's purchase of items used in conducting its exempt activities. In most states, the organization is still required to collect sales tax when it makes sales of taxable goods and services.

Local property tax exemptions may also be available. An organization owning real and personal property potentially subject to tax should seek the assistance of a person knowledgeable about the rules applicable to the area in which the organization is located. Some—but not all—§501(c)(3) organizations qualify for exemption under the Texas Property Tax Code, for example. The application for exemption is filed with the Appraisal District for the county in which the property is located and must be filed within a year from the time the property is acquired. YWCAs and YMCAs have faced challenges to their local property tax exemptions in California and in Oregon, with conflicting results. The primary issue has been the level of free services furnished

---

[1] 493 U.S. 378 (1990).

[2] 489 U.S. 1 (1989).

to the needy. In Utah, a hospital system conglomerate's local property tax exemption was revoked. Tax authorities in Pennsylvania tried to revoke property tax exemptions for private colleges.

Charitable solicitation registration is required in certain municipalities and states, depending upon the level of activity. Fortunately, National Association of State Charity Officials (NAAG/NASCO) has aided in the development of a form called the Unified Registration Statement that can be used to register in all states requiring registration except Alaska, Arizona, Colorado, and Florida. Some states require other forms in addition to the URS.[3]

---

[3]See Appendix J in this book.

1023 Book List of Appendices

Appendix A Suitability Checklist

Appendix A
SUITABILITY FOR TAX-EXEMPT STATUS

A predominance of "yes" answers to the following questions indicate the proposed organization is NOT a suitable candidate for tax-exempt status or that special rules may apply. Proposed transactions with creators and board members will be thoroughly scrutinized by IRS and for private foundations may be prohibited. Chapter sections cited below from Tax Planning & Compliance for Tax-Exempt Organizations can be studied for more discussion of each issue.

1 Is a new organization necessary, or could the project be carried out as a branch of an existing organization?   Yes   No

- Life of the project is short.
- It is a one-time project with no prospect for ongoing funding.
- Project could operate under auspices of another EO.
- Duplication of administrative effort is too costly.
- Cost of obtaining and maintaining independent exemption is excessive in relation to total budget. (Ch. 18)
- Group exemption is available through a national EO. (Sec. 18.2(j))

2 Which §501(c) category of exemption is appropriate to the goals and purposes of the project?   Yes   No

- The organization participates in efforts to influence elections or otherwise participate in political campaigns. (Ch. 23)
- Purposes of the organization only be accomplished through legislative and grassroots lobbying activity. (Ch. 6 and 23)
- The organization's activities benefit a group of business persons or a social group. (Ch. 7, 8, and 9)
- Persons benefitted by the proposed activities represent a limited group rather than a charitable class. (Sec. 2.2(a))

3. Are the sources of revenue suitable for an exempt organization?   Yes   No

- Organization plans to sell goods produced by members indicating a cooperative, benefitting members not charitable class. (Sec. 2.2(e))
- A significant amount of the revenues will come from services to be rendered in competition with nonexempt businesses, such as legal services or insurance. (Sec. 21.8)
- Over half of revenues will be from unrelated businesses operated in competition with for-profit companies. (Sec. 21.4(b))
- A majority of the funding will come from a particular individual, family, or limited group of people that may require classification as a private foundation. (Chs. 11–17)

Appendix A Suitability Checklist

Appendix A, Page 2

SUITABILITY FOR TAX-EXEMPT STATUS

		Yes	No
4.	**Do the creators desire economic benefits from the operation of the organization?**		

- Transactions with related parties are anticipated. (Chs. 14–20)   _____   _____
- Proposed financial arrangements with creators will pay portion of revenues to insiders as rent, royalty, or interest. (Ch. 6)   _____   _____
- Creators wish to be paid incentive compensation based upon funds raised or profitability of the organization. (Secs. 14.1 and 20.4)   _____   _____
- Assets will be purchased and/or debts of creators assumed. (Sec. 20.8)   _____   _____
- Project will be operated in partnership with for-profit investors. (Ch. 22)   _____   _____
- Services and activities will be available to a limited group of persons or members instead of a public class.   _____   _____
- Upon dissolution of the organization, assets can be returned to creators and/or major donors. (Sec. 2.1(c))   _____   _____

Chapter sections in parenthesis refer to Blazek, *Tax Planning & Compliance for Tax-Exempt Organizations 4th Edition*, 2004, John Wiley & Sons.

Form 1023 Checklist
(Revised October 2004)
Application for Recognition of Exemption under Section 501(c)(3) of the Internal Revenue Code

---

Note. *Retain a copy of the completed Form 1023 in your permanent records. Refer to the* General Instructions *regarding Public Inspection of approved applications.*

Check each box to finish your application (Form 1023). Send this completed Checklist with your filled-in application. If you have not answered all the items below, your application may be returned to you as incomplete.

☑ Assemble the application and materials in this order:
- Form 1023 Checklist
- Form 2848, *Power of Attorney and Declaration of Representative* (if filing)
- Form 8821, *Tax Information Authorization* (if filing)
- Expedite request (if requesting)
- Application (Form 1023 and Schedules A through H, as required)
- Articles of organization
- Amendments to articles of organization in chronological order
- Bylaws or other rules of operation and amendments
- Documentation of nondiscriminatory policy for schools, as required by Schedule B
- Form 5768, Election/Revocation of Election by an Eligible Section 501(c)(3) Organization To Make Expenditures To Influence Legislation (if filing)
- All other attachments, including explanations, financial data, and printed materials or publications. Label each page with name and EIN.

☑ User fee payment placed in envelope on top of checklist. DO NOT STAPLE or otherwise attach your check or money order to your application. Instead, just place it in the envelope.

☑ Employer Identification Number (EIN)

☑ Completed Parts I through XI of the application, including any requested information and any required Schedules A through H.
- You must provide specific details about your past, present, and planned activities.
- Generalizations or failure to answer questions in the Form 1023 application will prevent us from recognizing you as tax exempt.
- Describe your purposes and proposed activities in specific easily understood terms.
- Financial information should correspond with proposed activities.

☑ Schedules. Submit only those schedules that apply to you and check either "Yes" or "No" below.

Schedule A	Yes ___ No ✔		Schedule E	Yes ___ No ✔
Schedule B	Yes ___ No ✔		Schedule F	Yes ___ No ✔
Schedule C	Yes ___ No ✔		Schedule G	Yes ___ No ✔
Schedule D	Yes ___ No ✔		Schedule H	Yes ___ No ✔

Appendix B Form 1023 for a Public Charity

☑ An exact copy of your complete articles of organization (creating document). Absence of the proper purpose and dissolution clauses is the number one reason for delays in the issuance of determination letters.

- Location of Purpose Clause from Part III, line 1 (Page, Article and Paragraph Number) **Pg 1, Art 4, Sec 4.01**
- Location of Dissolution Clause from Part III, line 2b or 2c (Page, Article and Paragraph Number) or by operation of state law **Pg 2, Art 4, Sec 4.02C**

☑ Signature of an officer, director, trustee, or other official who is authorized to sign the application.
- Signature at Part XI of Form 1023.

☑ Your name on the application must be the same as your legal name as it appears in your articles of organization.

Send completed Form 1023, user fee payment, and all other required information, to:

Internal Revenue Service
P.O. Box 192
Covington, KY 41012-0192

If you are using express mail or a delivery service, send Form 1023, user fee payment, and attachments to:

Internal Revenue Service
201 West Rivercenter Blvd.
Attn: Extracting Stop 312
Covington, KY 41011

Printed on recycled paper

129

Appendix B Form 1023 for a Public Charity

Form **2848**	**Power of Attorney**	OMB No. 1545-0150

Form 2848
(Rev. March 2004)
Department of the Treasury
Internal Revenue Service

Power of Attorney
and Declaration of Representative

▶ Type or print. ▶ See the separate instructions.

OMB No. 1545-0150

For IRS Use Only

Received by:

Name _____
Telephone _____
Function _____
Date ____ / ____ / ____

Part I **Power of Attorney**
Caution: *Form 2848 will not be honored for any purpose other than representation before the IRS.*

1 Taxpayer information. Taxpayer(s) must sign and date this form on page 2, line 9.

Taxpayer name(s) and address	Social security number(s)	Employer identification number
Hometown Campaign to Clean Up America 1111 Any Street Hometown, XX 77777-7777		44 : 4444444
	Daytime telephone number (**444**) **444-4444**	Plan number (if applicable)

hereby appoint(s) the following representative(s) as attorney(s)-in-fact:

2 Representative(s) must sign and date this form on page 2, Part II.

Name and address	
A Good Accountant **1 Main Street** **Any Town, XX 77777**	CAF No. .... **5555-55555R** Telephone No. .... **555-555-5551** Fax No. .... **555-555-5552** Check if new: Address ☐ Telephone No. ☐ Fax No. ☐
Name and address	CAF No. .... Telephone No. .... Fax No. .... Check if new: Address ☐ Telephone No. ☐ Fax No. ☐
Name and address	CAF No. .... Telephone No. .... Fax No. .... Check if new: Address ☐ Telephone No. ☐ Fax No. ☐

to represent the taxpayer(s) before the Internal Revenue Service for the following tax matters:

3 Tax matters

Type of Tax (Income, Employment, Excise, etc.) or Civil Penalty (see the instructions for line 3)	Tax Form Number (1040, 941, 720, etc.)	Year(s) or Period(s) (see the instructions for line 3)
Income	1023	2005-2006

4 Specific use not recorded on Centralized Authorization File (CAF). If the power of attorney is for a specific use not recorded on CAF, check this box. See the instructions for **Line 4. Specific uses not recorded on CAF.** . . . . ▶ ☐

5 Acts authorized. The representatives are authorized to receive and inspect confidential tax information and to perform any and all acts that I (we) can perform with respect to the tax matters described on line 3, for example, the authority to sign any agreements, consents, or other documents. The authority does not include the power to receive refund checks (see line 6 below), the power to substitute another representative, the power to sign certain returns, or the power to execute a request for disclosure of tax returns or return information to a third party. See the line 5 instructions for more information.

Exceptions. An unenrolled return preparer cannot sign any document for a taxpayer and may only represent taxpayers in limited situations. See **Unenrolled Return Preparer** on page 2 of the instructions. An enrolled actuary may only represent taxpayers to the extent provided in section 10.3(d) of Circular 230. See the line 5 instructions for restrictions on tax matters partners.

List any specific additions or deletions to the acts otherwise authorized in this power of attorney: ....
....
....
....

6 Receipt of refund checks. If you want to authorize a representative named on line 2 to receive, **BUT NOT TO ENDORSE OR CASH**, refund checks, initial here _____ and list the name of that representative below.

Name of representative to receive refund check(s) ▶

For Privacy Act and Paperwork Reduction Notice, see page 4 of the instructions.   Cat. No. 11980J   Form **2848** (Rev. 3-2004)

Appendix B Form 1023 for a Public Charity

7 **Notices and communications.** Original notices and other written communications will be sent to you and a copy to the first representative listed on line 2.

a If you also want the second representative listed to receive a copy of notices and communications, check this box   . ▶ ☐

b If you do not want any notices or communications sent to your representative(s), check this box   . . . . ▶ ☐

8 **Retention/revocation of prior power(s) of attorney.** The filing of this power of attorney automatically revokes all earlier power(s) of attorney on file with the Internal Revenue Service for the same tax matters and years or periods covered by this document. If you **do not** want to revoke a prior power of attorney, check here. . . . . ▶ ☐

YOU MUST ATTACH A COPY OF ANY POWER OF ATTORNEY YOU WANT TO REMAIN IN EFFECT.

9 **Signature of taxpayer(s).** If a tax matter concerns a joint return, **both** husband and wife must sign if joint representation is requested, otherwise, see the instructions. If signed by a corporate officer, partner, guardian, tax matters partner, executor, receiver, administrator, or trustee on behalf of the taxpayer, I certify that I have the authority to execute this form on behalf of the taxpayer.

▶ **IF NOT SIGNED AND DATED, THIS POWER OF ATTORNEY WILL BE RETURNED.**

Signature	Date	Title (if applicable)
(signature)	7-10-05	President
John J. Environmentalist	PIN Number: 5 5 5 5 5	Hometown Campaign to Clean Up America
Print Name		Print name of taxpayer from line 1 if other than individual
	Date	Title (if applicable)
Signature		
Print Name	PIN Number: ☐ ☐ ☐ ☐ ☐	

Part II   Declaration of Representative

Caution: *Students with a special order to represent taxpayers in Qualified Low Income Taxpayer Clinics or the Student Tax Clinic Program, see the instructions for Part II.*

Under penalties of perjury, I declare that:

- I am not currently under suspension or disbarment from practice before the Internal Revenue Service;
- I am aware of regulations contained in Treasury Department Circular No. 230 (31 CFR, Part 10), as amended, concerning the practice of attorneys, certified public accountants, enrolled agents, enrolled actuaries, and others;
- I am authorized to represent the taxpayer(s) identified in Part I for the tax matter(s) specified there; and
- I am one of the following:

  a Attorney—a member in good standing of the bar of the highest court of the jurisdiction shown below.

  b Certified Public Accountant—duly qualified to practice as a certified public accountant in the jurisdiction shown below.

  c Enrolled Agent—enrolled as an agent under the requirements of Treasury Department Circular No. 230.

  d Officer—a bona fide officer of the taxpayer's organization.

  e Full-Time Employee—a full-time employee of the taxpayer.

  f Family Member—a member of the taxpayer's immediate family (i.e., spouse, parent, child, brother, or sister).

  g Enrolled Actuary—enrolled as an actuary by the Joint Board for the Enrollment of Actuaries under 29 U.S.C. 1242 (the authority to practice before the Service is limited by section 10.3(d) of Treasury Department Circular No. 230).

  h Unenrolled Return Preparer—the authority to practice before the Internal Revenue Service is limited by Treasury Department Circular No. 230, section 10.7(c)(1)(viii). You must have prepared the return in question and the return must be under examination by the IRS. See **Unenrolled Return Preparer** on page 2 of the instructions.

▶ **IF THIS DECLARATION OF REPRESENTATIVE IS NOT SIGNED AND DATED, THE POWER OF ATTORNEY WILL BE RETURNED.** See the Part II instructions.

Designation—Insert above letter **(a–h)**	Jurisdiction (state) or identification	Signature	Date
b	xx	*AB Accountant*	7/10/05

Form **2848** (Rev. 3-2004)

Appendix B Form 1023 for a Public Charity

Form **1023**	**Application for Recognition of Exemption**	OMB No. 1545-0056
(Rev. October 2004) Department of the Treasury Internal Revenue Service	**Under Section 501(c)(3) of the Internal Revenue Code**	**Note:** *If exempt status is approved, this application will be open for public inspection.*

*Use the instructions to complete this application and for a definition of all **bold** items.* For additional help, call IRS Exempt Organizations Customer Account Services toll-free at 1-877-829-5500. Visit our website at **www.irs.gov** for forms and publications. If the required information and documents are not submitted with payment of the appropriate user fee, the application may be returned to you.

Attach additional sheets to this application if you need more space to answer fully. Put your name and EIN on each sheet and identify each answer by Part and line number. Complete Parts I - XI of Form 1023 and submit only those Schedules (A through H) that apply to you.

Part I Identification of Applicant

1 Full name of organization (exactly as it appears in your **organizing document**) **Hometown Campaign to Clean Up America**		**2** c/o Name (if applicable)
3 **Mailing address** (Number and street) (see instructions) **1111 Any Street**	Room/Suite	**4** Employer Identification Number (EIN) **44-4444444**
City or town, state or country, and ZIP + 4 **Hometown, XX 77777-7777**		**5** Month the annual accounting period ends (01 – 12) **06**

6 Primary contact (officer, director, trustee, or **authorized representative**)

a Name: **A Good Accountant or Lawyer**	**b** Phone: **(444) 444-4444**
	c Fax: (optional) **(444) 444-4445**

7 Are you represented by an authorized representative, such as an attorney or accountant? If "Yes," provide the authorized representative's name, and the name and address of the authorized representative's firm. Include a completed Form 2848, *Power of Attorney and Declaration of Representative*, with your application if you would like us to communicate with your representative.   ☑ **Yes** ☐ **No**   **See Attachment**

8 Was a person who is not one of your officers, directors, trustees, employees, or an authorized representative listed in line 7, paid, or promised payment, to help plan, manage, or advise you about the structure or activities of your organization, or about your financial or tax matters? If "Yes," provide the person's name, the name and address of the person's firm, the amounts paid or promised to be paid, and describe that person's role.   ☑ **Yes** ☐ **No**   **See Attachment**

9a Organization's website: **www.hometowncleanup.org**

  b Organization's email: (optional) **info@hometowncleanup.org**

10 Certain organizations are not required to file an information return (Form 990 or Form 990-EZ). If you are granted tax-exemption, are you claiming to be excused from filing Form 990 or Form 990-EZ? If "Yes," explain. See the instructions for a description of organizations not required to file Form 990 or Form 990-EZ.   ☐ **Yes** ☑ **No**

11 Date incorporated if a corporation, or formed, if other than a corporation.   (MM/DD/YYYY)   **01** / **15** / **2005**

12 Were you formed under the laws of a **foreign country?**
If "Yes," state the country.   ☐ **Yes** ☑ **No**

For Paperwork Reduction Act Notice, see page 24 of the instructions.   Cat. No. 17133K   Form **1023** (Rev. 10-2004)

Appendix B Form 1023 for a Public Charity

Part II   Organizational Structure

You must be a corporation (including a limited liability company), an unincorporated association, or a trust to be tax exempt. (See instructions.) **DO NOT file this form unless you can check "Yes" on lines 1, 2, 3, or 4.**

1 Are you a **corporation**? If "Yes," attach a copy of your articles of incorporation showing **certification of filing** with the appropriate state agency. Include copies of any amendments to your articles and be sure they also show state filing certification.   ☑ **Yes**   ☐ **No**   *See Attachment*

2 Are you a **limited liability company (LLC)**? If "Yes," attach a copy of your articles of organization showing certification of filing with the appropriate state agency. Also, if you adopted an operating agreement, attach a copy. Include copies of any amendments to your articles and be sure they show state filing certification. Refer to the instructions for circumstances when an LLC should not file its own exemption application.   ☐ Yes   ☑ No

3 Are you an **unincorporated association**? If "Yes," attach a copy of your articles of association, constitution, or other similar organizing document that is dated and includes at least two signatures. Include signed and dated copies of any amendments.   ☐ Yes   ☑ No

4a Are you a **trust**? If "Yes," attach a signed and dated copy of your trust agreement. Include signed and dated copies of any amendments.   ☐ Yes   ☑ No

b Have you been funded? If "No," explain how you are formed without anything of value placed in trust.   ☐ Yes   ☑ No

5 Have you adopted **bylaws**? If "Yes," attach a current copy showing date of adoption. If "No," explain how your officers, directors, or trustees are selected.   ☑ **Yes**   ☐ No   *See Attachment*

Part III   Required Provisions in Your Organizing Document

The following questions are designed to ensure that when you file this application, your organizing document contains the required provisions to meet the organizational test under section 501(c)(3). Unless you can check the boxes in both lines 1 and 2, your organizing document does not meet the organizational test. **DO NOT file this application until you have amended your organizing document.** Submit your original and amended organizing documents (showing state filing certification if you are a corporation or an LLC) with your application.

1 Section 501(c)(3) requires that your organizing document state your exempt purpose(s), such as charitable, religious, educational, and/or scientific purposes. Check the box to confirm that your organizing document meets this requirement. Describe specifically where your organizing document meets this requirement, such as a reference to a particular article or section in your organizing document. Refer to the instructions for exempt purpose language. Location of Purpose Clause (Page, Article, and Paragraph): **Page 1, Article 4, Section 4.01**   ☑

2a Section 501(c)(3) requires that upon dissolution of your organization, your remaining assets must be used exclusively for exempt purposes, such as charitable, religious, educational, and/or scientific purposes. Check the box on line 2a to confirm that your organizing document meets this requirement by express provision for the distribution of assets upon dissolution. If you rely on state law for your dissolution provision, do not check the box on line 2a and go to line 2c.   ☑

2b If you checked the box on line 2a, specify the location of your dissolution clause (Page, Article, and Paragraph). Do not complete line 2c if you checked box 2a. **Page 2, Article 4, Section 4.02C**

2c See the instructions for information about the operation of state law in your particular state. Check this box if you rely on operation of state law for your dissolution provision and indicate the state: _____   ☐

Part IV   Narrative Description of Your Activities

Using an attachment, describe your *past*, *present*, and *planned* activities in a narrative. If you believe that you have already provided some of this information in response to other parts of this application, you may summarize that information here and refer to the specific parts of the application for supporting details. You may also attach representative copies of newsletters, brochures, or similar documents for supporting details to this narrative. Remember that if this application is approved, it will be open for public inspection. Therefore, your narrative description of activities should be thorough and accurate. Refer to the instructions for information that must be included in your description.

Part V   Compensation and Other Financial Arrangements With Your Officers, Directors, Trustees, Employees, and Independent Contractors

1a List the names, titles, and mailing addresses of all of your officers, directors, and trustees. For each person listed, state their total annual **compensation**, or proposed compensation, for all services to the organization, whether as an officer, employee, or other position. Use actual figures, if available. Enter "none" if no compensation is or will be paid. If additional space is needed, attach a separate sheet. Refer to the instructions for information on what to include as compensation.

Name	Title	Mailing address	Compensation amount (annual actual or estimated)
John J. Environmentalist	President	1111 Any Street Hometown, XX 77777-7777	None
Jane D. Environmentalist	Secretary/Treasurer	1111 Any Street Hometown, XX 77777-7777	None
James F. Friend	Vice President	1111 Any Street Hometown, XX 77777-7777	None
Jacob Thoughtful	Director	1111 Any Street Hometown, XX 77777-7777	None
Jennifer Scholar	Director	1111 Any Street Hometown, XX 77777-7777	None

Form **1023** (Rev. 10-2004)

Appendix B Form 1023 for a Public Charity

Part V	Compensation and Other Financial Arrangements With Your Officers, Directors, Trustees, Employees, and Independent Contractors *(Continued)*

b List the names, titles, and mailing addresses of each of your five highest compensated employees who receive or will receive compensation of more than $50,000 per year. Use the actual figure, if available. Refer to the instructions for information on what to include as compensation. Do not include officers, directors, or trustees listed in line 1a.

Name	Title	Mailing address	Compensation amount (annual actual or estimated)
Andrew Organized	Executive Director	1111 Any Street Hometown, XX 77777-7777	70,000
Joan Controller	Controller	1111 Any Street Hometown, XX 77777-7777	55,000

c List the names, names of businesses, and mailing addresses of your five highest compensated **independent contractors** that receive or will receive compensation of more than $50,000 per year. Use the actual figure, if available. Refer to the instructions for information on what to include as compensation.

Name	Title	Mailing address	Compensation amount (annual actual or estimated)
Ellen Organized	Development/Public Relations	2222 Main Street Hometown, XX 77777-7777	55,000

The following "Yes" or "No" questions relate to *past, present, or planned* relationships, transactions, or agreements with your officers, directors, trustees, highest compensated employees, and highest compensated independent contractors listed in lines 1a, 1b, and 1c.

2a Are any of your officers, directors, or trustees **related** to each other through **family** or **business relationships**? If "Yes," identify the individuals and explain the relationship.   ☑ **Yes** ☐ **No**   **See Attachment**

b Do you have a business relationship with any of your officers, directors, or trustees other than through their position as an officer, director, or trustee? If "Yes," identify the individuals and describe the business relationship with each of your officers, directors, or trustees.   ☐ **Yes** ☑ **No**

c Are any of your officers, directors, or trustees related to your highest compensated employees or highest compensated independent contractors listed on lines 1b or 1c through family or business relationships? If "Yes," identify the individuals and explain the relationship.   ☑ **Yes** ☐ **No**   **See Attachment**

3a For each of your officers, directors, trustees, highest compensated employees, and highest compensated independent contractors listed on lines 1a, 1b, or 1c, attach a list showing their name, qualifications, average hours worked, and duties.   **See Attachment**

b Do any of your officers, directors, trustees, highest compensated employees, and highest compensated independent contractors listed on lines 1a, 1b, or 1c receive compensation from any other organizations, whether tax exempt or taxable, that are related to you through **common control**? If "Yes," identify the individuals, explain the relationship between you and the other organization, and describe the compensation arrangement.   ☐ **Yes** ☑ **No**

4 In establishing the compensation for your officers, directors, trustees, highest compensated employees, and highest compensated independent contractors listed on lines 1a, 1b, and 1c, the following practices are recommended, although they are not required to obtain exemption. Answer "Yes" to all the practices you use.

a Do you or will the individuals that approve compensation arrangements follow a conflict of interest policy?   ☑ **Yes** ☐ **No**

b Do you or will you approve compensation arrangements in advance of paying compensation?   ☑ **Yes** ☐ **No**

c Do you or will you document in writing the date and terms of approved compensation arrangements?   ☑ **Yes** ☐ **No**

Form **1023** (Rev. 10-2004)

Appendix B Form 1023 for a Public Charity

| **Part V** | **Compensation and Other Financial Arrangements With Your Officers, Directors, Trustees, Employees, and Idenpendent Contractors** *(Continued)* |

d Do you or will you record in writing the decision made by each individual who decided or voted on compensation arrangements? ☑ Yes ☐ No

e Do you or will you approve compensation arrangements based on information about compensation paid by **similarly situated** taxable or tax-exempt organizations for similar services, current compensation surveys compiled by independent firms, or actual written offers from similarly situated organizations? Refer to the instructions for Part V, lines 1a, 1b, and 1c, for information on what to include as compensation. ☑ Yes ☐ No

f Do you or will you record in writing both the information on which you relied to base your decision and its source? ☑ Yes ☐ No

g If you answered "No" to any item on lines 4a through 4f, describe how you set compensation that is **reasonable** for your officers, directors, trustees, highest compensated employees, and highest compensated independent contractors listed in Part V, lines 1a, 1b, and 1c.

5a Have you adopted a **conflict of interest policy** consistent with the sample conflict of interest policy in Appendix A to the instructions? If "Yes," provide a copy of the policy and explain how the policy has been adopted, such as by resolution of your governing board. If "No," answer lines 5b and 5c. ☑ Yes ☐ No **See Attachment**

b What procedures will you follow to assure that persons who have a conflict of interest will not have influence over you for setting their own compensation?

c What procedures will you follow to assure that persons who have a conflict of interest will not have influence over you regarding business deals with themselves?

Note: A conflict of interest policy is recommended though it is not required to obtain exemption. Hospitals, see Schedule C, Section I, line 14.

6a Do you or will you compensate any of your officers, directors, trustees, highest compensated employees, and highest compensated independent contractors listed in lines 1a, 1b, or 1c through **non-fixed payments**, such as discretionary bonuses or revenue-based payments? If "Yes," describe all non-fixed compensation arrangements, including how the amounts are determined, who is eligible for such arrangements, whether you place a limitation on total compensation, and how you determine or will determine that you pay no more than reasonable compensation for services. Refer to the instructions for Part V, lines 1a, 1b, and 1c, for information on what to include as compensation. ☑ Yes ☐ No **See Attachment**

b Do you or will you compensate any of your employees, other than your officers, directors, trustees, or your five highest compensated employees who receive or will receive compensation of more than $50,000 per year, through non-fixed payments, such as discretionary bonuses or revenue-based payments? If "Yes," describe all non-fixed compensation arrangements, including how the amounts are or will be determined, who is or will be eligible for such arrangements, whether you place or will place a limitation on total compensation, and how you determine or will determine that you pay no more than reasonable compensation for services. Refer to the instructions for Part V, lines 1a, 1b, and 1c, for information on what to include as compensation. ☐ Yes ☑ No

7a Do you or will you purchase any goods, services, or assets from any of your officers, directors, trustees, highest compensated employees, or highest compensated independent contractors listed in lines 1a, 1b, or 1c? If "Yes," describe any such purchase that you made or intend to make, from whom you make or will make such purchases, how the terms are or will be negotiated at **arm's length**, and explain how you determine or will determine that you pay no more than **fair market value**. Attach copies of any written contracts or other agreements relating to such purchases. ☐ Yes ☑ No

b Do you or will you sell any goods, services, or assets to any of your officers, directors, trustees, highest compensated employees, or highest compensated independent contractors listed in lines 1a, 1b, or 1c? If "Yes," describe any such sales that you made or intend to make, to whom you make or will make such sales, how the terms are or will be negotiated at arm's length, and explain how you determine or will determine you are or will be paid at least fair market value. Attach copies of any written contracts or other agreements relating to such sales. ☐ Yes ☑ No

8a Do you or will you have any leases, contracts, loans, or other agreements with your officers, directors, trustees, highest compensated employees, or highest compensated independent contractors listed in lines 1a, 1b, or 1c? If "Yes," provide the information requested in lines 8b through 8f. ☐ Yes ☑ No

b Describe any written or oral arrangements that you made or intend to make.

c Identify with whom you have or will have such arrangements.

d Explain how the terms are or will be negotiated at arm's length.

e Explain how you determine you pay no more than fair market value or you are paid at least fair market value.

f Attach copies of any signed leases, contracts, loans, or other agreements relating to such arrangements.

9a Do you or will you have any leases, contracts, loans, or other agreements with any organization in which any of your officers, directors, or trustees are also officers, directors, or trustees, or in which any individual officer, director, or trustee owns more than a 35% interest? If "Yes," provide the information requested in lines 9b through 9f. ☐ Yes ☑ No

Appendix B Form 1023 for a Public Charity

Part V **Compensation and Other Financial Arrangements With Your Officers, Directors, Trustees, Employees, and Independent Contractors** *(Continued)*

   b Describe any written or oral arrangements you made or intend to make.

   c Identify with whom you have or will have such arrangements.

   d Explain how the terms are or will be negotiated at arm's length.

   e Explain how you determine or will determine you pay no more than fair market value or that you are paid at least fair market value.

   f Attach a copy of any signed leases, contracts, loans, or other agreements relating to such arrangements.

Part VI **Your Members and Other Individuals and Organizations That Receive Benefits From You**

The following "Yes" or "No" questions relate to goods, services, and funds you provide to individuals and organizations as part of your activities. Your answers should pertain to *past, present,* and *planned* activities. (See instructions.)

1a In carrying out your exempt purposes, do you provide goods, services, or funds to individuals? If "Yes," describe each program that provides goods, services, or funds to individuals.   ☑ **Yes** ☐ **No**
See Attachment

   b In carrying out your exempt purposes, do you provide goods, services, or funds to organizations? If "Yes," describe each program that provides goods, services, or funds to organizations.   ☐ **Yes** ☑ **No**

2 Do any of your programs limit the provision of goods, services, or funds to a specific individual or group of specific individuals? For example, answer "Yes," if goods, services, or funds are provided only for a particular individual, your members, individuals who work for a particular employer, or graduates of a particular school. If "Yes," explain the limitation and how recipients are selected for each program.   ☐ **Yes** ☑ **No**

3 Do any individuals who receive goods, services, or funds through your programs have a family or business relationship with any officer, director, trustee, or with any of your highest compensated employees or highest compensated independent contractors listed in Part V lines 1a, 1b, and 1c? If "Yes," explain how these related individuals are eligible for goods, services, or funds.   ☐ **Yes** ☑ **No**

Part VII **Your History**

The following "Yes" or "No" questions relate to your history. (See instructions.)

1 Are you a **successor** to another organization? Answer "Yes," if you have taken or will take over the activities of another organization; you took over 25% or more of the fair market value of the net assets of another organization; or you were established upon the conversion of an organization from for-profit to non-profit status. If "Yes," complete Schedule G.   ☐ **Yes** ☑ **No**

2 Are you submitting this application more than 27 months after the end of the month in which you were legally formed? If "Yes," complete Schedule E.   ☐ **Yes** ☑ **No**

Part VIII **Your Specific Activities**

The following "Yes" or "No" questions relate to specific activities that you may conduct. Check the appropriate box. Your answers should pertain to *past, present,* and *planned* activities. (See instructions.)

1 Do you support or oppose candidates in **political campaigns** in any way? If "Yes," explain.   ☐ **Yes** ☑ **No**

2a Do you attempt to **influence legislation**? If "Yes," explain how you attempt to influence legislation and complete line 2b. If "No," go to line 3a.   ☑ **Yes** ☐ **No**
See Attachment

   b Have you made or are you making an **election** to have your legislative activities measured by expenditures by filing Form 5768? If "Yes," attach a copy of the Form 5768 that was already filed or attach a completed Form 5768 that you are filing with this application. If "No," describe whether your attempts to influence legislation are a substantial part of your activities. Include the time and money spent on your attempts to influence legislation as compared to your total activities.   ☑ **Yes** ☐ **No**

3a Do you or will you operate bingo or **gaming** activities? If "Yes," describe who conducts them, and list all revenue received or expected to be received and expenses paid or expected to be paid in operating these activities. **Revenue and expenses** should be provided for the time periods specified in Part IX Financial Data.   ☐ **Yes** ☑ **No**

   b Do you or will you enter into contracts or other agreements with individuals or organizations to conduct bingo or gaming for you? If "Yes," describe any written or oral arrangements that you made or intend to make, identify with whom you have or will have such arrangements, explain how the terms are or will be negotiated at arm's length, and explain how you determine or will determine you pay no more than fair market value or you will be paid at least fair market value. Attach copies or any written contracts or other agreements relating to such arrangements.   ☐ **Yes** ☑ **No**

   c List the states and local jurisdictions, including Indian Reservations, in which you conduct or will conduct gaming or bingo.

Appendix B Form 1023 for a Public Charity

Part VIII   Your Specific Activities *(Continued)*

4a Do you or will you undertake **fundraising**? If "Yes," check all the fundraising programs you do or will conduct. (See instructions.)   ☑ Yes   ☐ No

- ☑ mail solicitations
- ☑ email solicitations
- ☑ personal solicitations
- ☐ vehicle, boat, plane, or similar donations
- ☑ foundation grant solicitations
- ☐ phone solicitations
- ☑ accept donations on your website
- ☐ receive donations from another organization's website
- ☐ government grant solicitations
- ☐ Other   **See Attachment**

Attach a description of each fundraising program.

b Do you or will you have written or oral contracts with any individuals or organizations to raise funds for you? If "Yes," describe these activities. Include all revenue and expenses from these activities and state who conducts them. Revenue and expenses should be provided for the time periods specified in Part IXFinancial Data. Also, attach a copy of any contracts or agreements.   ☑ Yes   ☐ No   **See Attachment**

c Do you or will you engage in fundraising activities for other organizations? If "Yes," describe these arrangements. Include a description of the organizations for which you raise funds and attach copies of all contracts or agreements.   ☐ Yes   ☑ No

d List all states and local jurisdictions in which you conduct fundraising. For each state or local jurisdiction listed, specify whether you fundraise for your own organization, you fundraise for another organization, or another organization fundraises for you.   **Texas, Oklahoma-Fundraising for own organization only**

e Do you or will you maintain separate accounts for any contributor under which the contributor has the right to advise on the use or distribution of funds? Answer "Yes" if the donor may provide advice on the types of investments, distributions from the types of investments, or the distribution from the donor's contribution account. If "Yes," describe this program, including the type of advice that may be provided and submit copies of any written materials provided to donors.   ☐ Yes   ☑ No

5 Are you **affiliated** with a governmental unit? If "Yes," explain.   ☐ Yes   ☑ No

6a Do you or will you engage in **economic development**? If "Yes," describe your program.   ☐ Yes   ☑ No
b Describe in full who benefits from your economic development activities and how the activities promote exempt purposes.

7a Do or will persons other than your employees or volunteers **develop** your facilities? If "Yes," describe each facility, the role of the developer, and any business or family relationship(s) between the developer and your officers, directors, or trustees.   ☐ Yes   ☑ No

b Do or will persons other than your employees or volunteers **manage** your activities or facilities? If "Yes," describe each activity and facility, the role of the manager, and any business or family relationship(s) between the manager and your officers, directors, or trustees.   ☐ Yes   ☑ No

c If there is a business or family relationship between any manager or developer and your officers, directors, or trustees, identify the individuals, explain the relationship, describe how contracts are negotiated at arm's length so that you pay no more than fair market value, and submit a copy of any contracts or other agreements.

8 Do you or will you enter into **joint ventures**, including partnerships or **limited liability companies** treated as partnerships, in which you share profits and losses with partners other than section 501(c)(3) organizations? If "Yes," describe the activities of these joint ventures in which you participate.   ☐ Yes   ☑ No

9a Are you applying for exemption as a childcare organization under section 501(k)? If "Yes," answer lines 9b through 9d. If "No," go to line 10.   ☐ Yes   ☑ No

b Do you provide child care so that parents or caretakers of children you care for can be **gainfully employed** (see instructions)? If "No," explain how you qualify as a childcare organization described in section 501(k).   ☐ Yes   ☐ No

c Of the children for whom you provide child care, are 85% or more of them cared for by you to enable their parents or caretakers to be gainfully employed (see instructions)? If "No," explain how you qualify as a childcare organization described in section 501(k).   ☐ Yes   ☐ No

d Are your services available to the general public? If "No," describe the specific group of people for whom your activities are available. Also, see the instructions and explain how you qualify as a childcare organization described in section 501(k).   ☐ Yes   ☐ No

10 Do you or will you publish, own, or have rights in music, literature, tapes, artworks, choreography, scientific discoveries, or other **intellectual property**? If "Yes," explain. Describe who owns or will own any copyrights, patents, or trademarks, whether fees are or will be charged, how the fees are determined, and how any items are or will be produced, distributed, and marketed.   ☐ Yes   ☑ No

Form **1023** (Rev. 10-2004)

Appendix B Form 1023 for a Public Charity

Part VIII	**Your Specific Activities** *(Continued)*

11 Do you or will you accept contributions of: real property; conservation easements; closely held securities; intellectual property such as patents, trademarks, and copyrights; works of music or art; licenses; royalties; automobiles, boats, planes, or other vehicles; or collectibles of any type? If "Yes," describe each type of contribution, any conditions imposed by the donor on the contribution, and any agreements with the donor regarding the contribution.   ☑ **Yes**   ☐ **No**
See Attachment

12a Do you or will you operate in a **foreign country** or **countries?** If "Yes," answer lines 12b through 12d. If "No," go to line 13a.   ☐ **Yes**   ☑ **No**

  b Name the foreign countries and regions within the countries in which you operate.

  c Describe your operations in each country and region in which you operate.

  d Describe how your operations in each country and region further your exempt purposes.

13a Do you or will you make grants, loans, or other distributions to organization(s)? If "Yes," answer lines 13b through 13g. If "No," go to line 14a.   ☐ **Yes**   ☑ **No**

  b Describe how your grants, loans, or other distributions to organizations further your exempt purposes.

  c Do you have written contracts with each of these organizations? If "Yes," attach a copy of each contract.   ☐ **Yes**   ☐ **No**

  d Identify each recipient organization and any **relationsip** between you and the recipient organization.

  e Describe the records you keep with respect to the grants, loans, or other distributions you make.

  f Describe your selection process, including whether you do any of the following:

  i) Do you require an application form? If "Yes," attach a copy of the form.   ☐ **Yes**   ☐ **No**

  (i) Do you require a grant proposal? If "Yes," describe whether the grant proposal specifies your responsibilities and those of the grantee, obligates the grantee to use the grant funds only for the purposes for which the grant was made, provides for periodic written reports concerning the use of grant funds, requires a final written report and an accounting of how grant funds were used, and acknowledges your authority to withhold and/or recover grant funds in case such funds are, or appear to be, misused.   ☐ **Yes**   ☐ **No**

  g Describe your procedures for oversight of distributions that assure you the resources are used to further your exempt purposes, including whether you require periodic and final reports on the use of resources.

14a Do you or will you make grants, loans, or other distributions to foreign organizations? If "Yes," answer lines 14b through 14f. If "No," go to line 15.   ☐ **Yes**   ☑ **No**

  b Provide the name of each foreign organization, the country and regions within a country in which each foreign organization operates, and describe any relationship you have with each foreign organization.

  c Does any foreign organization listed in line 14b accept contributions earmarked for a specific country or specific organization? If "Yes," list all earmarked organizations or countries.   ☐ **Yes**   ☐ **No**

  d Do your contributors know that you have ultimate authority to use contributions made to you at your discretion for purposes consistent with your exempt purposes? If "Yes," describe how you relay this information to contributors.   ☐ **Yes**   ☐ **No**

  e Do you or will you make pre-grant inquiries about the recipient organization? If "Yes," describe these inquiries, including whether you inquire about the recipient's financial status, its tax-exempt status under the Internal Revenue Code, its ability to accomplish the purpose for which the resources are provided, and other relevant information.   ☐ **Yes**   ☐ **No**

  f Do you or will you use any additional procedures to ensure that your distributions to foreign organizations are used in furtherance of your exempt purposes? If "Yes," describe these procedures, including site visits by your employees or compliance checks by impartial experts, to verify that grant funds are being used appropriately.   ☐ **Yes**   ☐ **No**

Form **1023** (Rev. 10-2004)

Appendix B Form 1023 for a Public Charity

Part VIII	**Your Specific Activities** *(Continued)*		
15	Do you have a **close connection** with any organizations? If "Yes," explain.	☐ Yes	☑ No
16	Are you applying for exemption as a **cooperative hospital service organization** under section 61(e)? If "Yes," explain.	☐ Yes	☑ No
17	Are you applying for exemption as a **cooperative service organization of operating educational organizations** under section 61(f)? If "Yes," explain.	☐ Yes	☑ No
18	Are you applying for exemption as a **charitable risk pool** under section 61(n)? If "Yes," explain.	☐ Yes	☑ No
19	Do you or will you operate a **school**? If "Yes," complete Schedule B. Answer "Yes," whether you operate a school as your main function or as a secondary activity.	☐ Yes	☑ No
20	Is your main function to provide **hospital** or **medical care**? If "Yes," complete Schedule C.	☐ Yes	☑ No
21	Do you or will you provide **low-income housing** or housing for the **elderly** or **handicapped**? If "Yes," complete Schedule F.	☐ Yes	☑ No
22	Do you or will you provide scholarships, fellowships, educational loans, or other educational grants to individuals, including grants for travel, study, or other similar purposes? If "Yes," complete Schedule H.	☐ Yes	☑ No

Note: Private foundations may use Schedule H to reqest advance approval of individual grant procedures.

Appendix B   Form 1023 for a Public Charity

Part IX	Financial Data

For purposes of this schedule, years in existence refer to completed tax years. If in existence 4 or more years, complete the schedule for the most recent 4 tax years. If in existence more than 1 year but less than 4 years, complete the statements for each year in existence and provide projections of your likely revenues and expenses based on a reasonable and good faith estimate of your future finances for a total of 3 years of financial information. If in existence less than 1 year, provide projections of your likely revenues and expenses for the current year and the 2 following years, based on a reasonable and good faith estimate of your future finances for a total of 3 years of financial information. (See instructions.)

A. Statement of Revenues and Expenses

	Type of revenue or expense	Current tax year (a) From 01/15/05 To 06/30/05	3 prior tax years or 2 succeeding tax years (b) From 07/01/05 To 06/30/06	(c) From 07/01/06 To 06/30/06	(d) From .... To	(e) Provide Total for (a) through (d)
Revenues	1 Gifts, grants, and contributions received (do not include unusual grants)	120,000	350,000	430,000		900,000
	2 Membership fees received	0	0	0		0
	3 Gross investment income	100	500	700		1,300
	4 Net unrelated business income	0	0	0		0
	5 Taxes levied for your benefit	0	0	0		0
	6 Value of services or facilities furnished by a governmental unit without charge (not including the value of services generally furnished to the public without charge)	0	0	0		0
	7 Any revenue not otherwise listed above or in lines 9–12 below (attach an itemized list)	0	0	0		0
	8 Total of lines 1 through 7	121,100	350,500	430,700		901,300
	9 Gross receipts from admissions, merchandise sold or services performed, or furnishing of facilities in any activity that is related to your exempt purposes (attach itemized list)	0	10,000	20,000		30,000
	10 Total of lines 8 and 9	121,100	360,500	450,700		931,300
	11 Net gain or loss on sale of capital assets (attach schedule and see instructions)	0	0	0		0
	12 Unusual grants	0	0	0		0
	13 Total Revenue Add lines 10 through 12	121,100	360,500	450,700		931,300
Expenses	14 Fundraising expenses	13,000	60,000	50,000		
	15 Contributions, gifts, grants, and similar amounts paid out (attach an itemized list)	1,000	1,200	1,200		
	16 Disbursements to or for the benefit of members (attach an itemized list)	0	0	0		
	17 Compensation of officers, directors, and trustees	0	0	0		
	18 Other salaries and wages	11,000	209,000	316,800		
	19 Interest expense	0	0	0		
	20 Occupancy (rent, utilities, etc.)	0	0	15,000		
	21 Depreciation and depletion	1,400	2,800	2,800		
	22 Professional fees	5,000	3,000	4,000		
	23 Any expense not otherwise classified, such as program services (attach itemized list)	20,000	25,000	32,000		
	24 Total Expenses Add lines 14 through 23	51,400	301,000	421,800		

Form **1023** (Rev. 10-2004)

Appendix B Form 1023 for a Public Charity

Part IX   Financial Data *(Continued)*

B. Balance Sheet (for your most recently completed tax year) | | **Year End: 06/30/05**

Assets		(Whole dollars)
1 Cash	1	57,100
2 Accounts receivable, net	2	0
3 Inventories	3	0
4 Bonds and notes receivable (attach an itemized list)	4	0
5 Corporate stocks (attach an itemized list)	5	0
6 Loans receivable (attach an itemized list)	6	0
7 Other investments (attach an itemized list)	7	0
8 Depreciable and depletable assets (attach an itemized list)	8	12,600
9 Land	9	0
10 Other assets (attach an itemized list)	10	0
11 Total Assets (add lines 1 through 10)	11	69,700
Liabilities		
12 Accounts payable	12	1,000
13 Contributions, gifts, grants, etc. payable	13	0
14 Mortgages and notes payable (attach an itemized list)	14	0
15 Other liabilities (attach an itemized list)	15	0
16 Total Liabilities (add lines 12 through 15)	16	1,000
Fund Balances or Net Assets		
17 Total fund balances or net assets	17	68,700
18 Total Liabilities and Fund Balances or Net Assets (add lines 16 and 17)	18	69,700

19 Have there been any substantial changes in your assets or liabilities since the end of the period shown above? If "Yes," explain.   ☐ Yes   ☑ No

Part X   Public Charity Status

Part X is designed to classify you as an organization that is either a **private foundation** or a **public charity** . Public charity status is a more favorable tax status than private foundation status. If you are a private foundation, Part X is designed to further determine whether you are a **private operating foundation.** (See instructions.)

1a Are you a private foundation? If "Yes," go to line 1b. If "No," go to line 5 and proceed as instructed. If you are unsure, see the instructions.   ☐ Yes   ☑ No

b As a private foundation, section 508(e) requires special provisions in your organizing document in addition to those that apply to all organizations described in section 501(c)(3). Check the box to confirm that your organizing document meets this requirement, whether by express provision or by reliance on operation of state law. Attach a statement that describes specifically where your organizing document meets this requirement, such as a reference to a particular article or section in your organizing document or by operation of state law. See the instructions, including Appendix B, for information about the special provisions that need to be contained in your organizing document. Go to line 2.

2 Are you a private operating foundation? To be a private operating foundation you must engage directly in the active conduct of charitable, religious, educational, and similar activities, as opposed to indirectly carrying out these activities by providing grants to individuals or other organizations. If "Yes," go to line 3. If "No," go to the signature section of Part XI.   ☐ Yes   ☐ No

3 Have you existed for one or more years? If "Yes," attach financial information showing that you are a private operating foundation; go to the signature section of Part XI. If "No," continue to line 4.   ☐ Yes   ☐ No

4 Have you attached either (1) an affidavit or opinion of counsel, (including a written affidavit or opinion from a certified public accountant or accounting firm with expertise regarding this tax law matter), that sets forth facts concerning your operations and support to demonstrate that you are likely to satisfy the requirements to be classified as a private operating foundation; or (2) a statement describing your proposed operations as a private operating foundation?   ☐ Yes   ☐ No

5 If you answered "No" to line 1a, indicate the type of public charity status you are requesting by checking one of the choices below. You may check only one box.

The organization is not a private foundation because it is:

a 509(a)(1) and 170(b)(1)(A)(i)—a church or a convention or association of churches. Complete and attach Schedule A.   ☐

b 509(a)(1) and 170(b)(1)(A)(ii)—a **school** . Complete and attach Schedule B.   ☐

c 509(a)(1) and 170(b)(1)(A)(iii)—a **hospital** , a cooperative hospital service organization, or a medical research organization operated in conjunction with a hospital. Complete and attach Schedule C.   ☐

d 509(a)(3)—an organization supporting either one or more organizations described in line 5a through c, f, g, or h or a publicly supported section 501(c)(4), (5), or (6) organization. Complete and attach Schedule D.   ☐

Form **1023** (Rev. 10-2004)

Appendix B Form 1023 for a Public Charity

Part X	**Public Charity Status** *(Continued)*

e 509(a)(4)—an organization organized and operated exclusively for testing for public safety. ☐

f 509(a)(1) and 170(b)(1)(A)(iv)—an organization operated for the benefit of a college or university that is owned or operated by a governmental unit. ☐

g 509(a)(1) and 170(b)(1)(A)(vi)—an organization that receives a substantial part of its financial support in the form of contributions from publicly supported organizations, from a governmental unit, or from the general public. ☑

h 509(a)(2)—an organization that normally receives not more than one-third of its financial support from gross **investment income** and receives more than one-third of its financial support from contributions, membership fees, and gross receipts from activities related to its exempt functions (subject to certain exceptions). ☐

i A publicly supported organization, but unsure if it is described in 5g or 5h. The organization would like the IRS to decide the correct status. ☐

6 If you checked box g, h, or i in question 5 above, you must request either an **advance** or a **definitive ruling** by selecting one of the boxes below. Refer to the instructions to determine which type of ruling you are eligible to receive.

a Reqest for Advance Ruling: By checking this box and signing the consent, pursuant to section 6501(c)(4) of the Code you request an advance ruling and agree to extend the statute of limitations on the assessment of excise tax under section 4940 of the Code. The tax will apply only if you do not establish public support status at the end of the 5-year advance ruling period. The assessment period will be extended for the 5 advance ruling years to 8 years, 4 months, and 15 days beyond the end of the first year. You have the right to refuse or limit the extension to a mutually agreed-upon period of time or issue(s). Publication 1035, *Extending the Tax Assessment Period,* provides a more detailed explanation of your rights and the consequences of the choices you make. You may obtain Publication 1035 free of charge from the IRS web site at *www.irs.gov* or by calling toll-free 1-800-829-3676. Signing this consent will not deprive you of any appeal rights to which you would otherwise be entitled. If you decide not to extend the statute of limitations, you are not eligible for an advance ruling. ☑

> Consent Fiing Period of Lmitations Upon Assessment of Tax Under Section 4940 of th Internal Revenue Code

For Organization

(Signature of Officer, Director, Trustee, or other authorized official)

John J. Environmentalist
(Type or print name of signer)

President
(Type or print title or authority of signer)

7.10.05
(Date)

For Director, Exempt Organizations

By .... Date ....

b Reqest for Definitive Ruling: Check this box if you have completed one tax year of at least 8 full months and you are requesting a definitive ruling. To confirm your public support status, answer line 6b(i) if you checked box g in line 5 above. Answer line 6b(ii) if you checked box h in line 5 above. If you checked box i in line 5 above, answer both lines 6b(i) and (ii). ☐

(i) (a) Enter 2% of line 8, column (e) on Part IX-A. Statement of Revenues and Expenses. _____

(b) Attach a list showing the name and amount contributed by each person, company, or organization whose gifts totaled more than the 2% amount. If the answer is "None," check this box. ☐

(ii) (a) For each year amounts are included on lines 1, 2, and 9 of Part IX-A. Statement of Revenues and Expenses, attach a list showing the name of and amount received from each **disqalified person.** If the answer is "None," check this box. ☐

(b) For each year amounts are included on line 9 of Part IX-A. Statement of Revenues and Expenses, attach a list showing the name of and amount received from each payer, other than a disqualified person, whose payments were more than the larger of (1) 1% of line 10, Part IX-A. Statement of Revenues and Expenses, or (2) $5,000. If the answer is "None," check this box. ☐

7 Did you receive any unusual grants during any of the years shown on Part IX-A. Statement of Revenues and Expenses? If "Yes," attach a list including the name of the contributor, the date and amount of the grant, a brief description of the grant, and explain why it is unusual. ☐ Yes ☑ No

Form **1023** (Rev. 10-2004)

Appendix B Form 1023 for a Public Charity

Part XI	**User Fee Information**

You must include a user fee payment with this application. It will not be processed without your paid user fee. If your average annual gross receipts have exceeded or will exceed $10,000 annually over a 4-year period, you must submit payment of $500. If your gross receipts have not exceeded or will not exceed $10,000 annually over a 4-year period, the required user fee payment is $150. See instructions for Part XI, for a definition of **gross receipts** over a 4-year period. Your check or money order must be made payable to the United States Treasury. *User fees are subject to change. Check our website at www.irs.gov and type "User Fee" in the keyword box, or call Customer Account Services at 1-877-829-5500 for current information.*

1	Have your annual gross receipts averaged or are they expected to average not more than $10,000? If "Yes," check the box on line 2 and enclose a user fee payment of $150 (Subject to change—see above). If "No," check the box on line 3 and enclose a user fee payment of $500 (Subject to change—see above).	☐ Yes	☑ No
2	Check the box if you have enclosed the reduced user fee payment of $150 (Subject to change).		☐
3	Check the box if you have enclosed the user fee payment of $500 (Subject to change).		☑

I declare under the penalties of perjury that I am authorized to sign this application on behalf of the above organization and that I have examined this application, including the accompanying schedules and attachments, and to the best of my knowledge it is true, correct, and complete.

Please Sign Here   ▶ _(signature)_
(Signature of Officer, Director, Trustee, or other authorized official)

John J. Environmentalist   7-10-05
(Type or print name of signer)   (Date)

President
(Type or print title or authority of signer)

Reminder: Send the completed Form 1023 Checklist with your filled-in-application.   Form **1023** (Rev. 10-2004)

Appendix B Form 1023 for a Public Charity

Corporations Section
P.O.Box 13697
Austin, Texas 78711-3697

Geoffrey S. Connor
Secretary of State

Office of the Secretary of State

CERTIFICATE OF INCORPORATION
OF

HOMETOWN CAMPAIGN TO CLEAN UP AMERICA

Filing Number: 212121

The undersigned, as Secretary of State of Texas, hereby certifies that Articles of Incorporation for the above named corporation have been received in this office and have been found to conform to law.

Accordingly, the undersigned, as Secretary of State, and by virtue of the authority vested in the Secretary by law, hereby issues this Certificate of Incorporation.

Issuance of this Certificate of Incorporation does not authorize the use of a name in this state in violation of the rights of another under the federal Trademark Act of 1946, the Texas trademark law, the Assumed Business or Professional Name Act, or the common law.

Dated: 01/15/05

Effective: 01/15/05

Geoffrey S. Connor
Secretary of State

PHONE(512) 463-5555
Prepared by: Dolores Kloore

Come visit us on the internet at http://www.sos.state.tx.us
FAX(512) 463-5709

TTY7-1-1

Appendix B Form 1023 for a Public Charity

Hometown Campaign to Clean Up America   44-4444444
Attachment to Form 1023

ARTICLES OF INCORPORATION
OF
Hometown Campaign to Clean Up America

I, the undersigned natural person of the age of eighteen (18) years or more, acting as incorporator of a corporation under the Texas Non-Profit Corporation Act, do hereby adopt the following Articles of Incorporation for such Corporation:

ARTICLE ONE
Name

The name of the Corporation is HOMETOWN CAMPAIGN TO CLEAN UP AMERICA

ARTICLE TWO
Nonprofit Corporation

The Corporation is a nonprofit corporation.

ARTICLE THREE
Duration

The period of the Corporation's duration is perpetual.

ARTICLE FOUR
Purposes

Section 4.01. The Corporation is organized exclusively for charitable, scientific and educational purposes as defined in Section 501(c)(3) of the Internal Revenue Code. These activities will include, but not be limited to acquiring by gifts and donations funds to be donated to other charitable entities as defined in Section 501(c)(3).

Section 4.02. Notwithstanding any other provision of these Articles of Incorporation:

a. No part of the net earnings of the Corporation shall inure to the benefit of any director of the Corporation, officer of the Corporation, or any private individual (except that reasonable compensation may be paid for services rendered to or for the Corporation affecting one or more of its purposes); and no director, officer or any private individual shall be entitled to share in the distribution of any of the corporate assets on dissolution of the Corporation. No substantial part of the activities of the Corporation shall be the carrying on of propaganda, or otherwise attempting to influence legislation, and the Corporation shall not participate in, or intervene in (including the publication or distribution of statements) any political campaign on behalf of any candidate for public office.

b. The corporation shall not conduct or carry on any activities not permitted to be conducted or carried on by an organization exempt from taxation under Section 501(c)(3) of the Internal Revenue Code and its Regulations as they now exist or as they may hereafter be amended, or by an organization, contributions to which are deductible under 170(c)(2) of the Internal Revenue Code and Regulations as they now exist or as they may hereafter be amended.

Appendix B Form 1023 for a Public Charity

c. Upon dissolution of the Corporation or the winding up of its affairs, the assets of the Corporation shall be distributed exclusively to charitable organizations which would then qualify under the provisions of Section 501(c)(3) of the Internal Revenue Code and its Regulations as they now exist or as they may be hereafter amended.

d. The Corporation is organized pursuant to the Texas Nonprofit Corporation Act and does not contemplate pecuniary gain or profit and is organized for nonprofit purposes which are consistent with the provisions of Section 501(c)(3) of the Internal Revenue Code and its Regulations as they now exist or as they may be hereafter amended.

ARTICLE FIVE
Membership

The Corporation shall have no voting members.

ARTICLE SIX
Initial Registration Office and Agent

The street address of the initial registered office of the Corporation is 1111 Any Street, Hometown, XX 77777-7777 and the name of the initial registered agent at such address is John J. Environmentalist.

ARTICLE SEVEN
Directors

The number of Directors constituting the initial Board of Directors of the Corporation is five (5), and the names and addresses of those people who are to serve as the initial Directors are:

Name	Address
John J. Environmentalist	1111 Any Street Hometown, XX 77777-7777
Jane D. Environmentalist	1111 Any Street Hometown, XX 77777-7777
James F. Friend	1111 Any Street Hometown, XX 77777-7777
Jacob Thoughtful	1111 Any Street Hometown, XX 77777-7777
Jennifer Scholar	1111 Any Street Hometown, XX 77777-7777

Appendix B Form 1023 for a Public Charity

ARTICLE EIGHT
Indemnification of Directors and Officers

Each Director and each officer or former Director or officer may be indemnified and may be advanced reasonable expenses by the Corporation against liabilities imposed upon him or her and expenses reasonably incurred by him or her in connection with any claim against him or her, or any action, suit or proceeding to which he or she may be a party by reason of his or being, or having been, such Director or officer and against such sum as independent counsel selected by the Directors shall deem reasonable payment made in settlement of any such claim, action, suit or proceeding primarily with the view of avoiding expenses of litigation; provided, however, that no Director or officer shall be indemnified (a) with respect to matters as to which he or she shall be adjudged in such action, suit or proceeding to be liable for negligence or misconduct in performance or duty, (b) with respect to any matters which shall be settled by the payment of sums which independent counsel selected by the Directors shall not deem reasonable payment made primarily with a view to avoiding expense of litigation, or (c) with respect to matters for which such indemnification would be against public policy. Such rights of indemnification shall be in addition to any other rights to which Directors or officers may be entitled under any bylaw, agreement, corporate resolution, vote of Directors or otherwise. The Corporation shall have the power to purchase and maintain at its cost and expense insurance on behalf of such persons to the fullest extent permitted by this Article and applicable state law.

ARTICLE NINE
Limitation On Scope Of Liability

No director shall be liable to the Corporation for monetary damages for an act or omission in the Director's capacity as a Director of the Corporation, except and only for the following:

a.   A breach of the Director's duty of loyalty to the Corporation;

b.   An act or omission not in good faith by the Director or an act or omission that involves the intentional misconduct or knowing violation of the law by the Director;

c.   A transaction from which the Director gained any improper benefit whether or not such benefit resulted from an action taken within the scope of the Director's office; or

d.   An act or omission by the Directors for which liability is expressly provided for by statute.

ARTICLE TEN
Informal Action by Directors

Any action required by law to be taken at a meeting of Directors, or any action which may be taken at a meeting of Directors, may be taken without a meeting if a consent in writing setting forth the action so taken shall be signed by a sufficient number of Directors as would be necessary to take that action at a meeting at which all of the Directors were present and voted. All consents signed in this manner must be delivered to the Secretary or other officer having custody of the minute book within sixty (60) days after the date of the earliest dated consent delivered to the Corporation in this manner. A facsimile transmission or other similar transmission shall be regarded as signed by the Director for purposes of this Article.

Appendix B Form 1023 for a Public Charity

ARTICLE ELEVEN
Incorporator

The name and address of the incorporator is:

Name	Address
John J. Environmentalist	1111 Any Street Hometown, TX 77777-7777

IN WITNESS WHEREOF, I have hereunto set my hand, this 15th day of January 2005.

John J. Environmentalist

Appendix B Form 1023 for a Public Charity

BYLAWS OF
HOMETOWN CAMPAIGN TO CLEAN UP AMERICA
a Texas Non-Profit Corporation
* * * * * * * * * * * * * * * *
ARTICLE ONE - OFFICES

Section 1.01.   Principal Office. The principal office of the Corporation in the State of Texas shall be located in the City of Hometown, County of Harris. The Corporation may have such other offices, either within or without the State of Texas, as the Board of Directors may determine or as the affairs of the Corporation may require from time to time.

Section 1.02.   Registered Office and Registered Agent. The Corporation shall have and continuously maintain in the State of Texas a registered office, and a registered agent whose office is identical with such registered office may be, but need not be, identical with the principal office of the Corporation in the State of Texas, and the address of the registered office may be changed from time to time by the Board of Directors.

ARTICLE TWO - PURPOSES

Section 2.01.   Organizational Purposes. The Corporation is organized exclusively for charitable, scientific and educational purposes. The corporation is established as a permanent organization in Texas seeking to enrich the local community through activities promoting such provision. The Corporation may engage in any activities that further its purpose.

No part of the net earnings of the Corporation shall inure to the benefit of any Director of the Corporation, officer of the Corporation, or any private individual (except that reasonable compensation may be paid for services rendered to or for the Corporation affecting one or more of its purposes), and no Director or officer of the Corporation, or any private individual shall be entitled to share in the distribution of any of the corporate assets on dissolution of the Corporation. No substantial part of the activities of the Corporation shall be the carrying on of propaganda, or otherwise attempting to influence legislation, and the Corporation shall not participate in, or intervene in (including the publication or distribution of statements) any political campaigning on behalf of any candidate for public office.

Notwithstanding any other provision of these Bylaws, the Corporation shall not conduct or carry on any activities not permitted to be conducted or carried on by an organization exempt from taxation under Section 501(c)(3) of the Internal Revenue Code and its Regulations as they now exist or as they may hereafter be amended, or by an organization, contributions to which are deductible under Section 170(c)(2) of the Internal Revenue Code and Regulations, as they now exist or as they may hereafter be amended.

Upon dissolution of the Corporation or the winding up of its affairs, the assets of the Corporation shall be distributed exclusively to charitable organizations which would then qualify under the provisions of Section 501(c)(3) of the Internal Revenue Code and its Regulations as they now exist or as they may hereafter be amended.

ARTICLE THREE - MEMBERS

Section 3.01.   The corporation shall have no voting members.

ARTICLE FOUR - BOARD OF DIRECTORS

Section 4.01.   General Powers. The affairs of the Corporation shall be managed by its Board of Directors. Directors need not be residents of Texas.

Section 4.02.   Number, Tenure and Qualifications. The number of Directors shall be not less than three (3) nor more than twenty (20). The initial Directors shall serve terms of one, two and three years, as provided by the Board. Afterwards, each director shall serve for three years, thereby providing for staggered terms. The initial terms of additional Directors shall be fixed to ensure than a disproportionate number of Directors (more than one-half) will not be up for election in any given year.

Section 4.03.   Regular Meetings. The Board of Directors shall provide for by resolution the time and place, either within or without the State of Texas, for the holding of the regular annual meeting(s) of the Board, and may provide by resolution the time and place for the holding of additional regular meetings of the Board, without other notice than such resolution. However, there shall never be less than one annual meeting of the Board of Directors.

1

Bylaws

This model provided by the Texas Accountants and Lawyers for the Arts.

149

Hometown Campaign to Clean Up America   44-4444444
Attachment to Form 1023

Section 4.04.   Annual Meetings. Beginning in 2005 an annual meeting of the Board of Directors shall be held at the date, time and place determined by the Board of Directors.

Section 4.05.   Special Meetings. Special meetings of the Board of Directors may be called by or at the request of the President, or any two Directors. The person or persons authorized to call special meetings of the Board may fix any place, either within or without the State of Texas, as the place for holding any special meetings of the Board called by them.

Section 4.06.   Meetings Utilizing Electronic Media. Members of the Board of Directors or members of any committee designated by the Board of Directors may participate in and hold a meeting of that Board or committee, respectively, by means of conference telephone or similar communication equipment, provided that all persons participating in such a meeting shall constitute presence in person at such meeting, except where a person participates in the meeting for the express purpose of objecting to the transaction of any business on the ground that the meeting is not lawfully created.

Section 4.07.   Notice. Notice of any special meeting of the Board of Directors shall be given at least (5) business days previously thereto by oral or written notice delivered personally or sent by mail, telegram, facsimile or messenger to each Director at his or her address as shown by the records of the Corporation. If mailed, such notice shall be deemed to be delivered when deposited in the United States mail so addressed with postage thereon prepaid. If notice be given by telegram, such notice shall be deemed to be delivered when the telegram is delivered to the telegram company. Any Director may waive notice of any meeting. The attendance of a Director at any meeting shall constitute a waiver or notice of such meeting, except when a Director attends a meeting for the express purpose of objecting to the transaction of any business because the meeting is not lawfully called or convened. Neither the business to be transacted at, nor the purpose of, any regular or special meeting of the Board need be specified in the notice or waiver of notice of such meeting, unless specifically required by law or by these Bylaws.

Section 4.08.   Quorum. A majority of the Board of Directors, but never less than three (3), shall constitute a quorum for the transaction of business at any meeting of the Board; but if less than a quorum of the Directors is present at said meeting, a majority of the Directors present may adjourn the meeting from time to time without further notice.

Section 4.09.   Manner of Acting. The act of a majority of the Directors present at a meeting at which a quorum is present shall be the act of the Board of Directors, unless the act of a greater number is required by law or by these Bylaws.

Section 4.10.   Vacancies. Any vacancy occurring in the Board of Directors, and any directorship to be filled by reason of an increase in the number of Directors, shall be filled by the Board of Directors. A Director elected to fill a vacancy shall be elected for the unexpired term of his or her predecessor in office. However, vacancies need not be filled unless such a vacancy would result in fewer than three directors remaining on the board.

Section 4.11.   Compensation. Directors as such shall not receive any stated salaries for their services, but by resolution of the Board of Directors a fixed sum and expenses of attendance, if any, may be allowed for attendance at each regular or special meeting of the Board; but nothing herein contained shall be construed to preclude any Director from serving the Corporation in any other capacity and receiving compensation therefor.

Section 4.12.   Informal Action by Directors. Any action required by law to be taken at a meeting of Directors, or any action which may be taken at a meeting of Directors, may be taken without a meeting if a consent in writing setting forth the action so taken shall be signed by a sufficient number of Directors as would be necessary to take that action at a meeting at which all the Directors were present and voted. Each such written consent shall be delivered, by hand or certified or registered mail, return receipt requested, to the Secretary or other officer or agent of the Corporation having custody of the Corporation's minute book. A written consent signed by less than all of the Directors is not effective to take the action that is the subject of the consent unless, within sixty (60) days after the date of the earliest dated consent delivered to the Corporation in the manner required by this Article, a consent or consents signed by the required number of Directors is delivered to the Corporation as provided in this Article. For purposes of this Article, a telegram, telex, cablegram, or similar transmission by a Director or a photographic, photostatic, facsimile or similar reproduction of a writing signed by a Director shall be regarded as signed by the Director.

Section 4.13.   Resignation. Any Director may resign by giving written notice to the President. The resignation shall be effective at the next called meeting of the Board of Directors, of which meeting the resigning Director shall receive notice.

Section 4.14.   Removal. Any Director may be removed with or without cause by a two thirds majority of the remaining Directors.

Section 4.15.   Indemnification. The Corporation may indemnify and advance reasonable expenses to directors, officers, employees and agents of the Corporation to the fullest extent required or permitted by Article 2.22A of the Texas Non-Profit Corporation Act,

2

Bylaws

Appendix B Form 1023 for a Public Charity

Hometown Campaign to Clean Up America   44-4444444
Attachment to Form 1023

subject to the restrictions, if any, contained in the Corporation's Articles of Incorporation. The Corporation shall have the power to purchase and maintain at its cost and expense insurance on behalf of such persons to the fullest extent permitted by Article 2.22A of the Texas Non-Profit Corporation Act.

ARTICLE FIVE - OFFICERS

Section 5.01.   Officers. The officers of the Corporation shall be a President, one or more Vice Presidents (the number thereof to be determined by the Board of Directors), a Secretary, a Treasurer, and such other officers as may be elected in accordance with the provisions of this Article. The Board of Directors may elect or appoint such other officers, including one or more Assistant Secretaries and one or more Assistant Treasurers, as it shall deem desirable, such officers to have the authority and perform the duties prescribed, from time to time, by the Board of Directors. Any two or more offices may be held by the same person, except the offices of President and Secretary.

Section 5.02.   Election and Term of Office. The officers of the Corporation shall be elected by the Board of Directors at the alternate Annual meeting of the Board of Directors and shall serve terms of two years duration. If the election of officers shall not be held at such meeting, such election shall be held as soon thereafter as conveniently may be. New offices may be created and filled at any meeting of the Board of Directors. Each officer shall hold office for two years, or until his or her successor shall have been duly elected and shall have qualified.

Section 5.03.   Removal. Any officer elected or appointed by the Board of Directors may be removed with or without cause by a majority vote of the Board of Directors, but such removal shall be without prejudice to the contract rights, if any, of the officer so removed.

Section 5.04.   Vacancies. A vacancy in any office because of death, resignation, disqualification, or otherwise, may be filled by the Board of Directors for the unexpired portion of the term.

Section 5.05.   President. The President shall be the principal executive officer of the Corporation and shall, in general, supervise and control all of the business and affairs of the Corporation. He or she shall preside at all meetings of the Board of Directors. The President may sign, with the Secretary or any other proper officer of the Corporation authorized by the Board of Directors, any deeds, mortgages, bonds, contracts, or other instruments which the Board of Directors has authorized to be executed, except in cases where the signing and execution thereof shall be expressly delegated by the Board of Directors or by these Bylaws or by statute to some other officer or agent of the Corporation; and in general he or she shall perform all duties as may be prescribed by the Board of Directors from time to time, including participating in various committee meetings as a member or chairperson thereof. He or she shall also be responsible for informing the Board of Directors of possible programs, meetings, and functions of the corporation.

Section 5.06.   Vice President. In the absence of the President or in the event of his or her inability or refusal to act, the Vice President (or in the event there be more than one Vice President, the Vice Presidents in order of their election) shall perform the duties of the President, and when so acting shall have all the powers of and be subject to all the restrictions upon the President. Any Vice President shall perform such other duties as from time to time may be assigned to him or her by the President or Board of Directors.

Section 5.07.   Treasurer. If required by the Board of Directors, the Treasurer shall give a bond for the faithful discharge of his or her duties in such sum and with such surety or sureties as the Board of Directors shall determine. He or she shall have charge and custody of and be responsible for all funds and securities of the Corporation; receive and give receipts for moneys due and payable to the Corporation from any source whatsoever, and deposit all such moneys in the name of the Corporation in such banks, trust companies, or other depositories as shall be selected in accordance with the provisions of these Bylaws; he or she shall keep proper books of account and other books showing at all times the amount of funds and other property belonging to the Corporation, all of which books shall be open at all times to the inspection of the Board of Directors; he or she shall also submit a report of the accounts and financial condition of the Corporation at each annual meeting of the Board of Directors; and in general perform all the duties incident to the office of Treasurer and such other duties as from time to time may be assigned to him or her by the President or by the Board of Directors.

Section 5.08.   Secretary. The Secretary shall keep the minutes of the meetings of the Board of Directors in one or more books provided for that purpose; give all notices in accordance with the provisions of these Bylaws or as required by law; be custodian of the corporate records and of the seal of the Corporation, and affix the seal of the Corporation to all documents, the execution of which on behalf of the Corporation under its seal is duly authorized in accordance with the provisions of these Bylaws; and, in general, perform all duties incident to the office of Secretary and such other duties as from time to time may be assigned to him or her by the President or Board of Directors. The Board of Directors and Officers shall give bonds of the faithful discharge of their duties in such sums and with such sureties as the Board of Directors shall determine. The Assistant Treasurer and Assistant Secretaries, in general, shall perform such duties as shall be assigned to them by the Treasurer or the Secretary or by the President or the Board of Directors.

ARTICLE SIX- COMMITTEES

3

Appendix B Form 1023 for a Public Charity

Hometown Campaign to Clean Up America   44-4444444
Attachment to Form 1023

Section 6.01.   Appointment. The Board of Directors shall appoint members of committees established by the Board of Directors. The Board of Directors shall appoint the chairperson of each committee. These committees shall perform such functions and make such reports as the President or Board of Directors shall determine. Both Directors and members of the Advisory Board may serve on all committees except the Executive Committee.

Section 6.02.   Committees of Directors. The Board of Directors, by resolution adopted by a majority of the Directors in office, may designate and appoint one or more committees, each of which shall consist of two or more persons, a majority of who are Directors, which committees, to the extent provided in said resolution shall have and exercise the authority in the management of the Corporation of the Board of Directors. However, no such committee shall have the authority of the Board of Directors in reference to amending, altering, or repealing the Bylaws; electing, appointing, or removing any member of any such committee or any Director or officer of the Corporation; amending the Articles of Incorporation; adopting a plan of merger or adopting a plan of consolidation with another Corporation; authorizing the sale, lease, exchange, or mortgage of all or substantially all of the property and assets of the Corporation; authorizing the voluntary dissolution of the Corporation or revoking proceedings therefor; adopting a plan for the distribution of the assets of the Corporation; or amending, altering, or repealing any resolution of the Board of Directors which by its terms provides that it shall not be amended, altered or repealed by such committee. The designation and appointment of any such committee and the delegation thereof of authority shall not operate to relieve the Board of Directors, or any individual Director, of any responsibility imposed on it or him or her by law.

Section 6.03.   Executive Committee. The Board of Directors may from among its members appoint an Executive Committee consisting of the officers and any additional members as deemed necessary by the Board to serve at the pleasure of the Board. The President, unless absent or otherwise unable to do so, shall preside as Chairperson of the Executive Committee. The Committee shall meet at the call of the President or the Board of Directors, or any two (2) members of the Committee, and shall have and may exercise when the Board of Directors is not in session the power to perform all duties, of every kind and character, not required by law or the charter of the Corporation to be performed solely by the Board of Directors. The Executive Committee shall have authority to make rules for the holding and conduct of its meetings, keep records thereof and regularly report its actions to the Board. A majority but never less than three of the members of the Committee in office shall be sufficient to constitute a quorum at any meeting of the Committee, and all action taken at such a meeting shall be by a majority of those present all acts performed by the Executive Committee in the exercise of its aforesaid authority shall be deemed to be, and may be certified as, acts performed under authority of the Board of Directors. Vacancies in the Executive committee shall be filled by appointment by the Board of Directors. All actions of the Executive Committee shall be recorded in writing in a minute book kept for that purpose and a report of all action shall be made to the Board of Directors at its next meeting. The minutes of the Board of Directors shall reflect that such a report was made along with any action taken by the Board of Directors with respect thereto.

Section 6.04.   Nominating Committee. The President shall, with thirty (30) days advance notice to the Board of Directors, appoint the members of the Nominating Committee created by the Board of Directors. The members shall be members of the Board of Directors and Advisory Board appointed to nominate candidates for officers and directors. Additional nominations may be made by Directors at the annual meeting.

Section 6.05.   Advisory Committee. The function and purpose of the Advisory Committee shall be to advise the Board of Directors on matters relating to the purpose of the organization and to suggest projects which the Corporation may undertake.

Section 6.06.   Other Committees. Other committees not having and exercising the authority of the Board of Directors in the management of the Corporation may be designated by a resolution adopted by a majority of the Directors present at a meeting at which a quorum is present. Except as otherwise provided in such resolution, the President of the Corporation shall appoint the members of each such committee. Any member thereof may be removed by the person or persons authorized to appoint such member whenever in their judgment the best interests of the Corporation shall be served by such removal. Members of such committee or committees may, but need not be, Directors.

Section 6.07.   Term of Office. Each member of a committee shall continue as such until the next annual meeting of the members of the Board of Directors and until his or her successor is appointed, unless the committee shall be sooner terminated, or unless such member be removed from such committee, or unless such member shall cease to qualify as a member thereof.

Section 6.08.   Chairperson. One member of each committee shall be appointed chairperson by the person or persons authorized to appoint the members thereof.

Section 6.09.   Vacancies. Vacancies in the membership of any committee may be filled by appointments made in the same manner as provided in the case of the original appointments.

Section 6.10.   Quorum. Unless otherwise provided in the resolution of the Board of Directors designating a committee, a majority of the whole committee shall constitute a quorum and the act of a majority of the members present at a meeting at which a quorum is present shall

4

Bylaws

This model provided by the Texas Accountants and Lawyers for the Arts.

152

Appendix B Form 1023 for a Public Charity

be the act of the committee.

Section 6.11.   Rules. Each committee may adopt rules for its government not inconsistent with these Bylaws or with rules adopted by the Board of Directors.

Section 6.12.   Committee Dissolution. The Board of Directors may, in its sole discretion, dissolve any committee with or without cause. Except for the Executive Committee, such dissolution shall require approval by a majority of the quorum. The Executive Committee shall only be dissolved by approval of   two-thirds or more of all members of the Board of Directors.

ARTICLE SEVEN - CONTRACTS, CHECKS, DEPOSITS, AND GIFTS

Section 7.01.   Contracts. The Board of Directors may authorize any officer or officers, agent or agents of the Corporation, in addition to the officers so authorized by these Bylaws, to enter into any contract or execute and deliver any instrument in the name of and on behalf of the Corporation. Such authority may be general or confined to specific instances.

Section 7.02.   Checks and Drafts, Etc. All checks, drafts, or orders for the payment of money, notes, or other evidence of indebtedness issued in the name of the Corporation shall be signed by such officer or officers, agent or agents of the Corporation and in such manner as shall from time to time be determined by resolution of the Board of Directors. In the absence of such determination by the Board of Directors, such instruments shall be signed by the Treasurer or an Assistant Treasurer and countersigned by the President or a Vice President of the Corporation.

Section 7.03.   Deposits. All funds of the Corporation shall be deposited from time to time to the credit of the Corporation in such banks, trust companies, or other depositories as the Board of Directors may select.

Section 7.04.   Gifts. The Board of Directors may accept on behalf of the Corporation any contribution, gift, bequest, or devise for the general purposes or for any special purpose of the Corporation.

ARTICLE EIGHT - BOOKS AND RECORDS

Section 8.01.   Books and Records. The Corporation shall keep correct and complete books and records of account of the activities and transactions of the Corporation including, a minute book which shall contain a copy of the Corporation's application for tax-exempt statue (IRS Form 1023), copies of the organization's IRS information and/or tax returns (For example, Form 990 and all schedules thereto), and a copy of the Articles of Incorporation, Bylaws, and Amendments. The Corporation shall also keep minutes of the proceedings of its Board of Directors and any committees having the authority of the Board of Directors. All books and records of the Corporation may be inspected by any Director or his or her agent or attorney for any proper purpose at any reasonable time. Representatives of the Internal Revenue Service may inspect these books and records as necessary to meet the requirements relating to federal tax form 990. All financial records of the Corporation shall be available to the public for inspection and copying to the fullest extent required by law.

ARTICLE NINE - FISCAL YEAR

Section 9.01.   Fiscal Year. The fiscal year of the Corporation shall begin on July 1 of each year and conclude on the last day of June 30 of the following year.

ARTICLE TEN - SEAL

Section 10.01. Seal. The Board of Directors may authorize a corporate seal.

ARTICLE ELEVEN - WAIVER OF NOTICE

Section 11.01. Waiver of Notice. Whenever any notice is required to be given under the provisions of the Texas Non-Profit Corporation Act or under the provisions of the Articles of Incorporation or the Bylaws of the Corporation, a waiver thereof in writing signed by the person or persons entitled to such notice, whether before or after the time therein, shall be deemed equivalent to the giving of such notice.

ARTICLE TWELVE - AMENDMENTS TO BYLAWS

Section 12.01. Amendments to Bylaws. These Bylaws may be altered, amended, or repealed and new Bylaws may be adopted by a two-

thirds majority of the Directors present at any regular meeting or at any special meeting, if at least one day's written notice is given of an intention to alter, amend, or repeal these Bylaws or to adopt new Bylaws at such meeting.

5

Bylaws
This model provided by the Texas Accountants and Lawyers for the Arts.

Appendix B Form 1023 for a Public Charity

Hometown Campaign to Clean Up America   **44-4444444**
Attachment to Form 1023

ARTICLE THIRTEEN - <u>AMENDMENTS TO ARTICLES</u>

Section 13.01. <u>Amendments to Articles</u>. The Articles of Incorporation of the Corporation may, to the extent allowed by law, be altered, amended, or restated and new Articles of Incorporation may be adopted by a two-thirds majority of the Directors present at any regular meeting or at any special meeting, if at least one day's written notice is given of an intention to alter, amend, or restate the Articles of Incorporation or to adopt new Articles of Incorporation at such meeting.

<u>CERTIFICATE</u>

I HEREBY CERTIFY that the foregoing is a true, complete and correct copy of the By Laws of Hometown Campaign to Clean Up America, a Texas non-profit corporation, in effect on the date hereof.

IN WITNESS WHEREOF, I hereunto set my hand, this 15th day of January, 2005.

<u>John J. Environmentalist, President</u>

6

Appendix B Form 1023 for a Public Charity

Hometown Campaign to Clean Up America   44-4444444
Attachment to Form 1023

Hometown Campaign to Clean Up America Conflict of Interest Policy

Article I
Purpose

The purpose of the conflict of interest policy is to protect Hometown Campaign to Clean Up America's interests when it contemplates entering into a transaction or arrangement that might benefit the private interest of an officer or director of the organization or might result in a possible excess benefit transaction. This policy is intended to supplement but not replace any applicable state and federal laws governing conflict of interest applicable to nonprofit and charitable organizations.

Article II
Definitions

1. Interested Person
Any director, principal officer, or member of a committee with governing board delegated powers, who has a direct or indirect financial interest, as defined below, is an interested person.

2. Financial Interest
A person has a financial interest if the person has, directly or indirectly, through business, investment, or family:

   a. An ownership or investment interest in any entity with which the organization has a transaction or arrangement,
   b. A compensation arrangement with the organization or with any entity or individual with which the organization has a transaction or arrangement, or
   c. A potential ownership or investment interest in, or compensation arrangement with, any entity or individual with which the organization is negotiating a transaction or arrangement.

   Compensation includes direct and indirect remuneration as well as gifts or favors that are not insubstantial.

   (A financial interest is not necessarily a conflict of interest. Under Article III, Section 2, a person who has a financial interest may have a conflict of interest only if the appropriate governing board or committee decides that a conflict of interest exists.)

Article III
Procedures

1. Duty to Disclose
In connection with any actual or possible conflict of interest, an interested person must disclose the existence of the financial interest and be given the opportunity to disclose all material facts to the directors and members of committees with governing board delegated powers considering the proposed transaction or arrangement.

2. Determining Whether a Conflict of Interest Exists
After disclosure of the financial interest and all material facts, and after any discussion with the interested person, he/she shall leave the governing board or committee meeting while the determination of a conflict of interest is discussed and voted upon. The remaining board or committee members shall decide if a conflict of interest exists.

3. Procedures for Addressing the Conflict of Interest
   a. An interested person may make a presentation at the governing board or committee meeting, but after the presentation, he/she shall leave the meeting during the discussion of, and the vote on, the transaction or arrangement involving the possible conflict of interest.
   b. The chairperson of the governing board or committee shall, if appropriate, appoint a disinterested person or committee to investigate alternatives to the proposed transaction or arrangement.
   c. After exercising due diligence, the governing board or committee shall determine whether the organization can obtain with reasonable efforts a more advantageous transaction or arrangement from a person or entity that would not give rise to a conflict of interest.

1   Attachment to Part V, Line 5a

d. If a more advantageous transaction or arrangement is not reasonably possible under circumstances not producing a conflict of interest, the governing board or committee shall determine by a majority vote of the disinterested directors whether the transaction or arrangement is in the organization's best interest, for its own benefit, and whether it is fair and reasonable. In conformity with the above determination it shall make its decision as to whether to enter into the transaction or arrangement.

4. Violations of the Conflicts of Interest Policy

a. If the governing board or committee has reasonable cause to believe a member has failed to disclose actual or possible conflicts of interest, it shall inform the member of the basis for such belief and afford the member an opportunity to explain the alleged failure to disclose.

b. If, after hearing the member's response and after making further investigation as warranted by the circumstances, the governing board or committee determines the member has failed to disclose an actual or possible conflict of interest, it shall take appropriate disciplinary and corrective action.

Article IV
Records of Proceedings

The minutes of the governing board and all committees with board delegated powers shall contain:

a. The names of the persons who disclosed or otherwise were found to have a financial interest in connection with an actual or possible conflict of interest, the nature of the financial interest, any action taken to determine whether a conflict of interest was present, and the governing board's or committee's decision as to whether a conflict of interest in fact existed.

b. The names of the persons who were present for discussions and votes relating to the transaction or arrangement, the content of the discussion, including any alternatives to the proposed transaction or arrangement, and a record of any votes taken in connection with the proceedings.

Article V
Compensation

a. A voting member of the governing board who receives compensation, directly or indirectly, from the Organization for services is precluded from voting on matters pertaining to that member's compensation.

b. A voting member of any committee whose jurisdiction includes compensation matters and who receives compensation, directly or indirectly, from the Organization for services is precluded from voting on matters pertaining to that member's compensation.

c. No voting member of the governing board or any committee whose jurisdiction includes compensation matters and who receives compensation, directly or indirectly, from the Organization, either individually or collectively, is prohibited from providing information to any committee regarding compensation.

Article VI
Annual Statements

Each director, principal officer and member of a committee with governing board-delegated powers shall annually sign a statement, which affirms such person:

a. Has received a copy of the conflicts of interest policy,

b. Has read and understands the policy,

c. Has agreed to comply with the policy, and

d. Understands the organization is charitable and in order to maintain its federal tax exemption it must engage primarily in activities that accomplish one or more of its tax-exempt purposes.

Appendix B Form 1023 for a Public Charity

Article VII
Periodic Reviews

To ensure the organization operates in a manner consistent with charitable purposes and does not engage in activities that could jeopardize its tax-exempt status, periodic reviews shall be conducted. The periodic reviews shall, at a minimum, include the following subjects:

a. Whether compensation arrangements and benefits are reasonable, based on competent survey information, and the result of arm's length bargaining.

b. Whether partnerships, joint ventures, and arrangements with management organizations conform to the organization's written policies, are properly recorded, reflect reasonable investment or payments for goods and services, further charitable purposes and do not result in inurement, impermissible private benefit or in an excess benefit transaction.

Article VIII
Use of Outside Experts

When conducting the periodic reviews as provided for in Article VII, the organization may, but need not, use outside advisors. If outside experts are used, their use shall not relieve the governing board of its responsibility for ensuring periodic reviews are conducted.

Adopted by Board of Directors on June 1, 2005

3   Attachment to Part V, Line 5a

Appendix B Form 1023 for a Public Charity

Form **5768**	Election/Revocation of Election by an Eligible	
(Rev. December 2004)	Section 501(c)(3) Organization To Make	
Department of the Treasury Internal Revenue Service	Expenditures To Influence Legislation (Under Section 501(h) of the Internal Revenue Code)	For IRS Use Only ▶

Name of organization **Hometown Campaign to Clean Up America**	Employer identification number 44 : 4444444
Number and street (or P.O. box no., if mail is not delivered to street address) **1111 Any Street**	Room/suite
City, town or post office, and state **Hometown, XX 77777-7777**	ZIP + 4

1 Election—As an eligible organization, we hereby elect to have the provisions of section 501(h) of the Code, relating to expenditures to influence legislation, apply to our tax year ending................ 06/30/06 ....and all subsequent tax years until revoked.

                                                                    (Month, day, and year)

Note: *This election must be signed and postmarked within the first taxable year to which it applies.*

2 Revocation—As an eligible organization, we hereby revoke our election to have the provisions of section 501(h) of the Code, relating to expenditures to influence legislation, apply to our tax year ending ....

                                                                    (Month, day, and year)

Note: *This revocation must be signed and postmarked before the first day of the tax year to which it applies.*

Under penalties of perjury, I declare that I am authorized to make this (check applicable box) ▶ ☑ election ☐ revocation on behalf of the above named organization.

(Signature of officer or trustee)	**John J. Environmentalist, President** (Type or print name and title)	7-10.05 (Date)

General Instructions

Section references are to the Internal Revenue Code.

Section 501(c)(3) states that an organization exempt under that section will lose its tax-exempt status and its qualification to receive deductible charitable contributions if a substantial part of its activities are carried on to influence legislation. Section 501(h), however, permits certain eligible 501(c)(3) organizations to elect to make limited expenditures to influence legislation. An organization making the election will, however, be subject to an excise tax under section 4911 if it spends more than the amounts permitted by that section. Also, the organization may lose its exempt status if its lobbying expenditures exceed the permitted amounts by more than 50% over a 4-year period. For any tax year in which an election under section 501(h) is in effect, an electing organization must report the actual and permitted amounts of its lobbying expenditures and grass roots expenditures (as defined in section 4911(c)) on its annual return required under section 6033. See Schedule A (Form 990 or Form 990-EZ). Each electing member of an affiliated group must report these amounts for both itself and the affiliated group as a whole.

To make or revoke the election, enter the ending date of the tax year to which the election or revocation applies in item 1 or **2**, as applicable, and sign and date the form in the spaces provided.

Eligible Organizations.—A section 501(c)(3) organization is permitted to make the election if it is not a disqualified organization (see below) and is described in:

1. Section 170(b)(1)(A)(ii) (relating to educational institutions),
2. Section 170(b)(1)(A)(iii) (relating to hospitals and medical research organizations),
3. Section 170(b)(1)(A)(iv) (relating to organizations supporting government schools),
4. Section 170(b)(1)(A)(vi) (relating to organizations publicly supported by charitable contributions),
5. Section 509(a)(2) (relating to organizations publicly supported by admissions, sales, etc.), or
6. Section 509(a)(3) (relating to organizations supporting certain types of public charities other than those section 509(a)(3) organizations that support section 501(c)(4), (5), or (6) organizations).

Disqualified Organizations.—The following types of organizations are not permitted to make the election:

a. Section 170(b)(1)(A)(i) organizations (relating to churches),

b. An integrated auxiliary of a church or of a convention or association of churches, or
c. A member of an affiliated group of organizations if one or more members of such group is described in **a** or **b** of this paragraph.

Affiliated Organizations.—Organizations are members of an affiliated group of organizations only if **(1)** the governing instrument of one such organization requires it to be bound by the decisions of the other organization on legislative issues, or **(2)** the governing board of one such organization includes persons (i) who are specifically designated representatives of another such organization or are members of the governing board, officers, or paid executive staff members of such other organization, and (ii) who, by aggregating their votes, have sufficient voting power to cause or prevent action on legislative issues by the first such organization.

For more details, see section 4911 and section 501(h).

Note: *A private foundation (including a private operating foundation) is not an eligible organization.*

Where To File.—Mail Form 5768 to the Internal Revenue Service Center, Ogden, UT 84201-0027.

Cat. No. 12125M

Form **5768** (Rev. 12-2004)

Appendix B Form 1023 for a Public Charity

Hometown Campaign to Clean Up America   44-4444444
Attachment to Form 1023

Part I, Line 7

A Good Accountant, Smith & Jones, LLP, 1 Main Street, Hometown, XX 77777

Part I, Line 8

A Good Accountant, Smith & Jones, LLP, 1 Main Street, Hometown, XX 77777.
The amount to be paid for the preparation of Form 1023 is approximately $2,500. The fee for future preparation of required Internal Revenue Service filings such as the Form 990 is expected to range between $1,500 – 2,000 per year. A Good Accountant will help the organization by preparing all required Internal Revenue Service filings.

Part IV

The purpose of Hometown Campaign to Clean Up America ("Campaign") is to rid the cities, towns, suburbs, and other areas of the United States of trash, debris, and other litter, as the name of the organization indicates. It is the vision of those who have formed the organization that the beauty of the landscape of this country should not be tarnished, or hidden, by accumulations of garbage and other trash.

It is the Campaign's belief that much of the solution to the nation's trash problem lies in individuals' attitudes and mindsets. An area that is clean is less likely to be trashed than one that is already littered. A community whose occupants are sensitized to the litter accumulation problem is less likely to be full of trash than the one whose occupants have subconsciously repressed the ugly sights. A community whose members are willing to rid the area of trash, and keep it that way, will be a far more beautiful place to live and work, and be proud of, than one that is constantly strewn with litter.

VOLUNTEER TEAMS: The Campaign will focus on the prevention of littering and the pick-up of litter where it is found. As to the latter, the Campaign will, on a community-by community basis, organize teams of volunteers who will pick up trash to keep their community clean and scenic. It will supply these teams with the equipment necessary to achieve this end, including rakes, shovels, gloves, trash bags, and safety signs to alert traffic that Clean Up America teams are at work in their community. If funding permits, the Campaign will provide members of these teams with *CLEAN UP AMERICA* T-shirts, to both stimulate spirit in their volunteer work and advertise the program of the Campaign.

The Campaign will provide these teams with information regarding organizational techniques, safety matters and ideas for coordinating their efforts with local governmental officials. This latter aspect will also be of importance in organizing means of trash disposal. The Campaign will also provide the teams with practical guidelines on matters such as trespassing, personal safety, and similar aspects that involve considerations of law.

PUBLIC EDUCATION PROGRAM: The Campaign will endeavor to prevent littering from occurring in the first instance through public education programs. These will consist of training seminars, the distribution of literature, media advertising, and community meetings. The public education aspect of the Campaign's program will be intertwined with its fundraising program. Essentially, the public education component of the Campaign's efforts will be directed to ways to sensitize individuals to the problems of litter accumulation, in the hope that they will not litter, be moved of to dispose of litter caused by others, and join the Campaign to make and keep their community trash-free.

It is the belief of the Campaign that a community that is physically attractive (litter-free) is a community that will have other desirable attributes that constitute a better way of life for its citizens.

LEGISLATIVE ACTIVITY: The Campaign expects to engage in some attempts to influence legislation, mostly at the local level, such as laws to toughen the fines for littering and to force trucks to travel with their loads covered. However, any such activities will be insubstantial in relation to total activities and less than 1% of the budget would be devoted to lobbying.

Attachment to Many Parts

Page 1 of 4

Appendix B Form 1023 for a Public Charity

UNRELATED BUSINESS ACTIVITY: The Campaign may engage in modest activities that may constitute unrelated business. For example, the Campaign may sell trash bags (bearing its name and an anti-litter message) to the general public. Unrelated business activities, if any, will be insubstantial in relation to total activities.

Part V, Line 2a

The President, John J. Environmentalist, is married to the Secretary/Treasurer, Jane D. Environmentalist.

Part V, Line 2c

The Executive Director Andrew Organized is married to one of the highest compensated independent contractors, Ellen Organized. Ellen Organized provides development and public relations for Hometown Campaign to Clean Up America.

Part V, Line 3a

John J. Environmentalist is the President. His qualifications include a degree in environmental sciences. He generally works 10 hours a week for the organization as a volunteer with no compensation. His duties include supervising and conducting the organization's activities and operations. He will preside at all meetings and shall keep the Board informed concerning activities of the Campaign. He may sign contracts and documents authorized by the Board. He can establish committees and appoint members to serve on committees.

Jane D. Environmentalist is the Secretary and Treasurer. Her qualifications include working at a law firm, which specializes in environmental issues. She generally works 5 hours a week for the organization as a volunteer with no compensation. Her duties include acting as Secretary of all meetings and keeping the minutes. She also serves all notices of the Campaign. In addition, she has custody of all funds and securities of the Campaign. She maintains a full and accurate account of receipts and disbursements of the Campaign and deposits all money and valuables in the bank or other depositories.

James F. Friend is the Vice President. His qualifications include an interest in saving the environment and experience as a business owner. He generally works 2 hours a week for the organization as a volunteer with no compensation.

Jacob Thoughtful is a Director. His qualifications include working at the local waste management processing plant. He is also an avid recycler. He generally works 1 hour a week for the organization as a volunteer with no compensation.

Jennifer Scholar is a Director. Her qualifications include a doctorate in environmental science. She is a professor at Hometown University. She generally works 1 hour a week for the organization as a volunteer with no compensation.

Andrew Organized is the Executive Director. His qualifications include formerly working at the United Way for the environmental issues department. He has lectured throughout the country on the importance of cleanliness in the environment. He works approximately 45 hours per week. His duties include daily management of the organization and its activities under the guidance of the Board of Directors.

Joan Controller is the Controller. Her qualifications include being a certified public accountant and working for ten years for another exempt organization in Hometown. She works approximately 30 hours per week. Her duties include all financial aspects of the organization including budgeting and financial management. She also assists the executive director with his duties as needed.

Ellen Organized is a highly compensated independent contractor who specializes in development and public relations for companies. She runs her own business called Organize and Optimize. She has a fixed fee agreement with Campaign from February to December, 2005, for $55,000.

Appendix B Form 1023 for a Public Charity

Hometown Campaign to Clean Up America   44-4444444
Attachment to Form 1023

Part V, Line 5a

The Board of Directors of Campaign adopted a conflict of interest policy consistent with the recommendations of the Internal Revenue Service instructions. Please find a copy of the policy attached.

Part V, Line 6a

The employment agreement with the Executive Director, Andrew Organized, provides he may be compensated through a non-fixed payment in the form of a discretionary bonus. The Board of Directors has the option of voting to give the executive director a non-fixed bonus if his work has been excellent for the previous year and all goals have been met or exceeded. The optional bonus must be less than 10% of his total compensation for the year. The bonus must be reviewed by the Board of Directors to ensure that the total compensation plus the optional bonus is reasonable compensation for his services.

Part V, Line 8a

Initially, Campaign will use donated space. As the programs expand, Campaign expects to rent office space from an unrelated party.

Part VI, Line 1a

Campaign plans to provide funds to individuals in its volunteer recognition program. This program will annually recognize volunteers who have provided exemplary services in advancing the organization's mission. The value of the volunteer awards ranges from $100 to $1,500. Campaign will sponsor training seminars for its volunteers and community leaders and conduct other educational efforts as described in Part IV. Modest charges for programs will be charged for those that can pay.

Part VIII, Line 2a

The Campaign expects to engage in limited attempts to influence legislation, mostly at the local level, such as laws to toughen the fines for littering and to force trucks to travel with their loads covered. However, any such activities will be insubstantial in relation to total activities and less than 1% of the budget would be devoted to lobbying. Form 5768 is attached.

Part VIII, Line 4a

Campaign will conduct fundraising activities to raise funds for the organization's programs. Possible activities conducted by the staff of the organization and its volunteers include: mail solicitations, email solicitations, personal solicitations, foundation grant solicitations and accepting donations on the organization's website. See attached sample solicitation letter. All activities will comply with the Internal Revenue Service requirements regarding donor acknowledgements.

Part VIII, Line 4b

Campaign will purchase promotional and public relations services from an independent contractor Ellen Organized. Campaign has negotiated these services at arm's length and the fees are at or below the fair market value as determined by bids from similar companies. A copy of the terminable-at-will contract is attached to this application.

Attachment to Many Parts

Appendix B Form 1023 for a Public Charity

Hometown Campaign to Clean Up America
Attachment to Form 1023

44-4444444

Part VIII, Line 11

Campaign has not accepted donations other than cash at this time. It is unknown if any property contributions may be given to Campaign in the future. If Campaign were offered a non-cash contribution, the Campaign would work with its tax advisors to make sure that it complied with all applicable Internal Revenue Services rules for the organization and the donor.

Appendix B Form 1023 for a Public Charity

MINIMAL INDEPENDENT CONTRACTOR AGREEMENT

> Agreements should be prepared in consultation with a nonprofit's legal
> counsel. This model is intended only as an illustration.

Name of   <u>Hometown Campaign to Clean Up America</u>
Organization _____

Contractor: <u>Ellen Organized</u>
             _____

Price:

Fixed fee for February –December, 2005	<u>$55,000</u>
Hourly rate $. per-hour times____ hours =	_____
Reimbursable expenses:	
_____	_____
_____	_____

Payments will be made monthly, based upon invoices submitted by you, along with
receipts and other documentation for reimbursable expenses described above. For
consideration, you agree to perform the following work:

<u>Public relations and promotion of Hometown Campaign to Clean Up Public
America</u>

The total fees and expense reimbursements paid to you during the calendar year will
be reported to the Internal Revenue Service on Form 1099Misc, Non-employee
compensation. By signing this agreement and providing us with a signed Form W-9,
you certify that you are an independent contractor, not an employee, agent, or
representative of the company. You are responsible for all federal and state payroll
taxes and insurance. You--on behalf of yourself, your assigns, and estate--waive and
release any and all claims or rights whatsoever you may have against us. This
agreement may be terminated by either party at any time, except that you will be paid
for any unpaid services properly chargeable to us prior to termination.   In
acknowledgment of our understandings, we have both signed below.

By: John J. Environmentalist   By: Ellen Organized

Date: _____   Date: _____
       6·30·05   6·30·05

Reprinted from Blazek, *Financial Planning for Nonprofit Organizations*, John Wiley & Sons, 1996.

Attachment to Part V, Line 4

Appendix B Form 1023 for a Public Charity

Hometown Campaign to Clean Up America   44-4444444
Attachment to Form 1023

HOMETOWN CAMPAIGN TO CLEAN UP AMERICA
1111 Any Street
Hometown, XX 77777

April 1, 20xx

Joe Goodman, President
XYZ FOUNDATION
Central National Bank Building
Norman, OK 33333

Dear Joe,

The HOMETOWN CAMPAIGN TO CLEAN UP AMERICA (Campaign) has been established to rid our cities, towns and countrysides of the trash, debris and other litter which defaces our land. It is our vision that the beauty of the landscapes of this country should not be tarnished, or hidden, by accumulations of garbage and other trash that can be reused.

Part of our strategy is to change people's attitudes towards trash. Our municipality's experience is that a clean area is less likely to be trashed than one that is already littered. A community whose occupants are sensitized to the litter accumulation problems is less likely to be full of trash than the one where its occupants have subconsciously repressed the ugly sights. A community whose members are willing to rid the area of trash, and keep it that way, will be a far more beautiful place to live and work, and be proud of, than one that is constantly strewn with litter.

We will initially target three towns in Texas and two in Oklahoma. We respectfully request that your foundation serve as our official Oklahoma sponsor. Your foundation's name will be featured on all of our educational materials and volunteer packs distributed in the State of Oklahoma for the fist two years. We are asking you to grant us one-third of the estimated cost of our Oklahoma activities, or $60,000 a year for two years.

The Campaign's efforts for the first three years will be focused upon:

PROJECT	ESTIMATED COST
VOLUNTEER TEAMS	$ 350,000
PUBLIC EDUCATION	150,000
PROGRAMS AND SEMINARS	70,000
GENERAL & ADMINISTRATIVE	100,000
FUNDRAISING	110,000
	$ 780,000

Attachment to Part VIII, Line 4a

Appendix B Form 1023 for a Public Charity

Hometown Campaign to Clean Up America   44-4444444
Attachment to Form 1023

　　A detailed budget and description of the Campaign's projects are enclosed for your reference. We would be happy to meet with you at your convenience to answer any questions or furnish more details. We would welcome your help by way of introductions to folks in Oklahoma as well.

　　Our long range plans for the Campaign, along with wiping out litter, include fostering nationwide recycling habits by elimination of disposable containers and toxic containers which pollute our air, land and waters.

　　We trust our purposes are in line with those of XYZ Foundation and hope you can decide to work with us in eliminating the environmental problems of our nation.

　　　　　　　　　　　Best regards,

　　　　　　　　　　　Jane D. Environmentalist

enclosures

Appendix B Form 1023 for a Public Charity

Hometown Campaign to Clean Up America   44-4444444
Attachment to Form 1023

Part IX-A Financial Data

	01/15/05- 06/30/05	7/1/05 - 06/30/06	7/1/06 - 06/30/07	TOTAL
Line 1 - Gifts, grants, and contributions				
Contributions/disqualified persons	100,000	50,000	50,000	200,000
Contributions/general public	20,000	150,000	200,000	370,000
Grants/corporations		50,000	50,000	100,000
Grants/private foundations		100,000	130,000	230,000
	120,000	350,000	430,000	900,000
Line 9 - Gross receipts from admissions, etc.				
Seminars	-	5,000	10,000	15,000
Publications	-	5,000	10,000	15,000
	-	10,000	20,000	30,000
Line 14 - Fundraising expenses				
Professional fees	10,000	55,000	40,000	105,000
Printing and mailing	3,000	5,000	10,000	18,000
	13,000	60,000	50,000	123,000
Line 18 - Other salaries and wages				
Executive Director		70,000	80,000	150,000
Controller		55,000	58,000	113,000
Senior staff (1-3)		40,000	120,000	160,000
Administrative staff	10,000	25,000	30,000	65,000
Payroll costs and fringes	1,000	19,000	28,800	48,800
	11,000	209,000	316,800	536,800
Line 22 - Professional fees				
Tax compliance/1023	3,000	2,000	3,000	8,000
Legal fees	2,000	1,000	1,000	4,000
	5,000	3,000	4,000	12,000
Line 23 - Other expenses:				
Printing public information	5,000	10,000	6,000	21,000
Meetings/travel/conferences	-	10,000	20,000	30,000
Supplies	5,000	3,000	4,000	12,000
Website design/maintenance	10,000	2,000	2,000	14,000
	20,000	25,000	32,000	77,000

Part IX-B Financial Data

Line 8 - Depreciable and depletable assets	Cost Basis	Accum Deprec	Book Value
Office equipment and furnishings (5 yr SL)	14,000	(1,400)	12,600

Attachment to Part IX

166

Form 1023 Checklist
(Revised October 2004)
Application for Recognition of Exemption under Section 501(c)(3) of the Internal Revenue Code

Note. *Retain a copy of the completed Form 1023 in your permanent records. Refer to the* General Instructions *regarding Public Inspection of approved applications.*

Check each box to finish your application (Form 1023). Send this completed Checklist with your filled in application. If you have not answered all the items below your application may be returned to you as incomplete.

☑ Assemble the application and materials in this order:
- Form 1023 Checklist
- Form 2848, *Power of Attorney and Declaration of Representative* (if filing)
- Form 8821, *Tax Information Authorization* (if filing)
- Expedite request (if requesting)
- Application (Form 1023 and Schedules A through H, as required)
- Articles of organization
- Amendments to articles of organization in chronological order
- Bylaws or other rules of operation and amendments
- Documentation of nondiscriminatory policy for schools, as required by Schedule B
- Form 5768, Election/Revocation of Election by an Eligible Section 501(c)(3) Organization To Make Expenditures To Influence Legislation (if filing)
- All other attachments, including explanations, financial data, and printed materials or publications. Label each page with name and EIN.

☑ User fee payment placed in envelope on top of checklist. DO NOT STAPLE or otherwise attach your check or money order to your application. Instead, just place it in the envelope.

☑ Employer Identification Number (EIN)

☑ Completed Parts I through XI of the application, including any requested information and any required Schedules A through H.

- You must provide specific details about your past, present, and planned activities.
- Generalizations or failure to answer questions in the Form 1023 application will prevent us from recognizing you as tax exempt.
- Describe your purposes and proposed activities in specific easily understood terms.
- Financial information should correspond with proposed activities.

☑ Schedules. Submit only those schedules that apply to you and check either "Yes" or "No" below.

Schedule A Yes ___ No ✔		Schedule E Yes ___ No ✔	
Schedule B Yes ___ No ✔		Schedule F Yes ___ No ✔	
Schedule C Yes ___ No ✔		Schedule G Yes ___ No ✔	
Schedule D Yes ___ No ✔		Schedule H Yes ___ No ✔	

Appendix C   Form 1023 for a Private Operating Foundation

☑ An exact copy of your complete articles of organization (creating document). Absence of the proper purpose and dissolution clauses is the number one reason for delays in the issuance of determination letters.

  • Location of Purpose Clause from Part III, line 1 (Page, Article and Paragraph Number) **Pg 1, Art. 4, Sec 4.01**
  • Location of Dissolution Clause from Part III, line 2b or 2c (Page, Article and Paragraph Number) or by operation of state law **Pg 2, Art. 4, Sec. 4.02c**

☑ Signature of an officer, director, trustee, or other official who is authorized to sign the application.
  • Signature at Part XI of Form 1023.

☑ Your name on the application must be the same as your legal name as it appears in your articles of organization.

Send completed Form 1023, user fee payment, and all other required information, to:

Internal Revenue Service
P.O. Box 192
Covington, KY 41012-0192

If you are using express mail or a delivery service, send Form 1023, user fee payment, and attachments to:

Internal Revenue Service
201 West Rivercenter Blvd.
Attn: Extracting Stop 312
Covington, KY 41011

♻ *Printed on recycled paper*

Appendix C Form 1023 for a Private Operating Foundation

Form **2848** (Rev. March 2004) Department of the Treasury Internal Revenue Service	**Power of Attorney and Declaration of Representative** ▶ Type or print. ▶ See the separate instructions.	OMB No. 1545-0150 **For IRS Use Only** Received by:

Received by:
Name _____
Telephone _____
Function _____
Date ___ / ___ / ___

Part I **Power of Attorney**
Caution: *Form 2848 will not be honored for any purpose other than representation before the IRS.*

1 Taxpayer information. Taxpayer(s) must sign and date this form on page 2, line 9.

Taxpayer name(s) and address	Social security number(s)	Employer identification number
Active Project Fund **1010 Main Street** **Any Town, XX 77777**		**44 ː 4444444**
	Daytime telephone number (**444**) **444-4444**	Plan number (if applicable)

hereby appoint(s) the following representative(s) as attorney(s)-in-fact:

2 Representative(s) must sign and date this form on page 2, Part II.

Name and address	
A Good Accountant **1 Main Street** **Any Town, XX 77777**	CAF No. .... **5555-55555R** Telephone No. ...... **555-555-5551** Fax No. .... **555-555-5552** Check if new: Address ☐ Telephone No. ☐ Fax No. ☐
Name and address	CAF No. .... Telephone No. .... Fax No. .... Check if new: Address ☐ Telephone No. ☐ Fax No. ☐
Name and address	CAF No. .... Telephone No. .... Fax No. .... Check if new: Address ☐ Telephone No. ☐ Fax No. ☐

to represent the taxpayer(s) before the Internal Revenue Service for the following tax matters:

3 Tax matters

Type of Tax (Income, Employment, Excise, etc.) or Civil Penalty (see the instructions for line 3)	Tax Form Number (1040, 941, 720, etc.)	Year(s) or Period(s) (see the instructions for line 3)
Income	1023	2005-2006

4 Specific use not recorded on Centralized Authorization File (CAF). If the power of attorney is for a specific use not recorded on CAF, check this box. See the instructions for **Line 4. Specific uses not recorded on CAF.** . . . . ▶ ☐

5 Acts authorized. The representatives are authorized to receive and inspect confidential tax information and to perform any and all acts that I (we) can perform with respect to the tax matters described on line 3, for example, the authority to sign any agreements, consents, or other documents. The authority does not include the power to receive refund checks (see line 6 below), the power to substitute another representative, the power to sign certain returns, or the power to execute a request for disclosure of tax returns or return information to a third party. See the line 5 instructions for more information.

Exceptions. An unenrolled return preparer cannot sign any document for a taxpayer and may only represent taxpayers in limited situations. See **Unenrolled Return Preparer** on page 2 of the instructions. An enrolled actuary may only represent taxpayers to the extent provided in section 10.3(d) of Circular 230. See the line 5 instructions for restrictions on tax matters partners.

List any specific additions or deletions to the acts otherwise authorized in this power of attorney: ....
....
....
....

6 Receipt of refund checks. If you want to authorize a representative named on line 2 to receive, **BUT NOT TO ENDORSE OR CASH,** refund checks, initial here _____ and list the name of that representative below.

Name of representative to receive refund check(s) ▶

For Privacy Act and Paperwork Reduction Notice, see page 4 of the instructions.   Cat. No. 11980J   Form **2848** (Rev. 3-2004)

Appendix C Form 1023 for a Private Operating Foundation

7   **Notices and communications.** Original notices and other written communications will be sent to you and a copy to the first representative listed on line 2.

  a   If you also want the second representative listed to receive a copy of notices and communications, check this box . . ▶ ☐

  b   If you do not want any notices or communications sent to your representative(s), check this box . . . .▶ ☐

8   **Retention/revocation of prior power(s) of attorney.** The filing of this power of attorney automatically revokes all earlier power(s) of attorney on file with the Internal Revenue Service for the same tax matters and years or periods covered by this document. If you **do not** want to revoke a prior power of attorney, check here. . . . .▶ ☐

    YOU MUST ATTACH A COPY OF ANY POWER OF ATTORNEY YOU WANT TO REMAIN IN EFFECT.

9   **Signature of taxpayer(s).** If a tax matter concerns a joint return, **both** husband and wife must sign if joint representation is requested, otherwise, see the instructions. If signed by a corporate officer, partner, guardian, tax matters partner, executor, receiver, administrator, or trustee on behalf of the taxpayer, I certify that I have the authority to execute this form on behalf of the taxpayer.

    ▶ **IF NOT SIGNED AND DATED, THIS POWER OF ATTORNEY WILL BE RETURNED.**

(signature)	**5.2.05**	President
Signature	Date	Title (if applicable)
A.B. Sample	5 5 5 5 5	Active Project Fund
Print Name	PIN Number	Print name of taxpayer from line 1 if other than individual
Signature	Date	Title (if applicable)
	☐ ☐ ☐ ☐ ☐	
Print Name	PIN Number	

Part II   **Declaration of Representative**

Caution: *Students with a special order to represent taxpayers in Qualified Low Income Taxpayer Clinics or the Student Tax Clinic Program, see the instructions for Part II.*

Under penalties of perjury, I declare that:

- I am not currently under suspension or disbarment from practice before the Internal Revenue Service;
- I am aware of regulations contained in Treasury Department Circular No. 230 (31 CFR, Part 10), as amended, concerning the practice of attorneys, certified public accountants, enrolled agents, enrolled actuaries, and others;
- I am authorized to represent the taxpayer(s) identified in Part I for the tax matter(s) specified there; and
- I am one of the following:

  a   Attorney—a member in good standing of the bar of the highest court of the jurisdiction shown below.

  b   Certified Public Accountant—duly qualified to practice as a certified public accountant in the jurisdiction shown below.

  c   Enrolled Agent—enrolled as an agent under the requirements of Treasury Department Circular No. 230.

  d   Officer—a bona fide officer of the taxpayer's organization.

  e   Full-Time Employee—a full-time employee of the taxpayer.

  f   Family Member—a member of the taxpayer's immediate family (i.e., spouse, parent, child, brother, or sister).

  g   Enrolled Actuary—enrolled as an actuary by the Joint Board for the Enrollment of Actuaries under 29 U.S.C. 1242 (the authority to practice before the Service is limited by section 10.3(d) of Treasury Department Circular No. 230).

  h   Unenrolled Return Preparer—the authority to practice before the Internal Revenue Service is limited by Treasury Department Circular No. 230, section 10.7(c)(1)(viii). You must have prepared the return in question and the return must be under examination by the IRS. See **Unenrolled Return Preparer** on page 2 of the instructions.

▶ **IF THIS DECLARATION OF REPRESENTATIVE IS NOT SIGNED AND DATED, THE POWER OF ATTORNEY WILL BE RETURNED.** See the Part II instructions.

Designation—Insert above letter **(a–h)**	Jurisdiction (state) or identification	Signature	Date
b	XX	*(signature)* Accountant	5.1.05

Appendix C Form 1023 for a Private Operating Foundation

<table>
<tr><td>Form 1023
(Rev. October 2004)
Department of the Treasury
Internal Revenue Service</td><td align="center">Application for Recognition of Exemption
Under Section 501(c)(3) of the Internal Revenue Code</td><td>OMB No. 1545-0056
Note: If exempt status is approved, this application will be open for public inspection.</td></tr>
</table>

*Use the instructions to complete this application and for a definition of all **bold** items.* For additional help, call IRS Exempt Organizations Customer Account Services toll-free at 1-877-829-5500. Visit our website at **www.irs.gov** for forms and publications. If the required information and documents are not submitted with payment of the appropriate user fee, the application may be returned to you.

Attach additional sheets to this application if you need more space to answer fully. Put your name and EIN on each sheet and identify each answer by Part and line number. Complete Parts I - XI of Form 1023 and submit only those Schedules (A through H) that apply to you.

Part I   Identification of Applicant

1 Full name of organization (exactly as it appears in your **organizing document**) **Active Project Fund**	**2** c/o Name (if applicable)

3 **Mailing address** (Number and street) (see instructions) **1010 Main Street**	Room/Suite	**4** Employer Identification Number (EIN) **33-3333333**
City or town, state or country, and ZIP + 4 **Any Town, XX 77777**		**5** Month the annual accounting period ends (01 – 12) **12**

6 Primary contact (officer, director, trustee, or **authorized representative**) **a** Name: **A Good Accountant or Lawyer**	**b** Phone: **(323) 222-3333**
	c Fax: (optional) **(323) 222-3334**

7 Are you represented by an authorized representative, such as an attorney or accountant? If "Yes," provide the authorized representative's name, and the name and address of the authorized representative's firm. Include a completed Form 2848, *Power of Attorney and Declaration of Representative,* with your application if you would like us to communicate with your representative. ☑ Yes ☐ No

See attachment

8 Was a person who is not one of your officers, directors, trustees, employees, or an authorized representative listed in line 7, paid, or promised payment, to help plan, manage, or advise you about the structure or activities of your organization, or about your financial or tax matters? If "Yes," provide the person's name, the name and address of the person's firm, the amounts paid or promised to be paid, and describe that person's role. ☑ Yes ☐ No

See attachment

9a Organization's website: **www.activeprojectfund.org**

b Organization's email: (optional) **info@activeprojectfund.org**

10 Certain organizations are not required to file an information return (Form 990 or Form 990-EZ). If you are granted tax-exemption, are you claiming to be excused from filing Form 990 or Form 990-EZ? If "Yes," explain. See the instructions for a description of organizations not required to file Form 990 or Form 990-EZ. ☐ Yes ☑ No

11 Date incorporated if a corporation, or formed, if other than a corporation. (MM/DD/YYYY) **01** / **15** / **2005**

12 Were you formed under the laws of a **foreign country**? ☐ Yes ☑ No
If "Yes," state the country.

For Paperwork Reduction Act Notice, see page 24 of the instructions.	Cat. No. 17133K	Form **1023** (Rev. 10-2004)

Appendix C Form 1023 for a Private Operating Foundation

Part II Organizational Structure

You must be a corporation (including a limited liability company), an unincorporated association, or a trust to be tax exempt. (See instructions.) **DO NOT file this form unless you can check "Yes" on lines 1, 2, 3, or 4.**

1 Are you a **corporation**? If "Yes," attach a copy of your articles of incorporation showing **certification of filing** with the appropriate state agency. Include copies of any amendments to your articles and be sure they also show state filing certification. ☑ Yes ☐ No
See attachment

2 Are you a **limited liability company (LLC)**? If "Yes," attach a copy of your articles of organization showing certification of filing with the appropriate state agency. Also, if you adopted an operating agreement, attach a copy. Include copies of any amendments to your articles and be sure they show state filing certification. Refer to the instructions for circumstances when an LLC should not file its own exemption application. ☐ Yes ☑ No

3 Are you an **unincorporated association**? If "Yes," attach a copy of your articles of association, constitution, or other similar organizing document that is dated and includes at least two signatures. Include signed and dated copies of any amendments. ☐ Yes ☑ No

4a Are you a **trust**? If "Yes," attach a signed and dated copy of your trust agreement. Include signed and dated copies of any amendments. ☐ Yes ☑ No

b Have you been funded? If "No," explain how you are formed without anything of value placed in trust. ☐ Yes ☑ No

5 Have you adopted **bylaws**? If "Yes," attach a current copy showing date of adoption. If "No," explain how your officers, directors, or trustees are selected. ☑ Yes ☐ No
See attachment

Part III Required Provisions in Your Organizing Document

The following questions are designed to ensure that when you file this application, your organizing document contains the required provisions to meet the organizational test under section 501(c)(3). Unless you can check the boxes in both lines 1 and 2, your organizing document does not meet the organizational test. **DO NOT file this application until you have amended your organizing document**. Submit your original and amended organizing documents (showing state filing certification if you are a corporation or an LLC) with your application.

1 Section 501(c)(3) requires that your organizing document state your exempt purpose(s), such as charitable, religious, educational, and/or scientific purposes. Check the box to confirm that your organizing document meets this requirement. Describe specifically where your organizing document meets this requirement, such as a reference to a particular article or section in your organizing document. Refer to the instructions for exempt purpose language. Location of Purpose Clause (Page, Article, and Paragraph): <u>Pg 1, Art. 4, Sec. 4.01</u> ☑

2a Section 501(c)(3) requires that upon dissolution of your organization, your remaining assets must be used exclusively for exempt purposes, such as charitable, religious, educational, and/or scientific purposes. Check the box on line 2a to confirm that your organizing document meets this requirement by express provision for the distribution of assets upon dissolution. If you rely on state law for your dissolution provision, do not check the box on line 2a and go to line 2c. ☑

2b If you checked the box on line 2a, specify the location of your dissolution clause (Page, Article, and Paragraph). Do not complete line 2c if you checked box 2a. <u>Pg 2, Art. 4, Sec. 4.02 c</u>

2c See the instructions for information about the operation of state law in your particular state. Check this box if you rely on operation of state law for your dissolution provision and indicate the state: _____ ☐

Part IV Narrative Description of Your Activities **See attachment**

Using an attachment, describe your *past, present,* and *planned* activities in a narrative. If you believe that you have already provided some of this information in response to other parts of this application, you may summarize that information here and refer to the specific parts of the application for supporting details. You may also attach representative copies of newsletters, brochures, or similar documents for supporting details to this narrative. Remember that if this application is approved, it will be open for public inspection. Therefore, your narrative description of activities should be thorough and accurate. Refer to the instructions for information that must be included in your description.

Part V Compensation and Other Financial Arrangements With Your Officers, Directors, Trustees, Employees, and Independent Contractors

1a List the names, titles, and mailing addresses of all of your officers, directors, and trustees. For each person listed, state their total annual **compensation**, or proposed compensation, for all services to the organization, whether as an officer, employee, or other position. Use actual figures, if available. Enter "none" if no compensation is or will be paid. If additional space is needed, attach a separate sheet. Refer to the instructions for information on what to include as compensation.

Name	Title	Mailing address	Compensation amount (annual actual or estimated)
A.B. Sample	President	1010 Main Street Any Town, XX 77777	None
C.D. Sample	Secretary/Treasurer	1010 Main Street Any Town, XX 77777	None
E.F. Sample	Vice President	1010 Main Street Any Town, XX 77777	None

Form **1023** (Rev. 10-2004)

Appendix C Form 1023 for a Private Operating Foundation

Part V	**Compensation and Other Financial Arrangements With Your Officers, Directors, Trustees, Employees, and Independent Contractors** *(Continued)*

b List the names, titles, and mailing addresses of each of your five highest compensated employees who receive or will receive compensation of more than $50,000 per year. Use the actual figure, if available. Refer to the instructions for information on what to include as compensation. Do not include officers, directors, or trustees listed in line 1a.

Name	Title	Mailing address	Compensation amount (annual actual or estimated)
Jane Smith	Executive Director	1010 Main Street Any Town, XX 77777	52,000

c List the names, names of businesses, and mailing addresses of your five highest compensated **independent contractors** that receive or will receive compensation of more than $50,000 per year. Use the actual figure, if available. Refer to the instructions for information on what to include as compensation.

Name	Title	Mailing address	Compensation amount (annual actual or estimated)
None			None

The following "Yes" or "No" questions relate to *past, present, or planned* relationships, transactions, or agreements with your officers, directors, trustees, highest compensated employees, and highest compensated independent contractors listed in lines 1a, 1b, and 1c.

2a Are any of your officers, directors, or trustees **related** to each other through **family** or **business relationships**? If "Yes," identify the individuals and explain the relationship. ☑ **Yes** ☐ **No** **See attachment**

b Do you have a business relationship with any of your officers, directors, or trustees other than through their position as an officer, director, or trustee? If "Yes," identify the individuals and describe the business relationship with each of your officers, directors, or trustees. ☐ **Yes** ☑ **No**

c Are any of your officers, directors, or trustees related to your highest compensated employees or highest compensated independent contractors listed on lines 1b or 1c through family or business relationships? If "Yes," identify the individuals and explain the relationship. ☐ **Yes** ☑ **No**

3a For each of your officers, directors, trustees, highest compensated employees, and highest compensated independent contractors listed on lines 1a, 1b, or 1c, attach a list showing their name, qualifications, average hours worked, and duties. **See attachment**

b Do any of your officers, directors, trustees, highest compensated employees, and highest compensated independent contractors listed on lines 1a, 1b, or 1c receive compensation from any other organizations, whether tax exempt or taxable, that are related to you through **common control**? If "Yes," identify the individuals, explain the relationship between you and the other organization, and describe the compensation arrangement. ☐ **Yes** ☑ **No**

4 In establishing the compensation for your officers, directors, trustees, highest compensated employees, and highest compensated independent contractors listed on lines 1a, 1b, and 1c, the following practices are recommended, although they are not required to obtain exemption. Answer "Yes" to all the practices you use.

a Do you or will the individuals that approve compensation arrangements follow a conflict of interest policy? ☑ **Yes** ☐ **No**

b Do you or will you approve compensation arrangements in advance of paying compensation? ☑ **Yes** ☐ **No**

c Do you or will you document in writing the date and terms of approved compensation arrangements? ☑ **Yes** ☐ **No**

Appendix C Form 1023 for a Private Operating Foundation

Part V	**Compensation and Other Financial Arrangements With Your Officers, Directors, Trustees, Employees, and Idenpendent Contractors** *(Continued)*

d Do you or will you record in writing the decision made by each individual who decided or voted on compensation arrangements? ☑ Yes ☐ No

e Do you or will you approve compensation arrangements based on information about compensation paid by **similarly situated** taxable or tax-exempt organizations for similar services, current compensation surveys compiled by independent firms, or actual written offers from similarly situated organizations? Refer to the instructions for Part V, lines 1a, 1b, and 1c, for information on what to include as compensation. ☑ Yes ☐ No

f Do you or will you record in writing both the information on which you relied to base your decision and its source? ☑ Yes ☐ No

g If you answered "No" to any item on lines 4a through 4f, describe how you set compensation that is **reasonable** for your officers, directors, trustees, highest compensated employees, and highest compensated independent contractors listed in Part V, lines 1a, 1b, and 1c.

5a Have you adopted a **conflict of interest policy** consistent with the sample conflict of interest policy in Appendix A to the instructions? If "Yes," provide a copy of the policy and explain how the policy has been adopted, such as by resolution of your governing board. If "No," answer lines 5b and 5c. ☑ Yes ☐ No

See attachment

b What procedures will you follow to assure that persons who have a conflict of interest will not have influence over you for setting their own compensation?

c What procedures will you follow to assure that persons who have a conflict of interest will not have influence over you regarding business deals with themselves?

Note: A conflict of interest policy is recommended though it is not required to obtain exemption. Hospitals, see Schedule C, Section I, line 14.

6a Do you or will you compensate any of your officers, directors, trustees, highest compensated employees, and highest compensated independent contractors listed in lines 1a, 1b, or 1c through **non-fixed payments**, such as discretionary bonuses or revenue-based payments? If "Yes," describe all non-fixed compensation arrangements, including how the amounts are determined, who is eligible for such arrangements, whether you place a limitation on total compensation, and how you determine or will determine that you pay no more than reasonable compensation for services. Refer to the instructions for Part V, lines 1a, 1b, and 1c, for information on what to include as compensation. ☑ Yes ☐ No

See attachment

b Do you or will you compensate any of your employees, other than your officers, directors, trustees, or your five highest compensated employees who receive or will receive compensation of more than $50,000 per year, through non-fixed payments, such as discretionary bonuses or revenue-based payments? If "Yes," describe all non-fixed compensation arrangements, including how the amounts are or will be determined, who is or will be eligible for such arrangements, whether you place or will place a limitation on total compensation, and how you determine or will determine that you pay no more than reasonable compensation for services. Refer to the instructions for Part V, lines 1a, 1b, and 1c, for information on what to include as compensation. ☐ Yes ☑ No

7a Do you or will you purchase any goods, services, or assets from any of your officers, directors, trustees, highest compensated employees, or highest compensated independent contractors listed in lines 1a, 1b, or 1c? If "Yes," describe any such purchase that you made or intend to make, from whom you make or will make such purchases, how the terms are or will be negotiated at **arm's length**, and explain how you determine or will determine that you pay no more than **fair market value**. Attach copies of any written contracts or other agreements relating to such purchases. ☐ Yes ☑ No

b Do you or will you sell any goods, services, or assets to any of your officers, directors, trustees, highest compensated employees, or highest compensated independent contractors listed in lines 1a, 1b, or 1c? If "Yes," describe any such sales that you made or intend to make, to whom you make or will make such sales, how the terms are or will be negotiated at arm's length, and explain how you determine or will determine you are or will be paid at least fair market value. Attach copies of any written contracts or other agreements relating to such sales. ☐ Yes ☑ No

8a Do you or will you have any leases, contracts, loans, or other agreements with your officers, directors, trustees, highest compensated employees, or highest compensated independent contractors listed in lines 1a, 1b, or 1c? If "Yes," provide the information requested in lines 8b through 8f. ☐ Yes ☑ No

b Describe any written or oral arrangements that you made or intend to make.

c Identify with whom you have or will have such arrangements.

d Explain how the terms are or will be negotiated at arm's length.

e Explain how you determine you pay no more than fair market value or you are paid at least fair market value.

f Attach copies of any signed leases, contracts, loans, or other agreements relating to such arrangements.

9a Do you or will you have any leases, contracts, loans, or other agreements with any organization in which any of your officers, directors, or trustees are also officers, directors, or trustees, or in which any individual officer, director, or trustee owns more than a 35% interest? If "Yes," provide the information requested in lines 9b through 9f. ☐ Yes ☑ No

Appendix C Form 1023 for a Private Operating Foundation

Part V **Compensation and Other Financial Arrangements With Your Officers, Directors, Trustees, Employees, and Independent Contractors** *(Continued)*

b Describe any written or oral arrangements you made or intend to make.

c Identify with whom you have or will have such arrangements.

d Explain how the terms are or will be negotiated at arm's length.

e Explain how you determine or will determine you pay no more than fair market value or that you are paid at least fair market value.

f Attach a copy of any signed leases, contracts, loans, or other agreements relating to such arrangements.

Part VI **Your Members and Other Individuals and Organizations That Receive Benefits From You**

The following "Yes" or "No" questions relate to goods, services, and funds you provide to individuals and organizations as part of your activities. Your answers should pertain to *past, present,* and *planned* activities. (See instructions.)

1a In carrying out your exempt purposes, do you provide goods, services, or funds to individuals? If "Yes," describe each program that provides goods, services, or funds to individuals.	☐ Yes	☑ No
b In carrying out your exempt purposes, do you provide goods, services, or funds to organizations? If "Yes," describe each program that provides goods, services, or funds to organizations.	☑ Yes **See attachment**	☐ No
2 Do any of your programs limit the provision of goods, services, or funds to a specific individual or group of specific individuals? For example, answer "Yes," if goods, services, or funds are provided only for a particular individual, your members, individuals who work for a particular employer, or graduates of a particular school. If "Yes," explain the limitation and how recipients are selected for each program.	☐ Yes	☑ No
3 Do any individuals who receive goods, services, or funds through your programs have a family or business relationship with any officer, director, trustee, or with any of your highest compensated employees or highest compensated independent contractors listed in Part V, lines 1a, 1b, and 1c? If "Yes," explain how these related individuals are eligible for goods, services, or funds.	☐ Yes	☑ No

Part VII **Your History**

The following "Yes" or "No" questions relate to your history. (See instructions.)

1 Are you a **successor** to another organization? Answer "Yes," if you have taken or will take over the activities of another organization; you took over 25% or more of the fair market value of the net assets of another organization; or you were established upon the conversion of an organization from for-profit to non-profit status. If "Yes," complete Schedule G.	☐ Yes	☑ No
2 Are you submitting this application more than 27 months after the end of the month in which you were legally formed? If "Yes," complete Schedule E.	☐ Yes	☑ No

Part VIII **Your Specific Activities**

The following "Yes" or "No" questions relate to specific activities that you may conduct. Check the appropriate box. Your answers should pertain to *past, present,* and *planned* activities. (See instructions.)

1 Do you support or oppose candidates in **political campaigns** in any way? If "Yes," explain.	☐ Yes	☑ No
2a Do you attempt to **influence legislation**? If "Yes," explain how you attempt to influence legislation and complete 2b. If "No," go to line 3a.	☐ Yes	☑ No
b Have you made or are you making an **election** to have your legislative activities measured by expenditures by filing Form 5768? If "Yes," attach a copy of the Form 5768 that was already filed or attach a completed Form 5768 that you are filing with this application. If "No," describe whether your attempts to influence legislation are a substantial part of your activities. Include the time and money spent on your attempts to influence legislation as compared to your total activities.	☐ Yes	☐ No
3a Do you or will you operate bingo or **gaming** activities? If "Yes," describe who conducts them, and list all revenue received or expected to be received and expenses paid or expected to be paid in operating these activities. **Revenue and expenses** should be provided for the time periods specified in Part IXFinancial Data.	☐ Yes	☑ No
b Do you or will you enter into contracts or other agreements with individuals or organizations to conduct bingo or gaming for you? If "Yes," describe any written or oral arrangements that you made or intend to make, identify with whom you have or will have such arrangements, explain how the terms are or will be negotiated at arm's length, and explain how you determine or will determine you pay no more than fair market value or you will be paid at least fair market value. Attach copies or any written contracts or other agreements relating to such arrangements.	☐ Yes	☑ No
c List the states and local jurisdictions, including Indian Reservations, in which you conduct or will conduct gaming or bingo.		

Form **1023** (Rev. 10-2004)

Appendix C Form 1023 for a Private Operating Foundation

Part VIII	**Your Specific Activities** *(Continued)*

4a Do you or will you undertake **fundraising**? If "Yes," check all the fundraising programs you do or will conduct. (See instructions.) ☐ Yes ☑ No

    ☐ mail solicitations   ☐ phone solicitations
    ☐ email solicitations   ☐ accept donations on your website
    ☐ personal solicitations   ☐ receive donations from another organization's website
    ☐ vehicle, boat, plane, or similar donations   ☐ government grant solicitations
    ☐ foundation grant solicitations   ☐ Other

    Attach a description of each fundraising program.

b Do you or will you have written or oral contracts with any individuals or organizations to raise funds for you? If "Yes," describe these activities. Include all revenue and expenses from these activities and state who conducts them. Revenue and expenses should be provided for the time periods specified in Part IXFinancial Data. Also, attach a copy of any contracts or agreements. ☐ Yes ☑ No

c Do you or will you engage in fundraising activities for other organizations? If "Yes," describe these arrangements. Include a description of the organizations for which you raise funds and attach copies of all contracts or agreements. ☐ Yes ☑ No

d List all states and local jurisdictions in which you conduct fundraising. For each state or local jurisdiction listed, specify whether you fundraise for your own organization, you fundraise for another organization, or another organization fundraises for you.

e Do you or will you maintain separate accounts for any contributor under which the contributor has the right to advise on the use or distribution of funds? Answer "Yes" if the donor may provide advice on the types of investments, distributions from the types of investments, or the distribution from the donor's contribution account. If "Yes," describe this program, including the type of advice that may be provided and submit copies of any written materials provided to donors. ☐ Yes ☑ No

5 Are you **affiliated** with a governmental unit? If "Yes," explain. ☐ Yes ☑ No

6a Do you or will you engage in **economic development**? If "Yes," describe your program. ☐ Yes ☑ No
b Describe in full who benefits from your economic development activities and how the activities promote exempt purposes.

7a Do or will persons other than your employees or volunteers **develop** your facilities? If "Yes," describe each facility, the role of the developer, and any business or family relationship(s) between the developer and your officers, directors, or trustees. ☐ Yes ☑ No

b Do or will persons other than your employees or volunteers **manage** your activities or facilities? If "Yes," describe each activity and facility, the role of the manager, and any business or family relationship(s) between the manager and your officers, directors, or trustees. ☐ Yes ☑ No

c If there is a business or family relationship between any manager or developer and your officers, directors, or trustees, identify the individuals, explain the relationship, describe how contracts are negotiated at arm's length so that you pay no more than fair market value, and submit a copy of any contracts or other agreements.

8 Do you or will you enter into **joint ventures**, including partnerships or **limited liability companies** treated as partnerships, in which you share profits and losses with partners other than section 501(c)(3) organizations? If "Yes," describe the activities of these joint ventures in which you participate. ☐ Yes ☑ No

9a Are you applying for exemption as a childcare organization under section 501(k)? If "Yes," answer lines 9b through 9d. If "No," go to line 10. ☐ Yes ☑ No

b Do you provide child care so that parents or caretakers of children you care for can be **gainfully employed** (see instructions)? If "No," explain how you qualify as a childcare organization described in section 501(k). ☐ Yes ☐ No

c Of the children for whom you provide child care, are 85% or more of them cared for by you to enable their parents or caretakers to be gainfully employed (see instructions)? If "No," explain how you qualify as a childcare organization described in section 501(k). ☐ Yes ☐ No

d Are your services available to the general public? If "No," describe the specific group of people for whom your activities are available. Also, see the instructions and explain how you qualify as a childcare organization described in section 501(k). ☐ Yes ☐ No

10 Do you or will you publish, own, or have rights in music, literature, tapes, artworks, choreography, scientific discoveries, or other **intellectual property**? If "Yes," explain. Describe who owns or will own any copyrights, patents, or trademarks, whether fees are or will be charged, how the fees are determined, and how any items are or will be produced, distributed, and marketed. ☐ Yes ☑ No

Appendix C Form 1023 for a Private Operating Foundation

Part VIII	**Your Specific Activities** *(Continued)*

11 Do you or will you accept contributions of: real property; conservation easements; closely held securities; intellectual property such as patents, trademarks, and copyrights; works of music or art; licenses; royalties; automobiles, boats, planes, or other vehicles; or collectibles of any type? If "Yes," describe each type of contribution, any conditions imposed by the donor on the contribution, and any agreements with the donor regarding the contribution. ☑ Yes ☐ No
See attachment

12a Do you or will you operate in a **foreign country** or **countries?** If "Yes," answer lines 12b through 12d. If "No," go to line 13a. ☐ Yes ☑ No

  b Name the foreign countries and regions within the countries in which you operate.

  c Describe your operations in each country and region in which you operate.

  d Describe how your operations in each country and region further your exempt purposes.

13a Do you or will you make grants, loans, or other distributions to organization(s)? If "Yes," answer lines 13b through 13g. If "No," go to line 14a. ☑ Yes ☐ No
See attachment

  b Describe how your grants, loans, or other distributions to organizations further your exempt purposes.

  c Do you have written contracts with each of these organizations? If "Yes," attach a copy of each contract. ☐ Yes ☑ No

  d Identify each recipient organization and any **relationship** between you and the recipient organization.

  e Describe the records you keep with respect to the grants, loans, or other distributions you make.

  f Describe your selection process, including whether you do any of the following:

   (i) Do you require an application form? If "Yes," attach a copy of the form. ☐ Yes ☑ No

   (ii) Do you require a grant proposal? If "Yes," describe whether the grant proposal specifies your responsibilities and those of the grantee, obligates the grantee to use the grant funds only for the purposes for which the grant was made, provides for periodic written reports concerning the use of grant funds, requires a final written report and an accounting of how grant funds were used, and acknowledges your authority to withhold and/or recover grant funds in case such funds are, or appear to be, misused. ☐ Yes ☑ No

  g Describe your procedures for oversight of distributions that assure you the resources are used to further your exempt purposes, including whether you require periodic and final reports on the use of resources.

14a Do you or will you make grants, loans, or other distributions to foreign organizations? If "Yes," answer lines 14b through 14f. If "No," go to line 15. ☐ Yes ☑ No

  b Provide the name of each foreign organization, the country and regions within a country in which each foreign organization operates, and describe any relationship you have with each foreign organization.

  c Does any foreign organization listed in line 14b accept contributions earmarked for a specific country or specific organization? If "Yes," list all earmarked organizations or countries. ☐ Yes ☐ No

  d Do your contributors know that you have ultimate authority to use contributions made to you at your discretion for purposes consistent with your exempt purposes? If "Yes," describe how you relay this information to contributors. ☐ Yes ☐ No

  e Do you or will you make pre-grant inquiries about the recipient organization? If "Yes," describe these inquiries, including whether you inquire about the recipient's financial status, its tax-exempt status under the Internal Revenue Code, its ability to accomplish the purpose for which the resources are provided, and other relevant information. ☐ Yes ☐ No

  f Do you or will you use any additional procedures to ensure that your distributions to foreign organizations are used in furtherance of your exempt purposes? If "Yes," describe these procedures, including site visits by your employees or compliance checks by impartial experts, to verify that grant funds are being used appropriately. ☐ Yes ☐ No

Form **1023** (Rev. 10-2004)

Appendix C Form 1023 for a Private Operating Foundation

Part VIII Your Specific Activities *(Continued)*		
15 Do you have a **close connection** with any organizations? If "Yes," explain.	☐ Yes	☑ No
16 Are you applying for exemption as a **cooperative hospital service organization** under section 501(e)? If "Yes," explain.	☐ Yes	☑ No
17 Are you applying for exemption as a **cooperative service organization of operating educational organizations** under section 501(f)? If "Yes," explain.	☐ Yes	☑ No
18 Are you applying for exemption as a **charitable risk pool** under section 501(n)? If "Yes," explain.	☐ Yes	☑ No
19 Do you or will you operate a **school**? If "Yes," complete Schedule B. Answer "Yes," whether you operate a school as your main function or as a secondary activity.	☐ Yes	☑ No
20 Is your main function to provide **hospital** or **medical care**? If "Yes," complete Schedule C.	☐ Yes	☑ No
21 Do you or will you provide **low-income housing** or housing for the **elderly** or **handicapped**? If "Yes," complete Schedule F.	☐ Yes	☑ No
22 Do you or will you provide scholarships, fellowships, educational loans, or other educational grants to individuals, including grants for travel, study, or other similar purposes? If "Yes," complete Schedule H. **Note: Private foundations** may use Schedule H to request advance approval of individual grant procedures.	☐ Yes	☑ No

Appendix C Form 1023 for a Private Operating Foundation

Part IX	Financial Data

For purposes of this schedule, years in existence refer to completed tax years. If in existence 4 or more years, complete the schedule for the most recent 4 tax years. If in existence more than 1 year but less than 4 years, complete the statements for each year in existence and provide projections of your likely revenues and expenses based on a reasonable and good faith estimate of your future finances for a total of 3 years of financial information. If in existence less than 1 year, provide projections of your likely revenues and expenses for the current year and the 2 following years, based on a reasonable and good faith estimate of your future finances for a total of 3 years of financial information. (See instructions.)

A. Statement of Revenues and Expenses

	Type of revenue or expense	Current tax year	3 prior tax years or 2 succeeding tax years			(e) Provide Total for (a) through (d)
		(a) From 01/15/05 To 12/31/05	(b) From 01/01/06 To 12/31/06	(c) From 01/01/07 To 12/31/07	(d) From .... To	
Revenues	1 Gifts, grants, and contributions received (do not include unusual grants)	300,000	400,000	500,000		1,200,000
	2 Membership fees received	0	0	0		0
	3 Gross investment income	300	600	3,000		3,900
	4 Net unrelated business income	0	0	0		0
	5 Taxes levied for your benefit	0	0	0		0
	6 Value of services or facilities furnished by a governmental unit without charge (not including the value of services generally furnished to the public without charge)	0	0	0		0
	7 Any revenue not otherwise listed above or in lines 9–12 below (attach an itemized list)	0	0	0		0
	8 Total of lines 1 through 7	300,300	400,600	503,000		1,203,900
	9 Gross receipts from admissions, merchandise sold or services performed, or furnishing of facilities in any activity that is related to your exempt purposes (attach itemized list)	10,000	20,000	60,000		90,000
	10 Total of lines 8 and 9	310,300	420,600	563,000		1,293,900
	11 Net gain or loss on sale of capital assets (attach schedule and see instructions)	0	0	0		0
	12 **Unusual grants**	0	0	0		0
	13 Total Revenue Add lines 10 through 12	310,300	420,600	563,000		1,293,900
Expenses	14 Fundraising expenses	0	0	0		
	15 Contributions, gifts, grants, and similar amounts paid out (attach an itemized list)	0	2,000	2,000		
	16 Disbursements to or for the benefit of members (attach an itemized list)	0	0	0		
	17 Compensation of officers, directors, and trustees	0	0	0		
	18 Other salaries and wages	65,000	147,000	183,000		
	19 Interest expense	0	0	0		
	20 Occupancy (rent, utilities, etc.)	12,000	24,000	30,000		
	21 Depreciation and depletion	5,000	5,000	5,000		
	22 Professional fees	16,000	4,000	4,500		
	23 Any expense not otherwise classified, such as program services (attach itemized list)	77,000	64,000	50,000		
	24 Total Expenses Add lines 14 through 23	175,000	244,000	272,500		

Form **1023** (Rev. 10-2004)

Appendix C Form 1023 for a Private Operating Foundation

Form 1023 (Rev. 10-2004) Name: **Active Project Fund** EIN: 33 – 3333333 Page **10**

Part IX Financial Data (Continued)

B. Balance Sheet (for your most recently completed tax year) Year End: 06/30/05

The Foundation has no assets and has not completed a full year.

Assets (Whole dollars)

1	Cash	1	None
2	Accounts receivable, net	2	0
3	Inventories	3	0
4	Bonds and notes receivable (attach an itemized list)	4	0
5	Corporate stocks (attach an itemized list)	5	0
6	Loans receivable (attach an itemized list)	6	0
7	Other investments (attach an itemized list)	7	0
8	Depreciable and depletable assets (attach an itemized list)	8	0
9	Land	9	0
10	Other assets (attach an itemized list)	10	0
11	Total Assets (add lines 1 through 10)	11	0

Liabilities

12	Accounts payable	12	0
13	Contributions, gifts, grants, etc. payable	13	0
14	Mortgages and notes payable (attach an itemized list)	14	0
15	Other liabilities (attach an itemized list)	15	0
16	Total Liabilities (add lines 12 through 15)	16	0

Fund Balances or Net Assets

17	Total fund balances or net assets	17	0
18	Total Liabilities and Fund Balances or Net Assets (add lines 16 and 17)	18	None

19 Have there been any substantial changes in your assets or liabilities since the end of the period shown above? If "Yes," explain. ☐ Yes ☑ No

Part X Public Charity Status

Part X is designed to classify you as an organization that is either a **private foundation** or a **public charity**. Public charity status is a more favorable tax status than private foundation status. If you are a private foundation, Part X is designed to further determine whether you are a **private operating foundation**. (See instructions.)

1a Are you a private foundation? If "Yes," go to line 1b. If "No," go to line 5 and proceed as instructed. If you are unsure, see the instructions. ☑ Yes ☐ No

b As a private foundation, section 508(e) requires special provisions in your organizing document in addition to those that apply to all organizations described in section 501(c)(3). Check the box to confirm that your organizing document meets this requirement, whether by express provision or by reliance on operation of state law. Attach a statement that describes specifically where your organizing document meets this requirement, such as a reference to a particular article or section in your organizing document or by operation of state law. See the instructions, including Appendix B, for information about the special provisions that need to be contained in your organizing document. Go to line 2.

2 Are you a private operating foundation? To be a private operating foundation you must engage directly in the active conduct of charitable, religious, educational, and similar activities, as opposed to indirectly carrying out these activities by providing grants to individuals or other organizations. If "Yes," go to line 3. If "No," go to the signature section of Part XI. ☑ Yes ☐ No

3 Have you existed for one or more years? If "Yes," attach financial information showing that you are a private operating foundation; go to the signature section of Part XI. If "No," continue to line 4. ☐ Yes ☑ No

4 Have you attached either (1) an affidavit or opinion of counsel, (including a written affidavit or opinion from a certified public accountant or accounting firm with expertise regarding this tax law matter), that sets forth facts concerning your operations and support to demonstrate that you are likely to satisfy the requirements to be classified as a private operating foundation; or (2) a statement describing your proposed operations as a private operating foundation? ☑ Yes ☐ No **See attached affidavit**

5 If you answered "No" to line 1a, indicate the type of public charity status you are requesting by checking one of the choices below. You may check only one box.

The organization is not a private foundation because it is:

a 509(a)(1) and 170(b)(1)(A)(i)—a church or a convention or association of churches. Complete and attach Schedule A. ☐

b 509(a)(1) and 170(b)(1)(A)(ii)—a **school**. Complete and attach Schedule B. ☐

c 509(a)(1) and 170(b)(1)(A)(iii)—a **hospital**, a cooperative hospital service organization, or a medical research organization operated in conjunction with a hospital. Complete and attach Schedule C. ☐

d 509(a)(3)—an organization supporting either one or more organizations described in line 5a through c, f, g, or h or a publicly supported section 501(c)(4), (5), or (6) organization. Complete and attach Schedule D. ☐

Form **1023** (Rev. 10-2004)

Appendix C Form 1023 for a Private Operating Foundation

Part X   **Public Charity Status** *(Continued)*

e 509(a)(4)—an organization organized and operated exclusively for testing for public safety. ☐

f 509(a)(1) and 170(b)(1)(A)(iv)—an organization operated for the benefit of a college or university that is owned or operated by a governmental unit. ☐

g 509(a)(1) and 170(b)(1)(A)(vi)—an organization that receives a substantial part of its financial support in the form of contributions from publicly supported organizations, from a governmental unit, or from the general public. ☐

h 509(a)(2)—an organization that normally receives not more than one-third of its financial support from gross **investment income** and receives more than one-third of its financial support from contributions, membership fees, and gross receipts from activities related to its exempt functions (subject to certain exceptions). ☐

i A publicly supported organization, but unsure if it is described in 5g or 5h. The organization would like the IRS to decide the correct status. ☐

6 If you checked box g, h, or i in question 5 above, you must request either an **advance** or a **definitive ruling** by selecting one of the boxes below. Refer to the instructions to determine which type of ruling you are eligible to receive.

a **Request for Advance Ruling:** By checking this box and signing the consent, pursuant to section 6501(c)(4) of the Code you request an advance ruling and agree to extend the statute of limitations on the assessment of excise tax under section 4940 of the Code. The tax will apply only if you do not establish public support status at the end of the 5-year advance ruling period. The assessment period will be extended for the 5 advance ruling years to 8 years, 4 months, and 15 days beyond the end of the first year. You have the right to refuse or limit the extension to a mutually agreed-upon period of time or issue(s). Publication 1035, *Extending the Tax Assessment Period,* provides a more detailed explanation of your rights and the consequences of the choices you make. You may obtain Publication 1035 free of charge from the IRS web site at *www.irs.gov* or by calling toll-free 1-800-829-3676. Signing this consent will not deprive you of any appeal rights to which you would otherwise be entitled. If you decide not to extend the statute of limitations, you are not eligible for an advance ruling. ☐

Consent Fixing Period of Limitations Upon Assessment of Tax Under Section 4940 of the Internal Revenue Code

For Organization

....

(Signature of Officer, Director, Trustee, or other authorized official)   (Type or print name of signer)   (Date)

....
(Type or print title or authority of signer)

For Director, Exempt Organizations

By ....   Date ....

b **Request for Definitive Ruling:** Check this box if you have completed one tax year of at least 8 full months and you are requesting a definitive ruling. To confirm your public support status, answer line 6b(i) if you checked box g in line 5 above. Answer line 6b(ii) if you checked box h in line 5 above. If you checked box i in line 5 above, answer both lines 6b(i) and (ii). ☐

  (i) (a) Enter 2% of line 8, column (e) on Part IX-A. Statement of Revenues and Expenses. _____

      (b) Attach a list showing the name and amount contributed by each person, company, or organization whose gifts totaled more than the 2% amount. If the answer is "None," check this box. ☐

  (ii) (a) For each year amounts are included on lines 1, 2, and 9 of Part IX-A. Statement of Revenues and Expenses, attach a list showing the name of and amount received from each **disqualified person.** If the answer is "None," check this box. ☐

      (b) For each year amounts are included on line 9 of Part IX-A. Statement of Revenues and Expenses, attach a list showing the name of and amount received from each payer, other than a disqualified person, whose payments were more than the larger of (1) 1% of line 10, Part IX-A. Statement of Revenues and Expenses, or (2) $5,000. If the answer is "None," check this box. ☐

7 Did you receive any unusual grants during any of the years shown on Part IX-A. Statement of Revenues and Expenses? If "Yes," attach a list including the name of the contributor, the date and amount of the grant, a brief description of the grant, and explain why it is unusual. ☐ Yes ☑ No

Form **1023** (Rev. 10-2004)

Appendix C Form 1023 for a Private Operating Foundation

Part XI	**User Fee Information**

You must include a user fee payment with this application. It will not be processed without your paid user fee. If your average annual gross receipts have exceeded or will exceed $10,000 annually over a 4-year period, you must submit payment of $500. If your gross receipts have not exceeded or will not exceed $10,000 annually over a 4-year period, the required user fee payment is $150. See instructions for Part XI, for a definition of **gross receipts** over a 4-year period. Your check or money order must be made payable to the United States Treasury. *User fees are subject to change. Check our website at www.irs.gov and type "User Fee" in the keyword box, or call Customer Account Services at 1-877-829-5500 for current information.*

1	Have your annual gross receipts averaged or are they expected to average not more than $10,000?	☐ Yes	☑ No
	If "Yes," check the box on line 2 and enclose a user fee payment of $150 (Subject to change—see above).		
	If "No," check the box on line 3 and enclose a user fee payment of $500 (Subject to change—see above).		
2	Check the box if you have enclosed the reduced user fee payment of $150 (Subject to change).		☐
3	Check the box if you have enclosed the user fee payment of $500 (Subject to change).		☑

I declare under the penalties of perjury that I am authorized to sign this application on behalf of the above organization and that I have examined this application, including the accompanying schedules and attachments, and to the best of my knowledge it is true, correct, and complete.

Please Sign Here ▶

A.B. Sample   (Signature of Officer, Director, Trustee, or other authorized official)

A.B. Sample   (Type or print name of signer)

President   (Type or print title or authority of signer)

5. 2. 05   (Date)

Reminder: Send the completed Form 1023 Checklist with your filled-in-application.   Form **1023** (Rev. 10-2004)

Appendix C Form 1023 for a Private Operating Foundation

Active Project Fund
Attachment to Form 1023

33-3333333

Corporations Section
P.O.Box 13697
Austin, Texas 78711-3697
...

Geoffrey S. Connor
Secretary of State

Office of the Secretary of State

CERTIFICATE OF INCORPORATION
OF

ACTIVE PROJECT FUND

Filing Number: 151515

The undersigned, as Secretary of State of Texas, hereby certifies that Articles of Incorporation for the above named corporation have been received in this office and have been found to conform to law.

Accordingly, the undersigned, as Secretary of State, and by virtue of the authority vested in the Secretary by law, hereby issues this Certificate of Incorporation.

Issuance of this Certificate of Incorporation does not authorize the use of a name in this state in violation of the rights of another under the federal Trademark Act of 1946, the Texas trademark law, the Assumed Business or Professional Name Act, or the common law.

Dated: 01/15/05

Effective: 01/15/05

Geoffrey S. Connor
Secretary of State

PHONE(512) 463-5555
Prepared by Dolores Moore

Come visit us on the internet at http://www.sos.state.tx.us
FAX(512) 463-5709

TTY7-1-1

Certificate of Organization

183

Appendix C Form 1023 for a Private Operating Foundation

ARTICLES OF INCORPORATION
Of
Active Project Fund
(A Non-Profit Corporation)

I, the undersigned natural person of the age of eighteen (18) years or more, acting as incorporator of a corporation under the Texas Non-Profit Corporation Act, do hereby adopt the following Articles of Incorporation for such Corporation:

ARTICLE ONE
Name

The name of the Corporation is **Active Project Fund.**

ARTICLE TWO
Nonprofit Corporation

The Corporation is a nonprofit corporation.

ARTICLE THREE
Duration

The period of the Corporation's duration is perpetual.

ARTICLE FOUR
Purposes

Section 4.01. The Corporation is organized exclusively for charitable, literary, and educational purposes as defined in Section 501(c)(3) of the Internal Revenue Code. These activities will include, but not be limited to, improving the quality of management and operation of nonprofit organizations.

Section 4.02. Notwithstanding any other provision of these Articles of Incorporation:

a. No part of the net earnings of the Corporation shall inure to the benefit of any director of the Corporation, officer of the Corporation, or any private individual (except that reasonable compensation may be paid for services rendered to or for the Corporation affecting one or more of its purposes); and no director, officer or any private individual shall be entitled to share in the distribution of any of the corporate assets on dissolution of the Corporation. No substantial part of the activities of the Corporation shall be the carrying on of propaganda, or otherwise attempting to influence legislation, and the Corporation shall not participate in, or intervene in (including the publication or distribution of statements) any political campaign on behalf of any candidate for public office.

b. The corporation shall not conduct or carry on any activities not permitted to be conducted or carried on by an organization exempt from taxation under Section 501(c)(3) of the Internal Revenue Code and its Regulations as they now exist or as they may hereafter be amended, or by an organization, contributions to which are deductible under 170(c)(2) of the Internal Revenue Code and Regulations as they now exist or as they may hereafter be amended.

c. Upon dissolution of the Corporation or the winding up of its affairs, the assets of the Corporation shall be distributed exclusively to charitable organizations which would then qualify under the provisions of Section 501(c)(3) of the Internal Revenue Code and its Regulations as they now exist or as they may be hereafter amended.

d. The Corporation is organized pursuant to the Texas Nonprofit Corporation Act and does not contemplate pecuniary gain or profit and is organized for nonprofit purposes which are consistent with the provisions of Section 501(c)(3) of the Internal Revenue Code and its Regulations as they now exist or as they may hereafter be amended.

1

Articles of Organization

Appendix C Form 1023 for a Private Operating Foundation

ARTICLE FIVE
Membership

The Corporation shall have no voting members.

ARTICLE SIX
Initial Registration Office and Agent

The street address of the initial registered office of the Corporation is 1010 Main Street, Any Town, XX 77777, and the name of the initial registered agent at such address is A.B. Sample.

ARTICLE SEVEN
Directors

The number of Directors constituting the initial Board of Directors of the Corporation is three (3), and the names and addresses of those people who are to serve as the initial Directors are:

Name	Address
A.B. Sample	1010 Main Street, Any Town, XX, 77777
B.C. Sample	1010 Main Street, Any Town, XX, 77777
D.E. Sample	1010 Main Street, Any Town, XX, 77777

ARTICLE EIGHT
Indemnification of Directors and Officers

Each Director and each officer or former Director or officer may be indemnified and may be advanced reasonable expenses by the Corporation against liabilities imposed upon him or her and expenses reasonably incurred by him or her in connection with any claim against him or her, or any action, suit or proceeding to which he or she may be a party by reason of his or being, or having been, such Director or officer and against such sum as independent counsel selected by the Directors shall deem reasonable payment made in settlement of any such claim, action, suit or proceeding primarily with the view of avoiding expenses of litigation; provided, however, that no Director or officer shall be indemnified (a) with respect to matters as to which he or she shall be adjudged in such action, suit or proceeding to be liable for negligence or misconduct in performance or duty, (b) with respect to any matters which shall be settled by the payment of sums which independent counsel selected by the Directors shall not deem reasonable payment made primarily with a view to avoiding expense of litigation, or (c) with respect to matters for which such indemnification would be against public policy. Such rights of indemnification shall be in addition to any other rights to which Directors or officers may be entitled under any bylaw, agreement, corporate resolution, vote of Directors or otherwise. The Corporation shall have the power to purchase and maintain at its cost and expense insurance on behalf of such persons to the fullest extent permitted by this Article and applicable state law.

ARTICLE NINE
Limitation On Scope Of Liability

No director shall be liable to the Corporation for monetary damages for an act or omission in the Director's capacity as a Director of the Corporation, except and only for the following:

a.   A breach of the Director's duty of loyalty to the Corporation;

b.   An act or omission not in good faith by the Director or an act or omission that involves the intentional misconduct or knowing violation of the law by the Director;

c.   A transaction from which the Director gained any improper benefit whether or not such benefit resulted from an action taken within the scope of the Director's office; or

d.   An act or omission by the Directors for which liability is expressly provided for by statute.

This model provided by Texas Accountants and Lawyers for the Arts.

Appendix C Form 1023 for a Private Operating Foundation

ARTICLE TEN
Informal Action by Directors

Any action required by law to be taken at a meeting of Directors, or any action which may be taken at a meeting of Directors, may be taken without a meeting if a consent in writing setting forth the action so taken shall be signed by a sufficient number of Directors as would be necessary to take that action at a meeting at which all of the Directors were present and voted. All consents signed in this manner must be delivered to the Secretary or other officer having custody of the minute book within sixty (60) days after the date of the earliest dated consent delivered to the Corporation in this manner. A facsimile transmission or other similar transmission shall be regarded as signed by the Director for purposes of this Article.

ARTICLE ELEVEN
Incorporator

The name and address of the incorporator is:

Name	Address
A.B. Sample	1010 Main Street, Any Town, XX, 77777

IN WITNESS WHEREOF, I have hereunto set my hand, this 15th day of January, 2005.

Jane Smith
Jane Smith

3

Articles of Organization

Appendix C Form 1023 for a Private Operating Foundation

BYLAWS OF

Active Project Fund

a Texas Non-Profit Corporation
* * * * * * * * * * * * * * * *
ARTICLE ONE - OFFICES

Section 1.01.   Principal Office. The principal office of the Corporation in the State of Texas shall be located in the City of Any Town, County of Harris. The Corporation may have such other offices, either within or without the State of Texas, as the Board of Directors may determine or as the affairs of the Corporation may require from time to time.

Section 1.02.   Registered Office and Registered Agent. The Corporation shall have and continuously maintain in the State of Texas a registered office, and a registered agent whose office is identical with such registered office may be, but need not be, identical with the principal office of the Corporation in the State of Texas, and the address of the registered office may be changed from time to time by the Board of Directors.

ARTICLE TWO - PURPOSES

Section 2.01.   Organizational Purposes. The Corporation is organized exclusively for charitable, scientific and educational purposes. The corporation is established as a permanent organization in Texas seeking to enrich the local community through activities promoting such provision. The Corporation may engage in any activities that further its purpose.

No part of the net earnings of the Corporation shall inure to the benefit of any Director of the Corporation, officer of the Corporation, or any private individual (except that reasonable compensation may be paid for services rendered to or for the Corporation affecting one or more of its purposes), and no Director or officer of the Corporation, or any private individual shall be entitled to share in the distribution of any of the corporate assets on dissolution of the Corporation. No substantial part of the activities of the Corporation shall be the carrying on of propaganda, or otherwise attempting to influence legislation, and the Corporation shall not participate in, or intervene in (including the publication or distribution of statements) any political campaigning on behalf of any candidate for public office.

Notwithstanding any other provision of these Bylaws, the Corporation shall not conduct or carry on any activities not permitted to be conducted or carried on by an organization exempt from taxation under Section 501(c)(3) of the Internal Revenue Code and its Regulations as they now exist or as they may hereafter be amended, or by an organization, contributions to which are deductible under Section 170(c)(2) of the Internal Revenue Code and Regulations, as they now exist or as they may hereafter be amended.

Upon dissolution of the Corporation or the winding up of its affairs, the assets of the Corporation shall be distributed exclusively to charitable organizations which would then qualify under the provisions of Section 501(c)(3) of the Internal Revenue Code and its Regulations as they now exist or as they may hereafter be amended.

ARTICLE THREE - MEMBERS

Section 3.01.   The corporation shall have no voting members.

ARTICLE FOUR - BOARD OF DIRECTORS

Section 4.01.   General Powers. The affairs of the Corporation shall be managed by its Board of Directors. Directors need not be residents of Texas.

Section 4.02.   Number, Tenure and Qualifications. The number of Directors shall be not less than three (3) nor more than twenty (20). The initial Directors shall serve terms of one, two and three years, as provided by the Board. Afterwards, each director shall serve for three years, thereby providing for staggered terms. The initial terms of additional Directors shall be fixed to ensure than a disproportionate number of Directors (more than one-half) will not be up for election in any given year.

Section 4.03.   Regular Meetings. The Board of Directors shall provide for by resolution the time and place, either within or without the State of Texas, for the holding of the regular annual meeting(s) of the Board, and may provide by resolution the time and place for the holding of additional regular meetings of the Board, without other notice than such resolution. However, there shall never be less than one annual meeting of the Board of Directors.

1

Appendix C Form 1023 for a Private Operating Foundation

Active Project Fund   **33-3333333**
Attachment to Form 1023

Section 4.04. <u>Annual Meetings</u>. Beginning in 2005 an annual meeting of the Board of Directors shall be held at the date, time and place determined by the Board of Directors.

Section 4.05. <u>Special Meetings</u>. Special meetings of the Board of Directors may be called by or at the request of the President, or any two Directors. The person or persons authorized to call special meetings of the Board may fix any place, either within or without the State of Texas, as the place for holding any special meetings of the Board called by them.

Section 4.06. <u>Meetings Utilizing Electronic Media</u>. Members of the Board of Directors or members of any committee designated by the Board of Directors may participate in and hold a meeting of that Board or committee, respectively, by means of conference telephone or similar communication equipment, provided that all persons participating in such a meeting shall constitute presence in person at such meeting, except where a person participates in the meeting for the express purpose of objecting to the transaction of any business on the ground that the meeting is not lawfully created.

Section 4.07. <u>Notice</u>. Notice of any special meeting of the Board of Directors shall be given at least (5) business days previously thereto by oral or written notice delivered personally or sent by mail, telegram, facsimile or messenger to each Director at his or her address as shown by the records of the Corporation. If mailed, such notice shall be deemed to be delivered when deposited in the United States mail so addressed with postage thereon prepaid. If notice be given by telegram, such notice shall be deemed to be delivered when the telegram is delivered to the telegram company. Any Director may waive notice of any meeting. The attendance of a Director at any meeting shall constitute a waiver or notice of such meeting, except when a Director attends a meeting for the express purpose of objecting to the transaction of any business because the meeting is not lawfully called or convened. Neither the business to be transacted at, nor the purpose of, any regular or special meeting of the Board need be specified in the notice or waiver of notice of such meeting, unless specifically required by law or by these Bylaws.

Section 4.08. <u>Quorum</u>. A majority of the Board of Directors, but never less than three (3), shall constitute a quorum for the transaction of business at any meeting of the Board; but if less than a quorum of the Directors is present at said meeting, a majority of the Directors present may adjourn the meeting from time to time without further notice.

Section 4.09. <u>Manner of Acting</u>. The act of a majority of the Directors present at a meeting at which a quorum is present shall be the act of the Board of Directors, unless the act of a greater number is required by law or by these Bylaws.

Section 4.10. <u>Vacancies</u>. Any vacancy occurring in the Board of Directors, and any directorship to be filled by reason of an increase in the number of Directors, shall be filled by the Board of Directors. A Director elected to fill a vacancy shall be elected for the unexpired term of his or her predecessor in office. However, vacancies need not be filled unless such a vacancy would result in fewer than three directors remaining on the board.

Section 4.11. <u>Compensation</u>. Directors as such shall not receive any stated salaries for their services, but by resolution of the Board of Directors a fixed sum and expenses of attendance, if any, may be allowed for attendance at each regular or special meeting of the Board; but nothing herein contained shall be construed to preclude any Director from serving the Corporation in any other capacity and receiving compensation therefore.

Section 4.12. <u>Informal Action by Directors</u>. Any action required by law to be taken at a meeting of Directors, or any action which may be taken at a meeting of Directors, may be taken without a meeting if a consent in writing setting forth the action so taken shall be signed by a sufficient number of Directors as would be necessary to take that action at a meeting at which all the Directors were present and voted. Each such written consent shall be delivered, by hand or certified or registered mail, return receipt requested, to the Secretary or other officer or agent of the Corporation having custody of the Corporation's minute book. A written consent signed by less than all of the Directors is not effective to take the action that is the subject of the consent unless, within sixty (60) days after the date of the earliest dated consent delivered to the Corporation in the manner required by this Article, a consent or consents signed by the required number of Directors is delivered to the Corporation as provided in this Article. For purposes of this Article, a telegram, telex, cablegram, or similar transmission by a Director or a photographic, photostatic, facsimile or similar reproduction of a writing signed by a Director shall be regarded as signed by the Director.

Section 4.13. <u>Resignation</u>. Any Director may resign by giving written notice to the President. The resignation shall be effective at the next called meeting of the Board of Directors, of which meeting the resigning Director shall receive notice.

Section 4.14. <u>Removal</u>. Any Director may be removed with or without cause by a two thirds majority of the remaining Directors.

2
This model provided by the Texas Accountants and Lawyers for the Arts.   Bylaws

188

Appendix C Form 1023 for a Private Operating Foundation

Active Project Fund 33-3333333
Attachment to Form 1023

Section 4.15. <u>Indemnification</u>. The Corporation may indemnify and advance reasonable expenses to directors, officers, employees and agents of the Corporation to the fullest extent required or permitted by Article 2.22A of the Texas Non-Profit Corporation Act, subject to the restrictions, if any, contained in the Corporation's Articles of Incorporation. The Corporation shall have the power to purchase and maintain at its cost and expense insurance on behalf of such persons to the fullest extent permitted by Article 2.22A of the Texas Non-Profit Corporation Act.

ARTICLE FIVE - OFFICERS

Section 5.01. <u>Officers</u>. The officers of the Corporation shall be a President, one or more Vice Presidents (the number thereof to be determined by the Board of Directors), a Secretary, a Treasurer, and such other officers as may be elected in accordance with the provisions of this Article. The Board of Directors may elect or appoint such other officers, including one or more Assistant Secretaries and one or more Assistant Treasurers, as it shall deem desirable, such officers to have the authority and perform the duties prescribed, from time to time, by the Board of Directors. Any two or more offices may be held by the same person, except the offices of President and Secretary.

Section 5.02. <u>Election and Term of Office</u>. The officers of the Corporation shall be elected by the Board of Directors at the alternate Annual meeting of the Board of Directors and shall serve terms of two years duration. If the election of officers shall not be held at such meeting, such election shall be held as soon thereafter as conveniently may be. New offices may be created and filled at any meeting of the Board of Directors. Each officer shall hold office for two years, or until his or her successor shall have been duly elected and shall have qualified.

Section 5.03. <u>Removal</u>. Any officer elected or appointed by the Board of Directors may be removed with or without cause by a majority vote of the Board of Directors, but such removal shall be without prejudice to the contract rights, if any, of the officer so removed.

Section 5.04. <u>Vacancies</u>. A vacancy in any office because of death, resignation, disqualification, or otherwise, may be filled by the Board of Directors for the unexpired portion of the term.

Section 5.05. <u>President</u>. The President shall be the principal executive officer of the Corporation and shall, in general, supervise and control all of the business and affairs of the Corporation. He or she shall preside at all meetings of the Board of Directors. The President may sign, with the Secretary or any other proper officer of the Corporation authorized by the Board of Directors, any deeds, mortgages, bonds, contracts, or other instruments which the Board of Directors has authorized to be executed, except in cases where the signing and execution thereof shall be expressly delegated by the Board of Directors or by these Bylaws or by statute to some other officer or agent of the Corporation; and in general he or she shall perform all duties as may be prescribed by the Board of Directors from time to time, including participating in various committee meetings as a member or chairperson thereof. He or she shall also be responsible for informing the Board of Directors of possible programs, meetings, and functions of the corporation.

Section 5.06. <u>Vice President</u>. In the absence of the President or in the event of his or her inability or refusal to act, the Vice President (or in the event there be more than one Vice President, the Vice Presidents in order of their election) shall perform the duties of the President, and when so acting shall have all the powers of and be subject to all the restrictions upon the President. Any Vice President shall perform such other duties as from time to time may be assigned to him or her by the President or Board of Directors.

Section 5.07. <u>Treasurer</u>. If required by the Board of Directors, the Treasurer shall give a bond for the faithful discharge of his or her duties in such sum and with such surety or sureties as the Board of Directors shall determine. He or she shall have charge and custody of and be responsible for all funds and securities of the Corporation; receive and give receipts for moneys due and payable to the Corporation from any source whatsoever, and deposit all such moneys in the name of the Corporation in such banks, trust companies, or other depositories as shall be selected in accordance with the provisions of these Bylaws; he or she shall keep proper books of account and other books showing at all times the amount of funds and other property belonging to the Corporation, all of which books shall be open at all times to the inspection of the Board of Directors; he or she shall also submit a report of the accounts and financial condition of the Corporation at each annual meeting of the Board of Directors; and in general perform all the duties incident to the office of Treasurer and such other duties as from time to time may be assigned to him or her by the President or by the Board of Directors.

Section 5.08. <u>Secretary</u>. The Secretary shall keep the minutes of the meetings of the Board of Directors in one or more books provided for that purpose; give all notices in accordance with the provisions of these Bylaws or as required by law; be custodian of the corporate records and of the seal of the Corporation, and affix the seal of the Corporation to all documents, the execution of which on behalf of the Corporation under its seal is duly authorized in accordance with the provisions of these Bylaws; and, in general, perform all duties incident to the office of Secretary and such other duties as from time to time may be assigned to him or her by the President or Board of Directors. The Board of Directors and Officers shall give bonds of the faithful discharge of their duties in such sums and with such sureties as the Board of Directors shall determine. The Assistant Treasurer and Assistant Secretaries, in general, shall perform such duties as shall be assigned to them by the Treasurer or the Secretary or by the President or the Board of Directors.

3
This model provided by the Texas Accountants and Lawyers for the Arts.   Bylaws

189

Appendix C Form 1023 for a Private Operating Foundation

Active Project Fund   33-3333333
Attachment to Form 1023

ARTICLE SIX- COMMITTEES

Section 6.01.   Appointment. The Board of Directors shall appoint members of committees established by the Board of Directors. The Board of Directors shall appoint the chairperson of each committee. These committees shall perform such functions and make such reports as the President or Board of Directors shall determine. Both Directors and members of the Advisory Board may serve on all committees except the Executive Committee.

Section 6.02.   Committees of Directors. The Board of Directors, by resolution adopted by a majority of the Directors in office, may designate and appoint one or more committees, each of which shall consist of two or more persons, a majority of who are Directors, which committees, to the extent provided in said resolution shall have and exercise the authority in the management of the Corporation of the Board of Directors. However, no such committee shall have the authority of the Board of Directors in reference to amending, altering, or repealing the Bylaws; electing, appointing, or removing any member of any such committee or any Director or officer of the Corporation; amending the Articles of Incorporation; adopting a plan of merger or adopting a plan of consolidation with another Corporation; authorizing the sale, lease, exchange, or mortgage of all or substantially all of the property and assets of the Corporation; authorizing the voluntary dissolution of the Corporation or revoking proceedings therefor; adopting a plan for the distribution of the assets of the Corporation; or amending, altering, or repealing any resolution of the Board of Directors which by its terms provides that it shall not be amended, altered or repealed by such committee. The designation and appointment of any such committee and the delegation thereof of authority shall not operate to relieve the Board of Directors, or any individual Director, of any responsibility imposed on it or him or her by law.

Section 6.03.   Executive Committee. The Board of Directors may from among its members appoint an Executive Committee consisting of the officers and any additional members as deemed necessary by the Board to serve at the pleasure of the Board. The President, unless absent or otherwise unable to do so, shall preside as Chairperson of the Executive Committee. The Committee shall meet at the call of the President or the Board of Directors, or any two (2) members of the Committee, and shall have and may exercise when the Board of Directors is not in session the power to perform all duties, of every kind and character, not required by law or the charter of the Corporation to be performed solely by the Board of Directors. The Executive Committee shall have authority to make rules for the holding and conduct of its meetings, keep records thereof and regularly report its actions to the Board. A majority but never less than three of the members of the Committee in office shall be sufficient to constitute a quorum at any meeting of the Committee, and all action taken at such a meeting shall be by a majority of those present all acts performed by the Executive Committee in the exercise of its aforesaid authority shall be deemed to be, and may be certified as, acts performed under authority of the Board of Directors. Vacancies in the Executive committee shall be filled by appointment by the Board of Directors. All actions of the Executive Committee shall be recorded in writing in a minute book kept for that purpose and a report of all action shall be made to the Board of Directors at its next meeting. The minutes of the Board of Directors shall reflect that such a report was made along with any action taken by the Board of Directors with respect thereto.

Section 6.04.   Nominating Committee. The President shall, with thirty (30) days advance notice to the Board of Directors, appoint the members of the Nominating Committee created by the Board of Directors. The members shall be members of the Board of Directors and Advisory Board appointed to nominate candidates for officers and directors. Additional nominations may be made by Directors at the annual meeting.

Section 6.05.   Advisory Committee. The function and purpose of the Advisory Committee shall be to advise the Board of Directors on matters relating to the purpose of the organization and to suggest projects, which the Corporation may undertake.

Section 6.06.   Other Committees. Other committees not having and exercising the authority of the Board of Directors in the management of the Corporation may be designated by a resolution adopted by a majority of the Directors present at a meeting at which a quorum is present. Except as otherwise provided in such resolution, the President of the Corporation shall appoint the members of each such committee. Any member thereof may be removed by the person or persons authorized to appoint such member whenever in their judgment the best interests of the Corporation shall be served by such removal. Members of such committee or committees may, but need not be, Directors.

Section 6.07.   Term of Office. Each member of a committee shall continue as such until the next annual meeting of the members of the Board of Directors and until his or her successor is appointed, unless the committee shall be sooner terminated, or unless such member be removed from such committee, or unless such member shall cease to qualify as a member thereof.

Section 6.08.   Chairperson. One member of each committee shall be appointed chairperson by the person or persons authorized to appoint the members thereof.

Section 6.09.   Vacancies. Vacancies in the membership of any committee may be filled by appointments made in the same manner as provided in the case of the original appointments.

4
This model provided by the Texas Accountants and Lawyers for the Arts.   Bylaws

190

Appendix C Form 1023 for a Private Operating Foundation

Section 6.10.   Quorum. Unless otherwise provided in the resolution of the Board of Directors designating a committee, a majority of the whole committee shall constitute a quorum and the act of a majority of the members present at a meeting at which a quorum is present shall be the act of the committee.

Section 6.11.   Rules. Each committee may adopt rules for its government not inconsistent with these Bylaws or with rules adopted by the Board of Directors.

Section 6.12.   Committee Dissolution. The Board of Directors may, in its sole discretion, dissolve any committee with or without cause. Except for the Executive Committee, such dissolution shall require approval by a majority of the quorum. The Executive Committee shall only be dissolved by approval of   two-thirds or more of all members of the Board of Directors.

ARTICLE SEVEN - CONTRACTS, CHECKS, DEPOSITS, AND GIFTS

Section 7.01.   Contracts. The Board of Directors may authorize any officer or officers, agent or agents of the Corporation, in addition to the officers so authorized by these Bylaws, to enter into any contract or execute and deliver any instrument in the name of and on behalf of the Corporation. Such authority may be general or confined to specific instances.

Section 7.02.   Checks and Drafts, Etc. All checks, drafts, or orders for the payment of money, notes, or other evidence of indebtedness issued in the name of the Corporation shall be signed by such officer or officers, agent or agents of the Corporation and in such manner as shall from time to time be determined by resolution of the Board of Directors. In the absence of such determination by the Board of Directors, such instruments shall be signed by the Treasurer or an Assistant Treasurer and countersigned by the President or a Vice President of the Corporation.

Section 7.03.   Deposits. All funds of the Corporation shall be deposited from time to time to the credit of the Corporation in such banks, trust companies, or other depositories as the Board of Directors may select.

Section 7.04.   Gifts. The Board of Directors may accept on behalf of the Corporation any contribution, gift, bequest, or devise for the general purposes or for any special purpose of the Corporation.

ARTICLE EIGHT - BOOKS AND RECORDS

Section 8.01.   Books and Records. The Corporation shall keep correct and complete books and records of account of the activities and transactions of the Corporation including, a minute book which shall contain a copy of the Corporation's application for tax-exempt statue (IRS Form 1023), copies of the organization's IRS information and/or tax returns (For example, Form 990 and all schedules thereto), and a copy of the Articles of Incorporation, Bylaws, and Amendments. The Corporation shall also keep minutes of the proceedings of its Board of Directors and any committees having the authority of the Board of Directors. All books and records of the Corporation may be inspected by any Director or his or her agent or attorney for any proper purpose at any reasonable time. Representatives of the Internal Revenue Service may inspect these books and records as necessary to meet the requirements relating to federal tax form 990. All financial records of the Corporation shall be available to the public for inspection and copying to the fullest extent required by law.

ARTICLE NINE - FISCAL YEAR

Section 9.01.   Fiscal Year. The fiscal year of the Corporation shall begin on January 1 of each year and conclude on the last day of December of the following year.

ARTICLE TEN - SEAL

Section 10.01. Seal. The Board of Directors may authorize a corporate seal.

ARTICLE ELEVEN - WAIVER OF NOTICE

Section 11.01. Waiver of Notice. Whenever any notice is required to be given under the provisions of the Texas Non-Profit Corporation Act or under the provisions of the Articles of Incorporation or the Bylaws of the Corporation, a waiver thereof in writing signed by the person or persons entitled to such notice, whether before or after the time therein, shall be deemed equivalent to the giving of such notice.

5
This model provided by the Texas Accountants and Lawyers for the Arts.   Bylaws

191

Appendix C Form 1023 for a Private Operating Foundation

Active Project Fund   33-3333333
Attachment to Form 1023

ARTICLE TWELVE - <u>AMENDMENTS TO BYLAWS</u>

Section 12.01. <u>Amendments to Bylaws</u>. These Bylaws may be altered, amended, or repealed and new Bylaws may be adopted by a two-thirds majority of the Directors present at any regular meeting or at any special meeting, if at least one day's written notice is given of an intention to alter, amend, or repeal these Bylaws or to adopt new Bylaws at such meeting.

ARTICLE THIRTEEN - <u>AMENDMENTS TO ARTICLES</u>

Section 13.01. <u>Amendments to Articles</u>. The Articles of Incorporation of the Corporation may, to the extent allowed by law, be altered, amended, or restated and new Articles of Incorporation may be adopted by a two-thirds majority of the Directors present at any regular meeting or at any special meeting, if at least one day's written notice is given of an intention to alter, amend, or restate the Articles of Incorporation or to adopt new Articles of Incorporation at such meeting.

CERTIFICATE

I HEREBY CERTIFY that the foregoing is a true, complete and correct copy of the By Laws of Active Project Fund, a Texas non-profit corporation, in effect on the date hereof.

IN WITNESS WHEREOF, I hereunto set my hand, this 15th day of January, 2005.

_____   _____
                Signature   Title

6

This model provided by the Texas Accountants and Lawyers for the Arts.   Bylaws

192

Appendix C   Form 1023 for a Private Operating Foundation

Active Project Fund Conflict of Interest Policy

Article I
Purpose

The purpose of the conflict of interest policy is to protect Active Project Fund's interests when it contemplates entering into a transaction or arrangement that might benefit the private interest of an officer or director of the organization or might result in a possible excess benefit transaction. This policy is intended to supplement but not replace any applicable state and federal laws governing conflict of interest applicable to nonprofit and charitable organizations.

Article II
Definitions

1. Interested Person
Any director, principal officer, or member of a committee with governing board delegated powers, who has a direct or indirect financial interest, as defined below, is an interested person.

2. Financial Interest
A person has a financial interest if the person has, directly or indirectly, through business, investment, or family:
    a. An ownership or investment interest in any entity with which the organization has a transaction or arrangement,
    b. A compensation arrangement with the organization or with any entity or individual with which the organization has a transaction or arrangement, or
    c. A potential ownership or investment interest in, or compensation arrangement with, any entity or individual with which the organization is negotiating a transaction or arrangement.

Compensation includes direct and indirect remuneration as well as gifts or favors that are not insubstantial.

(A financial interest is not necessarily a conflict of interest. Under Article III, Section 2, a person who has a financial interest may have a conflict of interest only if the appropriate governing board or committee decides that a conflict of interest exists.)

Article III
Procedures

1. Duty to Disclose
In connection with any actual or possible conflict of interest, an interested person must disclose the existence of the financial interest and be given the opportunity to disclose all material facts to the directors and members of committees with governing board delegated powers considering the proposed transaction or arrangement.

2. Determining Whether a Conflict of Interest Exists
After disclosure of the financial interest and all material facts, and after any discussion with the interested person, he/she shall leave the governing board or committee meeting while the determination of a conflict of interest is discussed and voted upon. The remaining board or committee members shall decide if a conflict of interest exists.

3. Procedures for Addressing the Conflict of Interest
    a. An interested person may make a presentation at the governing board or committee meeting, but after the presentation, he/she shall leave the meeting during the discussion of, and the vote on, the transaction or arrangement involving the possible conflict of interest.
    b. The chairperson of the governing board or committee shall, if appropriate, appoint a disinterested person or committee to investigate alternatives to the proposed transaction or arrangement.
    c. After exercising due diligence, the governing board or committee shall determine whether the organization can obtain with reasonable efforts a more advantageous transaction or arrangement from a person or entity that would not give rise to a conflict of interest.

Appendix C Form 1023 for a Private Operating Foundation

d. If a more advantageous transaction or arrangement is not reasonably possible under circumstances not producing a conflict of interest, the governing board or committee shall determine by a majority vote of the disinterested directors whether the transaction or arrangement is in the organization's best interest, for its own benefit, and whether it is fair and reasonable. In conformity with the above determination it shall make its decision as to whether to enter into the transaction or arrangement.

4. Violations of the Conflicts of Interest Policy

a. If the governing board or committee has reasonable cause to believe a member has failed to disclose actual or possible conflicts of interest, it shall inform the member of the basis for such belief and afford the member an opportunity to explain the alleged failure to disclose.

b. If, after hearing the member's response and after making further investigation as warranted by the circumstances, the governing board or committee determines the member has failed to disclose an actual or possible conflict of interest, it shall take appropriate disciplinary and corrective action.

Article IV
Records of Proceedings

The minutes of the governing board and all committees with board delegated powers shall contain:

a. The names of the persons who disclosed or otherwise were found to have a financial interest in connection with an actual or possible conflict of interest, the nature of the financial interest, any action taken to determine whether a conflict of interest was present, and the governing board's or committee's decision as to whether a conflict of interest in fact existed.

b. The names of the persons who were present for discussions and votes relating to the transaction or arrangement, the content of the discussion, including any alternatives to the proposed transaction or arrangement, and a record of any votes taken in connection with the proceedings.

Article V
Compensation

a. A voting member of the governing board who receives compensation, directly or indirectly, from the Organization for services is precluded from voting on matters pertaining to that member's compensation.

b. A voting member of any committee whose jurisdiction includes compensation matters and who receives compensation, directly or indirectly, from the Organization for services is precluded from voting on matters pertaining to that member's compensation.

c. No voting member of the governing board or any committee whose jurisdiction includes compensation matters and who receives compensation, directly or indirectly, from the Organization, either individually or collectively, is prohibited from providing information to any committee regarding compensation.

Article VI
Annual Statements

Each director, principal officer and member of a committee with governing board-delegated powers shall annually sign a statement, which affirms such person:

a. Has received a copy of the conflicts of interest policy,

b. Has read and understands the policy,

c. Has agreed to comply with the policy, and

d. Understands the organization is charitable and in order to maintain its federal tax exemption it must engage primarily in activities that accomplish one or more of its tax-exempt purposes.

Article VII
Periodic Reviews

To ensure the organization operates in a manner consistent with charitable purposes and does not engage in activities that could jeopardize its tax-exempt status, periodic reviews shall be conducted. The periodic reviews shall, at a minimum, include the following subjects:

2   Attachment to Part V, Line 5a

Appendix C Form 1023 for a Private Operating Foundation

a. Whether compensation arrangements and benefits are reasonable, based on competent survey information, and the result of arm's length bargaining.

b. Whether partnerships, joint ventures, and arrangements with management organizations conform to the organization's written policies, are properly recorded, reflect reasonable investment or payments for goods and services, further charitable purposes and do not result in inurement, impermissible private benefit or in an excess benefit transaction.

Article VIII
Use of Outside Experts

When conducting the periodic reviews as provided for in Article VII, the organization may, but need not, use outside advisors. If outside experts are used, their use shall not relieve the governing board of its responsibility for ensuring periodic reviews are conducted.

Adopted by Board of Directors on June 1, 2005

Appendix C Form 1023 for a Private Operating Foundation

Active Project Fund   33-3333333
Attachment to Form 1023

<u>Part I, Line 7</u>

A Good Accountant, Smith & Jones, LLP, 1 Main Street, Any Town, XX 77777.

<u>Part I, Line 8</u>

A Good Accountant, Smith & Jones, LLP, 1 Main Street, Any Town, XX 77777.
The amount to be paid for the preparation of Form 1023 is approximately $2,500. The fee for future preparation of required Internal Revenue Service filings such as the Form 990PF may be $1,500 per year. A Good Accountant will help the organization by preparing all required Internal Revenue Service filings.

<u>Part IV</u>

Active Project Fund was created and will operate exclusively for charitable and educational purposes as defined in IRC §501(c)(3). Specifically, Active Project Fund (APF) is dedicated to improving the quality of management and operation of nonprofit organizations. APF will accomplish its purpose by conducting seminars, providing technical assistance, and writing and disseminating educational materials.

Seminars: APF has hired an executive director with significant experience in nonprofit management. She will develop courses on financial and management issues such as personnel policies, budgeting, fundraising, office efficiency, computer use, and other issues relevant to management of a nonprofit organization. APF will seek to identify qualified professionals in the community who will be willing to volunteer their time as teachers. APF also expects to hire instructors with special expertise. (20% of total activity)

Technical Assistance: APF plans to encourage effective management by facilitating solutions to problems nonprofits face. APF will develop, and keep open regularly, a library of technical books, publications, and computer programs on nonprofits. APF will seek to foster exchanges of information and encourage networking. For example, roundtable-type meetings will be held, possibly groups with similar concerns will be formed. APF will develop a database of problems faced and solutions found as a reference tool. APF also expects to develop, as a resource tool, lists of companies, professionals, and other information useful to its exempt constituents. (60% of total activity)

Publications: APF plans to publish an electronic newsletter that contains technical articles on topics of interest to nonprofits. The newsletter will also serve to announce seminars, roundtable meetings, library news and other information. The newsletter will be distributed free of charge and contain no advertising. APF will seek legal, accounting, and other types of professionals to donate articles and information. The newsletter will only be disseminated through the website to make it available to anyone. (20% of activity)

<u>Part V, Line 2a</u>

The President A.B. Sample is married to the Secretary/Treasurer C.D. Sample. E.F. Sample is their son.

<u>Part V, Line 3a</u>

A.B. Sample is the President. His qualifications include a degree in business. He expects to work 5-10 hours a week for the organization as a volunteer with no compensation. His duties include supervising and conducting APF's activities and operations. He will preside at all meetings and shall keep the Board informed concerning activities of the Fund. He may sign contracts and documents authorized by the Board. He will foster committees and appoint members to serve on committees.

Attachment to Many Parts

Appendix C Form 1023 for a Private Operating Foundation

Active Project Fund   33-3333333
Attachment to Form 1023

C.D. Sample is the Secretary and Treasurer. Her qualifications include working at an accounting firm that specializes in nonprofit issues. She plans to work 3-5 hours a week for the organization as a volunteer with no compensation. Her duties include acting as Secretary of all meetings and keeping the minutes. In addition, she will have custody of all funds and securities of APF. She will maintain a full and accurate account of receipts and disbursements of the Fund and deposits all money and valuables in the bank or other depositories.

E.F. Sample is the Vice President. His qualifications include an interest in aiding nonprofits. He plans to work 2 hours a week for the organization as a volunteer with no compensation.

Jane Smith is the Executive Director. She is unrelated to the Sample family. Her qualifications include working for ten years at The Big Foundation in a similar capacity. She has lectured throughout the country on the importance of structure within nonprofit organizations. She will work approximately 45 hours per week. Her duties will include managing the daily activities of APF under the guidance of the Board of Directors.

Part V, Line 5a

The Board of Directors of Active Project Fund has adopted a conflict of interest policy consistent with the recommendations of the Internal Revenue Service instructions. Please find a copy of the policy attached.

Part V, Line 6a

The employment agreement with the Executive Director Jane Smith provides that she may be compensated through a non-fixed payment in the form of a discretionary bonus. The Board of Directors has the option of voting to give the executive director a non-fixed bonus if her work has been excellent for the previous year and all goals have been met or exceeded. The optional bonus must be less than 10% of her total compensation for the year. The bonus must be reviewed by the Board of Directors to ensure that the total compensation plus the optional bonus is reasonable compensation for her services.

Part V, Line 7a

APF will purchase management services from highly compensated employee Jane Smith. APF has negotiated these services at arm's length and the fees are at or below the fair market value as determined by bids from similar companies.

Part VI, Line 1b

APF plans to provide an annual grant to a deserving organization that needs assistance in developing its management structure. Before making any grants, APF will verify that the grantee is listed in IRS Publication 78 as a public charity. See Part IV for a description of the services APF plans to provide to organizations.

Part VIII, Line 11

APF has not accepted donations other than cash at this time. It is unknown if any of such donations will be given to APF in the future. If APF were offered non-cash donations, it would work with its tax advisors to make sure that it complied with all applicable Internal Revenue Services rules for the organization and the donor.

Appendix C Form 1023 for a Private Operating Foundation

Active Project Fund   33-3333333
Attachment to Form 1023

Part VIII, Line 13b

APF plans to make one grant a year to a deserving organization that needs assistance in developing its management structure. APF's programs focus on improving management situations within nonprofits. The grant would serve to improve the organization's internal structure by providing funds for software, office equipment, necessary training, etc.

Part VIII, Line 13d

No recipients have been determined yet. However, no grants will be provided to organizations that have relationships with disqualified persons. Additionally, once an organization has received a grant, it becomes ineligible to receive further grants.

Part VIII, Line 13e

For each grant, APF plans to keep a file that includes a copy of the organization's IRS determination letter and APF's recommendation of the types of expenditures that would best improve the organization's internal structure.

Part VIII, Line 13f

The selection process will include recommendations from the Executive Director based upon organizations she has dealt with throughout the year during seminars or by providing technical assistance. The Board will then review the nominated organizations' most recent 990 and a letter that explains what the organization would do with the funds if granted them.

Part VIII, Line 13g

Once the organization has been granted the funds, it will be responsible for providing a report at the end of its next fiscal year that describes how the money was put to use.

Appendix C Form 1023 for a Private Operating Foundation

Active Project Fund   33-3333333
Attachment to Form 1023

Part IX - Financial Data	2005	2006	2007
Revenue, Line 1 - Contributions	$300,000	$400,000	$500,000

A.B. and C.D. Sample plan to donate shares of Clean Air Industries (listed on NYSE).
The shares will be sold upon receipt and used to support APF programs and provide working capital.

Revenue, Line 9 - Exempt Function Income

Seminar fees	5,000	10,000	30,000
Publication sales	5,000	10,000	30,000
	$ 10,000	$ 20,000	$ 60,000

Expenses, line 18 - Other salaries & wages

Executive Director (full time)	18,000	52,000	55,000
Administrator (full time)	20,000	30,000	32,000
Instructors (3-4 part-time)	10,000	20,000	24,000
Librarian/publicist (part time)	6,000	12,400	16,000
Assistants (2-3 part time)	5,000	20,000	40,000
	59,000	134,400	167,000
Fringe benefits and payroll tax	6,000	12,600	16,000
	$ 65,000	$ 147,000	$ 183,000

Expenses, Line 21 - Depreciation

Active Project Fund plans to spend up to $ 25,000 buying computers,
office furnishings, tables and chairs, projectors, and similar equipment.
The depreciation will be calculated on a five year straight-line basis.

Expenses, Line 21 -- Professional fees

Legal fees	4,000	1,000	1,000
Accounting fees	2,000	3,000	3,500
Website designer	10,000		
	$ 16,000	$ 4,000	$ 4,500

Expenses, Line 22 - Other Expense

Library books and publications	20,000	10,000	5,000
Computer programs for teaching purposes	22,000	18,000	7,000
Printing & design of seminar materials	10,000	6,000	4,000
Website fees and maintenance	12,000	14,000	16,000
Seminar refreshments	5,000	6,000	7,000
Office supplies & expenses	6,000	8,000	9,000
Insurance	2,000	2,000	2,000
	$ 77,000	$ 64,000	$ 50,000

Attachment to Part IX

Appendix C Form 1023 for a Private Operating Foundation

Active Project Fund   **33-3333333**
Attachment to Form 1023

Part X, Line 4

Active Project Fund projects the following information
that indicates it will meet the Income and Endowment Tests
and be eligible for classification as an operating foundation.

Income Test

		2005	2006	2007
Line 1a	Adjusted net income	300	600	3,000
Line 1b	Minimum investment return	9,000	12,500	13,000
Line 2a	Qualifying distributions *	170,000	239,000	267,500
Line 2b	Acquisition of exempt function assets	25,000		
Line 2d	Total qualifying distributions	$ 195,000	$ 239,000	$ 267,500
Line 3a	Percentage of qualifying distributions to ANI	> 100%	> 100%	>100%
Line 3b	Percentage of qualifying distribution to MDR	> 100%	> 100%	>100%

Endowment Test

Line 9	Value of assets not used directly in exempt activities.			
Line 9a	Projected monthly average of investment securities	0	0	0
Line 9b	Projected average of cash balances	180,000	250,000	260,000
Line 9c	Projected value of other investment property	-	0	0
Line 9d	Total	180,000	250,000	260,000
Line 10	Acquisition indebtedness		0	0
Line 11	Balance	180,000	250,000	260,000
Line 12	Multiply line 11 by 3-1/3%	$5,994	$8,325	$8,658

Note line 2d exceeds the amount on line 12.

*Depreciation expense is not included as a qualifying distribution here because the entire amount
paid at the time of the purchase of the assets was treated as a qualifying distribution.

Active Project Fund has made a good faith determination that it will satisfy the income test and
the endowment test set forth above for its first taxable year and the years thereafter based upon
projections of income and expenditures and the opinion of our counsel. See Part IV for a
description of the planned activities.

A Good Accountant

A Good Accountant

Attachment to Part X, Line 4

Appendix D Public Support Test Calculation for IRC 170(b)(1)(A)(vi) Organization

Sample Organization
Carryforward worksheet for schedule A: Public Support
509(a)(1) TEST

	08 return	07 return	06 return	05 return	Total	
Contributions p.1, line 1d	220,000	175,000	180,000	274,000		
Pledges rec'ble beginning	125,000	50,000	200,000	-		plus
Pledges rec'ble end	(75,000)	(125,000)	(50,000)	(200,000)		minus
Gov't contracts beginning						plus
Gov't contracts end						minus
Total Line 15 - Sch A Part IV-A	270,000	100,000	330,000	74,000	774,000	
Program service revenue (p.1 line 2)	55,000	60,000	20,000	40,000		
Gross receipts- p. 1 line 9	25,000	12,500	7,000	5,500		
Gross receipts- p.1, line 10	0	0	0	0		
Gross receipts- p.1, line 11	0	0	0	0		plus
Accounts rec'ble beginning	5,000	6,000	0	0		minus
Accounts rec'ble end	(1,500)	(5,000)	(6,000)	0		
Total Line 17 - Sch A, Part IV-A	83,500	73,500	21,000	45,500	223,500	
Interest p p. 1 line 4	500	375	250	125		
Dividends p.1, line 5	1,200	900	1,000	800		
Gross Rents p.1, line 6	-	-	-	-		
Other invtmt p.1, line 7	-	-	-	-		
Total Line 18	1,700	1,275	1,250	925	5,150	
Total Line 23	355,200	174,775	352,250	120,425	1,002,650	
Total Line 24 (lines23-17)	271,700	101,275	331,250	74,925	779,150	

	08 return	07 return	06 return	05 return	Total	2% Ln 24
						15,583
Major Donor 1	50,000	0	50,000	0	100,000	84,417
Major Donor 2	7,500	5,000	10,000	2,000	24,500	8,917
Major Donor 3	1,000	2,000	5,000	7,500	15,500	0
Major Donor 4	20,000	10,000	5,000	-	35,000	19,417
Major Donor 5	50,000	25,000	50,000	50,000	175,000	159,417
All other donors	141,500	58,000	210,000	14,500	424,000	
total cash donations	270,000	100,000	330,000	74,000	774,000	272,168
investment income	1,700	1,275	1,250	925	5,150	
Total support for 509(a)(1)	271,700	101,275	331,250	74,925	779,150	

less: donations considered private		(272,168)
less: investment income		(5,150)
Total Public Support		501,832
Public Support Ratio (Public Support/Total Support)		64.41%

Appendix E Public Support Test Calculation for IRC 509(a)(2)

Sample Organization
Carryforward worksheet for schedule A: Public Support
509(a)(2) TEST

	08 return	07 return	06 return	05 return	Total	
Contributions p.1, line 1d	150,000	125,000	75,000	100,000		
Pledges rec'ble beginning	25,000	50,000	10,000	-		plus
Pledges rec'ble end	(12,500)	(25,000)	(50,000)	(10,000)		minus
Gov't contracts beginning	-	-	-	-		
Gov't contracts end	-	-	-	-		
Total Line 15 - Sch A Part IV-A	162,500	150,000	35,000	90,000	437,500	
Program service revenue (p.1 line 2)	300,000	275,000	282,000	294,000		
Gross receipts- p. 1 line 9	· 5,200	7,500	10,000	5,000		
Gross receipts- p.1, line 10	-	-	-	-		plus
Gross receipts- p.1, line 11		-	-	-		minus
Accounts rec'ble beginning	75,000	80,000	50,000	100,000		
Accounts rec'ble end	(50,000)	(75,000)	(80,000)	(50,000)		
Total Line 17 - Sch A, Part IV-A	330,200	287,500	262,000	349,000	1,228,700	
Interest p p. 1 line 4	1,000	800	750	800		
Dividends p.1, line 5	2,500	2,200	2,000	1,750		
Gross Rents p.1, line 6	-	-	-	-		
Other invtmt p.1, line 7	-	-	-	-		
Total Line 18	3,500	3,000	2,750	2,550	11,800	
Total Line 23	496,200	440,500	299,750	441,550	1,678,000	
Total Line 24 (lines23-17)	166,000	153,000	37,750	92,550	449,300	
Line 25 (1% of Line 23)	4,962	4,405	2,998	4,416		

DP Donations - Line 27a

	08 return	07 return	06 return	05 return	Total
Disqualified person 1	1,000	1,000	1,000	1,000	4,000
Disqualified person 2	50,000	50,000	25,000	25,000	150,000
Disqualified person 3	250	500	500	400	1,650
Disqualified person 4	· 300	1,000	700	500	2,500
Disqualified person 5	25,000	23,000	25,000	25,000	98,000
Disqualified person 6	1,000	1,500	2,000	4,000	8,500
Total Line 27a	77,550	77,000	54,200	55,900	264,650

Major Vendors - Line 27b

	08 return	07 return	06 return	05 return	Total
Vendor 1	6,500	6,500	5,150	5,300	
Vendor 2	10,000	5,300	5,100	0	
Vendor 3	5,200	5,200	0	0	
less 1% of line 23 x number of EFP	(15,000)	(15,000)	(10,000)	(5,000)	
Total Line 27b	6,700	2,000	250	300	9,250

Line 27c (Lines 15, 16, 17, 20, & 21)	1,666,200
Line 27d (Private Support)	273,900
Line 27e (Public Support)	1,392,300
Line 27f (Total Support)	1,678,000
Line 27g (Public Support %)	82.97%
Line 27h (Investment Income %)	0.70%

Appendix F The Schedules

Schedule A. Churches

1a Do you have a written creed, statement of faith, or summary of beliefs? If "Yes," attach copies of relevant documents. ☐ Yes ☐ No

b Do you have a form of worship? If "Yes," describe your form of worship. ☐ Yes ☐ No

2a Do you have a formal code of doctrine and discipline? If "Yes," describe your code of doctrine and discipline. ☐ Yes ☐ No

b Do you have a distinct religious history? If "Yes," describe your religious history. ☐ Yes ☐ No

c Do you have a literature of your own? If "Yes," describe your literature. ☐ Yes ☐ No

3 Describe the organization's religious hierarchy or ecclesiastical government.

4a Do you have regularly scheduled religious services? If "Yes," describe the nature of the services and provide representative copies of relevant literature such as church bulletins. ☐ Yes ☐ No

b What is the average attendance at your regularly scheduled religious services? _____

5a Do you have an established place of worship? If "Yes," refer to the instructions for the information required. ☐ Yes ☐ No

b Do you own the property where you have an established place of worship? ☐ Yes ☐ No

6 Do you have an established congregation or other regular membership group? If "No," refer to the instructions. ☐ Yes ☐ No

7 How many members do you have? _____

8a Do you have a process by which an individual becomes a member? If "Yes," describe the process and complete lines 8b–8d, below. ☐ Yes ☐ No

b If you have members, do your members have voting rights, rights to participate in religious functions, or other rights? If "Yes," describe the rights your members have. ☐ Yes ☐ No

c May your members be associated with another denomination or church? ☐ Yes ☐ No

d Are all of your members part of the same **family**? ☐ Yes ☐ No

9 Do you conduct baptisms, weddings, funerals, etc.? ☐ Yes ☐ No

10 Do you have a school for the religious instruction of the young? ☐ Yes ☐ No

11a Do you have a minister or religious leader? If "Yes," describe this person's role and explain whether the minister or religious leader was ordained, commissioned, or licensed after a prescribed course of study. ☐ Yes ☐ No

b Do you have schools for the preparation of your ordained ministers or religious leaders? ☐ Yes ☐ No

12 Is your minister or religious leader also one of your officers, directors, or trustees? ☐ Yes ☐ No

13 Do you ordain, commission, or license ministers or religious leaders? If "Yes," describe the requirements for ordination, commission, or licensure. ☐ Yes ☐ No

14 Are you part of a group of churches with similar beliefs and structures? If "Yes," explain. Include the name of the group of churches. ☐ Yes ☐ No

15 Do you issue church charters? If "Yes," describe the requirements for issuing a charter. ☐ Yes ☐ No

16 Did you pay a fee for a church charter? If "Yes," attach a copy of the charter. ☐ Yes ☐ No

17 Do you have other information you believe should be considered regarding your status as a church? If "Yes," explain. ☐ Yes ☐ No

Form **1023** (Rev. 10-2004)

Appendix F The Schedules

Schedule B. Schools, Colleges, and Universities

If you operate a school as an activity, complete Schedule B

Section I	Operational Information

1a Do you normally have a regularly scheduled curriculum, a regular faculty of qualified teachers, a regularly enrolled student body, and facilities where your educational activities are regularly carried on? If "No," do not complete the remainder of Schedule B. ☐ Yes ☐ No

b Is the primary function of your school the presentation of formal instruction? If "Yes," describe your school in terms of whether it is an elementary, secondary, college, technical, or other type of school. If "No," do not complete the remainder of Schedule B. ☐ Yes ☐ No

2a Are you a public school because you are operated by a state or subdivision of a state? If "Yes," explain how you are operated by a state or subdivision of a state. Do not complete the remainder of Schedule B. ☐ Yes ☐ No

b Are you a public school because you are operated wholly or predominantly from government funds or property? If "Yes," explain how you are operated wholly or predominantly from government funds or property. Submit a copy of your funding agreement regarding government funding. Do not complete the remainder of Schedule B. ☐ Yes ☐ No

3 In what public school district, county, and state are you located?

4 Were you formed or substantially expanded at the time of public school desegregation in the above school district or county? ☐ Yes ☐ No

5 Has a state or federal administrative agency or judicial body ever determined that you are racially discriminatory? If "Yes," explain. ☐ Yes ☐ No

6 Has your right to receive financial aid or assistance from a governmental agency ever been revoked or suspended? If "Yes," explain. ☐ Yes ☐ No

7 Do you or will you contract with another organization to develop, build, market, or finance your facilities? If "Yes," explain how that entity is selected, explain how the terms of any contracts or other agreements are negotiated at arm's length, and explain how you determine that you will pay no more than fair market value for services. ☐ Yes ☐ No

Note. Make sure your answer is consistent with the information provided in Part VI, line 7a.

8 Do you or will you manage your activities or facilities through your own employees or volunteers? If "No," attach a statement describing the activities that will be managed by others, the names of the persons or organizations that manage or will manage your activities or facilities, and how these managers were or will be selected. Also, submit copies of any contracts, proposed contracts, or other agreements regarding the provision of management services for your activities or facilities. Explain how the terms of any contracts or other agreements were or will be negotiated, and explain how you determine you will pay no more than fair market value for services. ☐ Yes ☐ No

Note. Answer "Yes" if you manage or intend to manage your programs through your own employees or by using volunteers. Answer "No" if you engage or intend to engage a separate organization or independent contractor. Make sure your answer is consistent with the information provided in Part VI, line 7b.

Section II	Establishment of Racially Nondiscriminatory Policy

Information required by **Revenue Procedure 75-50.**

1 Have you adopted a racially nondiscriminatory policy as to students in your organizing document, bylaws, or by resolution of your governing body? If "Yes," state where the policy can be found or supply a copy of the policy. If "No," you must adopt a nondiscriminatory policy as to students before submitting this application. See Publication 557. ☐ Yes ☐ No

2 Do your brochures, application forms, advertisements, and catalogues dealing with student admissions, programs, and scholarships contain a statement of your racially nondiscriminatory policy? ☐ Yes ☐ No

a If "Yes," attach a representative sample of each document.
b If "No," by checking the box to the right you agree that all future printed materials, including website content, will contain the required nondiscriminatory policy statement. ► ☐

3 Have you published a notice of your nondiscriminatory policy in a newspaper of general circulation that serves all racial segments of the community? (See the instructions for specific requirements.) If "No," explain. ☐ Yes ☐ No

4 Does or will the organization (or any department or division within it) discriminate in any way on the basis of race with respect to admissions; use of facilities or exercise of student privileges; faculty or administrative staff; or scholarship or loan programs? If "Yes," for any of the above, explain fully. ☐ Yes ☐ No

Form **1023** (Rev. 10-2004)

Appendix F The Schedules

Schedule B. Schools, Colleges, and Universities *(Continued)*

5 Complete the table below to show the racial composition for the current academic year and projected for the next academic year, of: (a) the student body, (b) the faculty, and (c) the administrative staff. Provide actual numbers rather than percentages for each racial category.

If you are not operational, submit an estimate based on the best information available (such as the racial composition of the community served).

Racial Category	(a) Student Body		(b) Faculty		(c) Administrative Staff	
	Current Year	Next Year	Current Year	Next Year	Current Year	Next Year
Total						

6 In the table below, provide the number and amount of loans and scholarships awarded to students enrolled by racial categories.

Racial Category	Number of Loans		Amount of Loans		Number of Scholarships		Amount of Scholarships	
	Current Year	Next Year	Current Year	Next Year	Current Year	Next Year	Current Year	Next Year
Total								

7a Attach a list of your incorporators, founders, board members, and donors of land or buildings, whether individuals or organizations.

b Do any of these individuals or organizations have an objective to maintain segregated public or private school education? If "Yes," explain. ☐ Yes ☐ No

8 Will you maintain records according to the non-discrimination provisions contained in Revenue Procedure 75-50? If "No," explain. (See instructions.) ☐ Yes ☐ No

Form **1023** (Rev. 10-2004)

Appendix F The Schedules

Schedule C. Hospitals and Medical Research Organizations

Check the box if you are a **hospital**. See the instructions for a definition of the term "hospital," which includes an organization whose principal purpose or function is providing **hospital** or **medical care**. Complete Section I below. ☐

Check the box if you are a **medical research organization** operated in conjunction with a hospital. See the instructions for a definition of the term "medical research organization," which refers to an organization whose principal purpose or function is medical research and which is directly engaged in the continuous active conduct of medical research in conjunction with a hospital. Complete Section II. ☐

Section I   Hospitals

1a Are all the doctors in the community eligible for staff privileges? If "No," give the reasons why and explain how the medical staff is selected.   ☐ Yes   ☐ No

2a Do you or will you provide medical services to all individuals in your community who can pay for themselves or have private health insurance? If "No," explain.   ☐ Yes   ☐ No

b Do you or will you provide medical services to all individuals in your community who participate in Medicare? If "No," explain.   ☐ Yes   ☐ No

c Do you or will you provide medical services to all individuals in your community who participate in Medicaid? If "No," explain.   ☐ Yes   ☐ No

3a Do you or will you require persons covered by Medicare or Medicaid to pay a deposit before receiving services? If "Yes," explain.   ☐ Yes   ☐ No

b Does the same deposit requirement, if any, apply to all other patients? If "No," explain.   ☐ Yes   ☐ No

4a Do you or will you maintain a full-time emergency room? If "No," explain why you do not maintain a full-time emergency room. Also, describe any emergency services that you provide.   ☐ Yes   ☐ No

b Do you have a policy on providing emergency services to persons without apparent means to pay? If "Yes," provide a copy of the policy.   ☐ Yes   ☐ No

c Do you have any arrangements with police, fire, and voluntary ambulance services for the delivery or admission of emergency cases? If "Yes," describe the arrangements, including whether they are written or oral agreements. If written, submit copies of all such agreements.   ☐ Yes   ☐ No

5a Do you provide for a portion of your services and facilities to be used for charity patients? If "Yes," answer 5b through 5e.   ☐ Yes   ☐ No

b Explain your policy regarding charity cases, including how you distinguish between charity care and bad debts. Submit a copy of your written policy.

c Provide data on your past experience in admitting charity patients, including amounts you expend for treating charity care patients and types of services you provide to charity care patients.

d Describe any arrangements you have with federal, state, or local governments or government agencies for paying for the cost of treating charity care patients. Submit copies of any written agreements.

e Do you provide services on a sliding fee schedule depending on financial ability to pay? If "Yes," submit your sliding fee schedule.   ☐ Yes   ☐ No

6a Do you or will you carry on a formal program of medical training or medical research? If "Yes," describe such programs, including the type of programs offered, the scope of such programs, and affiliations with other hospitals or medical care providers with which you carry on the medical training or research programs.   ☐ Yes   ☐ No

b Do you or will you carry on a formal program of community education? If "Yes," describe such programs, including the type of programs offered, the scope of such programs, and affiliation with other hospitals or medical care providers with which you offer community education programs.   ☐ Yes   ☐ No

7 Do you or will you provide office space to physicians carrying on their own medical practices? If "Yes," describe the criteria for who may use the space, explain the means used to determine that you are paid at least fair market value, and submit representative lease agreements.   ☐ Yes   ☐ No

8 Is your board of directors comprised of a majority of individuals who are representative of the community you serve? Include a list of each board member's name and business, financial, or professional relationship with the hospital. Also, identify each board member who is representative of the community and describe how that individual is a community representative.   ☐ Yes   ☐ No

9 Do you participate in any joint ventures? If "Yes," state your ownership percentage in each joint venture, list your investment in each joint venture, describe the tax status of other participants in each joint venture (including whether they are section 501(c)(3) organizations), describe the activities of each joint venture, describe how you exercise control over the activities of each joint venture, and describe how each joint venture furthers your exempt purposes. Also, submit copies of all agreements.
Note. Make sure your answer is consistent with the information provided in Part VIII, line 8.   ☐ Yes   ☐ No

Appendix F The Schedules

Schedule C. Hospitals and Medical Research Organizations (Continued)

Section I   Hospitals (Continued)

10 Do you or will you manage your activities or facilities through your own employees or volunteers? If ☐ **Yes** ☐ **No**
"No," attach a statement describing the activities that will be managed by others, the names of the
persons or organizations that manage or will manage your activities or facilities, and how these
managers were or will be selected. Also, submit copies of any contracts, proposed contracts, or
other agreements regarding the provision of management services for your activities or facilities.
Explain how the terms of any contracts or other agreements were or will be negotiated, and explain
how you determine you will pay no more than fair market value for services.

Note. Answer "Yes" if you do manage or intend to manage your programs through your own
employees or by using volunteers. Answer "No" if you engage or intend to engage a separate
organization or independent contractor. Make sure your answer is consistent with the information
provided in Part VIII, line 7b.

11 Do you or will you offer recruitment incentives to physicians? If "Yes," describe your recruitment ☐ **Yes** ☐ **No**
incentives and attach copies of all written recruitment incentive policies.

12 Do you or will you lease equipment, assets, or office space from physicians who have a financial or ☐ **Yes** ☐ **No**
professional relationship with you? If "Yes," explain how you establish a fair market value for the
lease.

13 Have you purchased medical practices, ambulatory surgery centers, or other business assets from ☐ **Yes** ☐ **No**
physicians or other persons with whom you have a business relationship, aside from the purchase? If
"Yes," submit a copy of each purchase and sales contract and describe how you arrived at fair
market value, including copies of appraisals.

14 Have you adopted a **conflict of interest policy** consistent with the sample health care organization ☐ **Yes** ☐ **No**
conflict of interest policy in Appendix A of the instructions? If "Yes," submit a copy of the policy and
explain how the policy has been adopted, such as by resolution of your governing board. If "No,"
explain how you will avoid any conflicts of interest in your business dealings.

Section II   Medical Research Organizations

1 Name the hospitals with which you have a relationship and describe the relationship. Attach copies
of written agreements with each hospital that demonstrate continuing relationships between you and
the hospital(s).

2 Attach a schedule describing your present and proposed activities for the direct conduct of medical
research; describe the nature of the activities, and the amount of money that has been or will be
spent in carrying them out.

3 Attach a schedule of assets showing their fair market value and the portion of your assets directly
devoted to medical research.

Form **1023** (Rev. 10-2004)

Appendix F The Schedules

Form 1023 (Rev. 10-2004)   Name:

Schedule D. Section 509(a)(3) Supporting Organizations

Section I	**Identifying Information About the Supported Organization(s)**

1 State the names, addresses, and EINs of the supported organizations. If additional space is needed, attach a separate sheet.

Name	Address	EIN
		–
		–

2 Are all supported organizations listed in line 1 public charities under section 509(a)(1) or (2)? If "Yes," go to Section II. If "No," go to line 3.   ☐ Yes   ☐ No

3 Do the supported organizations have tax-exempt status under section 501(c)(4), 501(c)(5), or 501(c)(6)?   ☐ Yes   ☐ No

If "Yes," for each 501(c)(4), (5), or (6) organization supported, provide the following financial information:

- Part IX-A. Statement of Revenues and Expenses, lines 1–13 and
- Part X, lines 6b(ii)(a), 6b(ii)(b), and 7.

If "No," attach a statement describing how each organization you support is a public charity under section 509(a)(1) or (2).

Section II	**Relationship with Supported Organization(s)—Three Tests**

To be classified as a supporting organization, an organization must meet one of three relationship tests:

Test 1: "Operated, supervised, or controlled by" one or more publicly supported organizations, or

Test 2: "Supervised or controlled in connection with" one or more publicly supported organizations, or

Test 3: "Operated in connection with" one or more publicly supported organizations.

1 Information to establish the "operated, supervised, or controlled by" relationship (Test 1)
Is a majority of your governing board or officers elected or appointed by the supported organization(s)? If "Yes," describe the process by which your governing board is appointed and elected; go to Section III. If "No," continue to line 2.   ☐ Yes   ☐ No

2 Information to establish the "supervised or controlled in connection with" relationship (Test 2)
Does a majority of your governing board consist of individuals who also serve on the governing board of the supported organization(s)? If "Yes," describe the process by which your governing board is appointed and elected; go to Section III. If "No," go to line 3.   ☐ Yes   ☐ No

3 Information to establish the "operated in connection with" responsiveness test (Test 3)
Are you a trust from which the named supported organization(s) can enforce and compel an accounting under state law? If "Yes," explain whether you advised the supported organization(s) in writing of these rights and provide a copy of the written communication documenting this; go to Section II, line 5. If "No," go to line 4a.   ☐ Yes   ☐ No

4 Information to establish the alternative "operated in connection with" responsiveness test (Test 3)

a Do the officers, directors, trustees, or members of the supported organization(s) elect or appoint one or more of your officers, directors, or trustees? If "Yes," explain and provide documentation; go to line 4d, below. If "No," go to line 4b.   ☐ Yes   ☐ No

b Do one or more members of the governing body of the supported organization(s) also serve as your officers, directors, or trustees or hold other important offices with respect to you? If "Yes," explain and provide documentation; go to line 4d, below. If "No," go to line 4c.   ☐ Yes   ☐ No

c Do your officers, directors, or trustees maintain a close and continuous working relationship with the officers, directors, or trustees of the supported organization(s)? If "Yes," explain and provide documentation.   ☐ Yes   ☐ No

d Do the supported organization(s) have a significant voice in your investment policies, in the making and timing of grants, and in otherwise directing the use of your income or assets? If "Yes," explain and provide documentation.   ☐ Yes   ☐ No

e Describe and provide copies of written communications documenting how you made the supported organization(s) aware of your supporting activities.

Form **1023** (Rev. 10-2004)

Appendix F The Schedules

Schedule D. Section 509(a)(3) Supporting Organizations *(Continued)*

Section II Relationship with Supported Organization(s)—Three Tests *(Continued)*

5 Information to establish the "operated in connection with" integral part test (Test 3)

Do you conduct activities that would otherwise be carried out by the supported organization(s)? If "Yes," explain and go to Section III. If "No," continue to line 6a.   ☐ Yes   ☐ No

6 Information to establish the alternative "operated in connection with" integral part test (Test 3)

a Do you distribute at least 85% of your annual **net income** to the supported organization(s)? If "Yes," go to line 6b. (See instructions.)   ☐ Yes   ☐ No

If "No," state the percentage of your income that you distribute to each supported organization. Also explain how you ensure that the supported organization(s) are attentive to your operations.

b How much do you contribute annually to each supported organization? Attach a schedule.

c What is the total annual revenue of each supported organization? If you need additional space, attach a list.

d Do you or the supported organization(s) **earmark** your funds for support of a particular program or activity? If "Yes," explain.   ☐ Yes   ☐ No

7a Does your organizing document specify the supported organization(s) by name? If "Yes," state the article and paragraph number and go to Section III. If "No," answer line 7b.   ☐ Yes   ☐ No

b Attach a statement describing whether there has been an historic and continuing relationship between you and the supported organization(s).

Section III Organizational Test

1a If you met relationship Test 1 or Test 2 in Section II, your organizing document must specify the supported organization(s) by name, or by naming a similar purpose or charitable class of beneficiaries. If your organizing document complies with this requirement, answer "Yes." If your organizing document does not comply with this requirement, answer "No," and see the instructions.   ☐ Yes   ☐ No

b If you met relationship Test 3 in Section II, your organizing document must generally specify the supported organization(s) by name. If your organizing document complies with this requirement, answer "Yes," and go to Section IV. If your organizing document does not comply with this requirement, answer "No," and see the instructions.   ☐ Yes   ☐ No

Section IV Disqualified Person Test

You do not qualify as a supporting organization if you are **controlled** directly or indirectly by one or more **disqualified persons** (as defined in section 4946) other than **foundation managers** or one or more organizations that you support. Foundation managers who are also disqualified persons for another reason are disqualified persons with respect to you.

1a Do any persons who are disqualified persons with respect to you, (except individuals who are disqualified persons only because they are foundation managers), appoint any of your foundation managers? If "Yes," (1) describe the process by which disqualified persons appoint any of your foundation managers, (2) provide the names of these disqualified persons and the foundation managers they appoint, and (3) explain how control is vested over your operations (including assets and activities) by persons other than disqualified persons.   ☐ Yes   ☐ No

b Do any persons who have a family or business relationship with any disqualified persons with respect to you, (except individuals who are disqualified persons only because they are foundation managers), appoint any of your foundation managers? If "Yes," (1) describe the process by which individuals with a family or business relationship with disqualified persons appoint any of your foundation managers, (2) provide the names of these disqualified persons, the individuals with a family or business relationship with disqualified persons, and the foundation managers appointed, and (3) explain how control is vested over your operations (including assets and activities) in individuals other than disqualified persons.   ☐ Yes   ☐ No

c Do any persons who are disqualified persons, (except individuals who are disqualified persons only because they are foundation managers), have any influence regarding your operations, including your assets or activities? If "Yes," (1) provide the names of these disqualified persons, (2) explain how influence is exerted over your operations (including assets and activities), and (3) explain how control is vested over your operations (including assets and activities) by individuals other than disqualified persons.   ☐ Yes   ☐ No

Form **1023** (Rev. 10-2004)

Appendix F The Schedules

Schedule E. Organizations Not Filing Form 1023 Within 27 Months of Formation

Schedule E is intended to determine whether you are eligible for tax exemption under section 501(c)(3) from the postmark date of your application or from your date of incorporation or formation, whichever is earlier. If you are not eligible for tax exemption under section 501(c)(3) from your date of incorporation or formation, Schedule E is also intended to determine whether you are eligible for tax exemption under section 501(c)(4) for the period between your date of incorporation or formation and the postmark date of your application.

1	Are you a church, association of churches, or integrated auxiliary of a church? If "Yes," complete Schedule A and stop here. Do not complete the remainder of Schedule E.	☐ **Yes**	☐ **No**
2a	Are you a public charity with annual **gross receipts** that are normally are $5,000 or less? If "Yes," stop here. Answer "No" if you are a private foundation, regardless of your gross receipts.	☐ **Yes**	☐ **No**
b	If your gross receipts were normally more than $5,000, are you filing this application within 90 days from the end of the tax year in which your gross receipts were normally more than $5,000? If "Yes," stop here.	☐ **Yes**	☐ **No**
3a	Were you included as a subordinate in a group exemption application or letter? If "No," go to line 4.	☐ **Yes**	☐ **No**
b	If you were included as a subordinate in a group exemption letter, are you filing this application within 27 months from the date you were notified by the organization holding the group exemption letter or the Internal Revenue Service that you cease to be covered by the group exemption letter? If "Yes," stop here.	☐ **Yes**	☐ **No**
c	If you were included as a subordinate in a timely filed group exemption request that was denied, are you filing this application within 27 months from the postmark date of the Internal Revenue Service final adverse ruling letter? If "Yes," stop here.	☐ **Yes**	☐ **No**
4	Were you created on or before October 9, 1969? If "Yes," stop here. Do not complete the remainder of this schedule.	☐ **Yes**	☐ **No**
5	If you answered "No" to lines 1 through 4, we cannot recognize you as tax exempt from your date of formation unless you qualify for an extension of time to apply for exemption. Do you wish to request an extension of time to apply to be recognized as exempt from the date you were formed? If "Yes," attach a statement explaining why you did not file this application within the 27-month period. Do not answer lines 6, 7, or 8. If "No," go to line 6a.	☐ **Yes**	☐ **No**
6a	If you answered "No" to line 5, you can only be exempt under section 501(c)(3) from the postmark date of this application. Therefore, do you want us to treat this application as a request for tax exemption from the postmark date? If "Yes," you are eligible for an advance ruling. Complete Part X, line 6a. If "No," you will be treated as a private foundation.	☐ **Yes**	☐ **No**
	Note. Be sure your ruling eligibility agrees with your answer to Part X, line 6.		
b	Do you anticipate significant changes in your sources of support in the future? If "Yes," complete line 7 below.	☐ **Yes**	☐ **No**

Form **1023** (Rev. 10-2004)

Appendix F The Schedules

Schedule E. Organizations Not Filing Form 1023 Within 27 Months of Formation *(Continued)*

7 Complete this item only if you answered "Yes" to line 6b. Include projected revenue for the first two full years following the current tax year.

Type of Revenue	Projected revenue for 2 years following current tax year		
	(a) From .... To	**(b)** From .... To	**(c)** Total
1 Gifts, grants, and contributions received (do not include unusual grants)			
2 Membership fees received			
3 Gross investment income			
4 Net unrelated business income			
5 Taxes levied for your benefit			
6 Value of services or facilities furnished by a governmental unit without charge (not including the value of services generally furnished to the public without charge)			
7 Any revenue not otherwise listed above or in lines 9–12 below (attach an itemized list)			
8 Total of lines 1 through 7			
9 Gross receipts from admissions, merchandise sold, or services performed, or furnishing of facilities in any activity that is related to your exempt purposes (attach itemized list)			
10 Total of lines 8 and 9			
11 Net gain or loss on sale of capital assets (attach an itemized list)			
12 Unusual grants			
13 Total revenue. Add lines 10 through 12			

8 According to your answers, you are only eligible for tax exemption under section 501(c)(3) from the postmark date of your application. However, you may be eligible for tax exemption under section 501(c)(4) from your date of formation to the postmark date of the Form 1023. Tax exemption under section 501(c)(4) allows exemption from federal income tax, but generally not deductibility of contributions under Code section 170. Check the box at right if you want us to treat this as a request for exemption under 501(c)(4) from your date of formation to the postmark date.   ▶ ☐

Attach a completed Page 1 of Form 1024, Application for Recognition of Exemption Under Section 501(a), to this application.

Form **1023** (Rev. 10-2004)

Appendix F The Schedules

Schedule F. Homes for the Elderly or Handicapped and Low-Income Housing

Section I   General Information About Your Housing

1   Describe the type of housing you provide.

2   Provide copies of any application forms you use for admission.

3   Explain how the public is made aware of your facility.

4a Provide a description of each facility.
b What is the total number of residents each facility can accommodate?
c What is your current number of residents in each facility?
d Describe each facility in terms of whether residents rent or purchase housing from you.

5   Attach a sample copy of your residency or homeownership contract or agreement.

6   Do you participate in any joint ventures? If "Yes," state your ownership percentage in each joint venture, list your investment in each joint venture, describe the tax status of other participants in each joint venture (including whether they are section 501(c)(3) organizations), describe the activities of each joint venture, describe how you exercise control over the activities of each joint venture, and describe how each joint venture furthers your exempt purposes. Also, submit copies of all joint venture agreements.   ☐ Yes ☐ No

Note. Make sure your answer is consistent with the information provided in Part VIII, line 8.

7   Do you or will you contract with another organization to develop, build, market, or finance your housing? If "Yes," explain how that entity is selected, explain how the terms of any contract(s) are negotiated at arm's length, and explain how you determine you will pay no more than fair market value for services.   ☐ Yes ☐ No

Note. Make sure your answer is consistent with the information provided in Part VIII, line 7a.

8   Do you or will you manage your activities or facilities through your own employees or volunteers? If "No," attach a statement describing the activities that will be managed by others, the names of the persons or organizations that manage or will manage your activities or facilities, and how these managers were or will be selected. Also, submit copies of any contracts, proposed contracts, or other agreements regarding the provision of management services for your activities or facilities. Explain how the terms of any contracts or other agreements were or will be negotiated, and explain how you determine you will pay no more than fair market value for services.   ☐ Yes ☐ No

Note. Answer "Yes" if you do manage or intend to manage your programs through your own employees or by using volunteers. Answer "No" if you engage or intend to engage a separate organization or independent contractor. Make sure your answer is consistent with the information provided in Part VIII, line 7b.

9   Do you participate in any government housing programs? If "Yes," describe these programs.   ☐ Yes ☐ No

10a Do you own the facility? If "No," describe any enforceable rights you possess to purchase the facility in the future; go to line 10c. If "Yes," answer line 10b.   ☐ Yes ☐ No

b How did you acquire the facility? For example, did you develop it yourself, purchase a project, etc. Attach all contracts, transfer agreements, or other documents connected with the acquisition of the facility.

c Do you lease the facility or the land on which it is located? If "Yes," describe the parties to the lease(s) and provide copies of all leases.   ☐ Yes ☐ No

Appendix F The Schedules

Schedule F. Homes for the Elderly or Handicapped and Low-Income Housing *(Continued)*

Section II	Homes for the Elderly or Handicapped

1a Do you provide housing for the elderly? If "Yes," describe who qualifies for your housing in terms of age, infirmity, or other criteria and explain how you select persons for your housing.   ☐ **Yes**   ☐ **No**

  b Do you provide housing for the handicapped? If "Yes," describe who qualifies for your housing in terms of disability, income levels, or other criteria and explain how you select persons for your housing.   ☐ **Yes**   ☐ **No**

2a Do you charge an entrance or founder's fee? If "Yes," describe what this charge covers, whether it is a one-time fee, how the fee is determined, whether it is payable in a lump sum or on an installment basis, whether it is refundable, and the circumstances, if any, under which it may be waived.   ☐ **Yes**   ☐ **No**

  b Do you charge periodic fees or maintenance charges? If "Yes," describe what these charges cover and how they are determined.   ☐ **Yes**   ☐ **No**

  c Is your housing affordable to a significant segment of the elderly or handicapped persons in the community? Identify your **community**. Also, if "Yes," explain how you determine your housing is affordable.   ☐ **Yes**   ☐ **No**

3a Do you have an established policy concerning residents who become unable to pay their regular charges? If "Yes," describe your established policy.   ☐ **Yes**   ☐ **No**

  b Do you have any arrangements with government welfare agencies or others to absorb all or part of the cost of maintaining residents who become unable to pay their regular charges? If "Yes," describe these arrangements.   ☐ **Yes**   ☐ **No**

4 Do you have arrangements for the healthcare needs of your residents? If "Yes," describe these arrangements.   ☐ **Yes**   ☐ **No**

5 Are your facilities designed to meet the physical, emotional, recreational, social, religious, and/or other similar needs of the elderly or handicapped? If "Yes," describe these design features.   ☐ **Yes**   ☐ **No**

Section III	Low-Income Housing

1 Do you provide low-income housing? If "Yes," describe who qualifies for your housing in terms of income levels or other criteria, and describe how you select persons for your housing.   ☐ **Yes**   ☐ **No**

2 In addition to rent or mortgage payments, do residents pay periodic fees or maintenance charges? If "Yes," describe what these charges cover and how they are determined.   ☐ **Yes**   ☐ **No**

3a Is your housing affordable to low income residents? If "Yes," describe how your housing is made affordable to low-income residents.   ☐ **Yes**   ☐ **No**

  Note. Revenue Procedure 96-32, 1996-1 C.B. 717, provides guidelines for providing low-income housing that will be treated as charitable. (At least 75% of the units are occupied by low-income tenants or 40% are occupied by tenants earning not more than 120% of the very low-income levels for the area.)

  b Do you impose any restrictions to make sure that your housing remains affordable to low-income residents? If "Yes," describe these restrictions.   ☐ **Yes**   ☐ **No**

4 Do you provide social services to residents? If "Yes," describe these services.   ☐ **Yes**   ☐ **No**

Appendix F The Schedules

Schedule G. Successors to Other Organizations

1a Are you a **successor** to a **for-profit organization**? If "Yes," explain the relationship with the **predecessor** organization that resulted in your creation and complete line 1b. ☐ Yes ☐ No

  b Explain why you took over the activities or assets of a for-profit organization or converted from for-profit to nonprofit status.

2a Are you a successor to an organization other than a for-profit organization? Answer "Yes" if you have taken or will take over the activities of another organization; or you have taken or will take over 25% or more of the fair market value of the net assets of another organization. If "Yes," explain the relationship with the other organzation that resulted in your creation. ☐ Yes ☐ No

  b Provide the tax status of the predecessor organization.

  c Did you or did an organization to which you are a successor previously apply for tax exemption under section 501(c)(3) or any other section of the Code? If "Yes," explain how the application was resolved. ☐ Yes ☐ No

  d Was your prior tax exemption or the tax exemption of an organization to which you are a successor revoked or suspended? If "Yes," explain. Include a description of the corrections you made to re-establish tax exemption. ☐ Yes ☐ No

  e Explain why you took over the activities or assets of another organization.

3 Provide the name, last address, and EIN of the predecessor organization and describe its activities.
Name: _____   EIN: ___ − _____
Address: _____

4 List the owners, partners, principal stockholders, officers, and governing board members of the predecessor organization. Attach a separate sheet if additional space is needed.

Name	Address	Share/Interest (If a for-profit)

5 Do or will any of the persons listed in line 4, maintain a working relationship with you? If "Yes," describe the relationship in detail and include copies of any agreements with any of these persons or with any for-profit organizations in which these persons own more than a 35% interest. ☐ Yes ☐ No

6a Were any assets transferred, whether by gift or sale, from the predecessor organization to you? ☐ Yes ☐ No
If "Yes," provide a list of assets, indicate the value of each asset, explain how the value was determined, and attach an appraisal, if available. For each asset listed, also explain if the transfer was by gift, sale, or combination thereof.

  b Were any restrictions placed on the use or sale of the assets? If "Yes," explain the restrictions. ☐ Yes ☐ No

  c Provide a copy of the agreement(s) of sale or transfer.

7 Were any debts or liabilities transferred from the predecessor for-profit organization to you? ☐ Yes ☐ No
If "Yes," provide a list of the debts or liabilities that were transferred to you, indicating the amount of each, how the amount was determined, and the name of the person to whom the debt or liability is owed.

8 Will you lease or rent any property or equipment previously owned or used by the predecessor for-profit organization, or from persons listed in line 4, or from for-profit organizations in which these persons own more than a 35% interest? If "Yes," submit a copy of the lease or rental agreement(s). Indicate how the lease or rental value of the property or equipment was determined. ☐ Yes ☐ No

9 Will you lease or rent property or equipment to persons listed in line 4, or to for-profit organizations in which these persons own more than a 35% interest? If "Yes," attach a list of the property or equipment, provide a copy of the lease or rental agreement(s), and indicate how the lease or rental value of the property or equipment was determined. ☐ Yes ☐ No

Form **1023** (Rev. 10-2004)

Appendix F The Schedules

Schedule H. Organizations Providing Scholarships, Fellowships, Educational Loans, or Other Educational Grants to Individuals and Private Foundations Requesting Advance Approval of Individual Grant Procedures

Section I	*Names of individual recipients are not required to be listed in Schedule H.*

Public charities and private foundations complete lines 1a through 7 of this section. See the instructions to Part X if you are not sure whether you are a public charity or a private foundation.

1a Describe the types of educational grants you provide to individuals, such as scholarships, fellowships, loans, etc.

  b Describe the purpose and amount of your scholarships, fellowships, and other educational grants and loans that you award.

  c If you award educational loans, explain the terms of the loans (interest rate, length, forgiveness, etc.).

  d Specify how your program is publicized.

  e Provide copies of any solicitation or announcement materials.

  f Provide a sample copy of the application used.

2 Do you maintain case histories showing recipients of your scholarships, fellowships, educational loans, or other educational grants, including names, addresses, purposes of awards, amount of each grant, manner of selection, and relationship (if any) to officers, trustees, or donors of funds to you? If "No," refer to the instructions.   ☐ Yes   ☐ No

3 Describe the specific criteria you use to determine who is eligible for your program. (For example, eligibility selection criteria could consist of graduating high school students from a particular high school who will attend college, writers of scholarly works about American history, etc.)

4a Describe the specific criteria you use to select recipients. (For example, specific selection criteria could consist of prior academic performance, financial need, etc.)

  b Describe how you determine the number of grants that will be made annually.

  c Describe how you determine the amount of each of your grants.

  d Describe any requirement or condition that you impose on recipients to obtain, maintain, or qualify for renewal of a grant. (For example, specific requirements or conditions could consist of attendance at a four-year college, maintaining a certain grade point average, teaching in public school after graduation from college, etc.)

5 Describe your procedures for supervising the scholarships, fellowships, educational loans, or other educational grants. Describe whether you obtain reports and grade transcripts from recipients, or you pay grants directly to a school under an arrangement whereby the school will apply the grant funds only for enrolled students who are in good standing. Also, describe your procedures for taking action if the terms of the award are violated.

6 Who is on the selection committee for the awards made under your program, including names of current committee members, criteria for committee membership, and the method of replacing committee members?

7 Are relatives of members of the selection committee, or of your officers, directors, or **substantial contributors** eligible for awards made under your program? If "Yes," what measures are taken to ensure unbiased selections?   ☐ Yes   ☐ No

  Note. If you are a private foundation, you are not permitted to provide educational grants to **disqualified persons.** Disqualified persons include your substantial contributors and foundation managers and certain family members of disqualified persons.

Section II	**Private foundations complete lines 1a through 4f of this section. Public charities do not complete this section.**

1a If we determine that you are a private foundation, do you want this application to be considered as a request for advance approval of grant making procedures?   ☐ Yes   ☐ No   ☐ N/A

  b For which section(s) do you wish to be considered?

    ● 4945(g)(1)—Scholarship or fellowship grant to an individual for study at an educational institution   ☐

    ● 4945(g)(3)—Other grants, including loans, to an individual for travel, study, or other similar purposes, to enhance a particular skill of the grantee or to produce a specific product   ☐

2 Do you represent that you will (1) arrange to receive and review grantee reports annually and upon completion of the purpose for which the grant was awarded, (2) investigate diversions of funds from their intended purposes, and (3) take all reasonable and appropriate steps to recover diverted funds, ensure other grant funds held by a grantee are used for their intended purposes, and withhold further payments to grantees until you obtain grantees' assurances that future diversions will not occur and that grantees will take extraordinary precautions to prevent future diversions from occurring?   ☐ Yes   ☐ No

3 Do you represent that you will maintain all records relating to individual grants, including information obtained to evaluate grantees, identify whether a grantee is a disqualified person, establish the amount and purpose of each grant, and establish that you undertook the supervision and investigation of grants described in line 2?   ☐ Yes   ☐ No

Appendix F The Schedules

Schedule H. Organizations Providing Scholarships, Fellowships, Educational Loans, or Other Educational Grants to Individuals and Private Foundations Requesting Advance Approval of Individual Grant Procedures *(Continued)*

Section II	Private foundations complete lines 1a through 4f of this section. Public charities do not complete this section. *(Continued)*

4a Do you or will you award scholarships, fellowships, and educational loans to attend an educational institution based on the status of an individual being an *employee of a particular employer?* If "Yes," complete lines 4b through 4f.   ☐ **Yes** ☐ **No**

b Will you comply with the seven conditions and either the percentage tests or facts and circumstances test for scholarships, fellowships, and educational loans to attend an educational institution as set forth in Revenue Procedures 76-47, 1976-2 C.B. 670, and 80-39, 1980-2 C.B. 772, which apply to inducement, selection committee, eligibility requirements, objective basis of selection, employment, course of study, and other objectives? (See lines 4c, 4d, and 4e, regarding the percentage tests.)   ☐ **Yes** ☐ **No**

c Do you or will you provide scholarships, fellowships, or educational loans to attend an educational institution to employees of a particular employer?   ☐ **Yes** ☐ **No** ☐ **N/A**

If "Yes," will you award grants to 10% or fewer of the eligible applicants who were actually considered by the selection committee in selecting recipients of grants in that year as provided by Revenue Procedures 76-47 and 80-39?   ☐ **Yes** ☐ **No**

d Do you provide scholarships, fellowships, or educational loans to attend an educational institution to children of employees of a particular employer?   ☐ **Yes** ☐ **No** ☐ **N/A**

If "Yes," will you award grants to 25% or fewer of the eligible applicants who were actually considered by the selection committee in selecting recipients of grants in that year as provided by Revenue Procedures 76-47 and 80-39? If "No," go to line 4e.   ☐ **Yes** ☐ **No**

e If you provide scholarships, fellowships, or educational loans to attend an educational institution to children of employees of a particular employer, will you award grants to 10% or fewer of the number of employees' children who can be shown to be eligible for grants (whether or not they submitted an application) in that year, as provided by Revenue Procedures 76-47 and 80-39?   ☐ **Yes** ☐ **No** ☐ **N/A**

If "Yes," describe how you will determine who can be shown to be eligible for grants without submitting an application, such as by obtaining written statements or other information about the expectations of employees' children to attend an educational institution. If "No," go to line 4f.

Note. Statistical or sampling techniques are not acceptable. See Revenue Procedure 85-51, 1985-2 C.B. 717, for additional information.

f If you provide scholarships, fellowships, or educational loans to attend an educational institution to *children of employees of a particular employer* without regard to either the 25% limitation described in line 4d, or the 10% limitation described in line 4e, will you award grants based on facts and circumstances that demonstrate that the grants will not be considered compensation for past, present, or future services or otherwise provide a significant benefit to the particular employer? If "Yes," describe the facts and circumstances that you believe will demonstrate that the grants are neither compensatory nor a significant benefit to the particular employer. In your explanation, describe why you cannot satisfy either the 25% test described in line 4d or the 10% test described in line 4e.   ☐ **Yes** ☐ **No**

Appendix G Form 5768, Election/Revocation of Election

Form **5768** (Rev. December 2004) Department of the Treasury Internal Revenue Service	Election/Revocation of Election by an Eligible Section 501(c)(3) Organization To Make Expenditures To Influence Legislation (Under Section 501(h) of the Internal Revenue Code)	For IRS Use Only ▶

Name of organization **Hometown Campaign to Clean Up America**	Employer identification number **44 : 4444444**

Number and street (or P.O. box no., if mail is not delivered to street address) **1111 Any Street**	Room/suite

City, town or post office, and state **Hometown, XX 77777-7777**	ZIP + 4

1 Election—As an eligible organization, we hereby elect to have the provisions of section 501(h) of the Code, relating to expenditures to influence legislation, apply to our tax year ending................. **06/30/06** .... and all subsequent tax years until revoked.
(Month, day, and year)

Note: *This election must be signed and postmarked within the first taxable year to which it applies.*

2 Revocation—As an eligible organization, we hereby revoke our election to have the provisions of section 501(h) of the Code, relating to expenditures to influence legislation, apply to our tax year ending.................
(Month, day, and year)

Note: *This revocation must be signed and postmarked before the first day of the tax year to which it applies.*

Under penalties of perjury, I declare that I am authorized to make this (check applicable box) ▶ ☑ election ☐ revocation on behalf of the above named organization.

John J. Environmentalist, President

(Signature of officer or trustee)	(Type or print name and title)	(Date)

General Instructions

Section references are to the Internal Revenue Code.

Section 501(c)(3) states that an organization exempt under that section will lose its tax-exempt status and its qualification to receive deductible charitable contributions if a substantial part of its activities are carried on to influence legislation. Section 501(h), however, permits certain eligible 501(c)(3) organizations to elect to make limited expenditures to influence legislation. An organization making the election will, however, be subject to an excise tax under section 4911 if it spends more than the amounts permitted by that section. Also, the organization may lose its exempt status if its lobbying expenditures exceed the permitted amounts by more than 50% over a 4-year period. For any tax year in which an election under section 501(h) is in effect, an electing organization must report the actual and permitted amounts of its lobbying expenditures and grass roots expenditures (as defined in section 4911(c)) on its annual return required under section 6033. See Schedule A (Form 990 or Form 990-EZ). Each electing member of an affiliated group must report these amounts for both itself and the affiliated group as a whole.

To make or revoke the election, enter the ending date of the tax year to which the election or revocation applies in item 1 or **2**, as applicable, and sign and date the form in the spaces provided.

Eligible Organizations.—A section 501(c)(3) organization is permitted to make the election if it is not a disqualified organization (see below) and is described in:

1. Section 170(b)(1)(A)(ii) (relating to educational institutions),
2. Section 170(b)(1)(A)(iii) (relating to hospitals and medical research organizations),
3. Section 170(b)(1)(A)(iv) (relating to organizations supporting government schools),
4. Section 170(b)(1)(A)(vi) (relating to organizations publicly supported by charitable contributions),
5. Section 509(a)(2) (relating to organizations publicly supported by admissions, sales, etc.), or
6. Section 509(a)(3) (relating to organizations supporting certain types of public charities other than those section 509(a)(3) organizations that support section 501(c)(4), (5), or (6) organizations).

Disqualified Organizations.—The following types of organizations are not permitted to make the election:

a. Section 170(b)(1)(A)(i) organizations (relating to churches),

b. An integrated auxiliary of a church or of a convention or association of churches, or

c. A member of an affiliated group of organizations if one or more members of such group is described in **a** or **b** of this paragraph.

Affiliated Organizations.—Organizations are members of an affiliated group of organizations only if **(1)** the governing instrument of one such organization requires it to be bound by the decisions of the other organization on legislative issues, or **(2)** the governing board of one such organization includes persons (i) who are specifically designated representatives of another such organization or are members of the governing board, officers, or paid executive staff members of such other organization, and (ii) who, by aggregating their votes, have sufficient voting power to cause or prevent action on legislative issues by the first such organization.

For more details, see section 4911 and section 501(h).

Note: *A private foundation (including a private operating foundation) is not an eligible organization.*

Where To File.—Mail Form 5768 to the Internal Revenue Service Center, Ogden, UT 84201-0027.

Cat. No. 12125M

Form **5768** (Rev. 12-2004)

Appendix H Notice 3367, Acknowledgment of Your Request

Internal Revenue Service
Director, EO Rulings & Agreements
P.O. Box 2508
Cincinnati, OH 45201

Date: November 4, 2004

JODY BLAZEK

Depa. ...nent to the Treasury

Employer Identification Number:
55 — 5555555
Document Locator Number:
55555 — 555 — 55555 - 5
Toll Free Number: 877-829-5500
FAX Number: 513-263-3756
Application Form: 1023
User Fee Paid: $500.00

RE: APPLICANT NAME

Acknowledgement of Your Request

We received your application for exemption from federal income tax. When communicating with us, please refer to the employer identification number and document locator number shown above.

What Happens Next?

Your application was entered into our computer system at our processing center in Covington, Kentucky, and has been sent to our Cincinnati office for initial review. We approve some applications based on this review. If this is the case, you will receive a letter stating that you are exempt from federal income tax.

If the initial review indicates that additional information or changes are necessary, your application will be assigned to an Exempt Organization Specialist who will call or write you. We assign applications in the order we receive them.

If the additional information indicates that you qualify for exemption, you will receive a letter stating that you are exempt from federal income tax. If you do not qualify for exemption, we will send you a letter telling you why we believe you do not qualify and will include a complete explanation of your appeal rights.

The IRS does not issue "tax exempt numbers" or "tax exempt certificates" for state or local sales or income taxes. If you need exemption from these taxes, contact your state or local tax offices.

How long will this process take?

Normally, you may expect to hear from us within 120 days. If you do not, call our toll free number between the hours of 8 a.m. and 6:30 p.m. Eastern Time. Please have your identification numbers available so that we can identify your application. If you would rather write than call, please include a copy of this notice with your correspondence.

Notice 3367 (cg)(poa) - (Rev. 12/20

Appendix I Determination Letters Recognizing Exemption

INTERNAL REVENUE SERVICE
P. O. BOX 2508
CINCINNATI, OH 45201

DEPARTMENT OF THE TREASURY

Date: **JAN 1 8 2005**

C/O JODY BLAZEK
2900 WESLAYAN STE 200
HOUSTON, TX 77027-0000

Employer Identification Number:

DLN:
 17053335121004
Contact Person:
 RONALD D BELL   ID# 31185
Contact Telephone Number:
 (877) 829-5500
Accounting Period Ending:
 DECEMBER 31
Public Charity Status:
 170(b)(1)(A)(vi)
Form 990 Required:
 YES
Effective Date of Exemption:
 OCTOBER 12, 2004
Contribution Deductibility:
 YES
Advance Ruling Ending Date:
 DECEMBER 31, 2008

Dear Applicant:

We are pleased to inform you that upon review of your application for tax
exempt status we have determined that you are exempt from Federal income tax
under section 501(c)(3) of the Internal Revenue Code. Contributions to you are
deductible under section 170 of the Code. You are also qualified to receive
tax deductible bequests, devises, transfers or gifts under section 2055, 2106
or 2522 of the Code. Because this letter could help resolve any questions
regarding your exempt status, you should keep it in your permanent records.

Organizations exempt under section 501(c)(3) of the Code are further classified
as either public charities or private foundations. During your advance ruling
period, you will be treated as a public charity. Your advance ruling period
begins with the effective date of your exemption and ends with advance ruling
ending date shown in the heading of the letter.

Shortly before the end of your advance ruling period, we will send you Form
8734, Support Schedule for Advance Ruling Period. You will have 90 days after
the end of your advance ruling period to return the completed form. We will
then notify you, in writing, about your public charity status.

Please see enclosed Information for Exempt Organizations Under Section
501(c)(3) for some helpful information about your responsibilities as an exempt
organization.

Letter 1045 (DO/CG)

219

Appendix I Determination Letters Recognizing Exemption

-2-

We have sent a copy of this letter to your representative as indicated in your power of attorney.

Sincerely,

Lois G. Lerner
Director, Exempt Organizations
Rulings and Agreements

Enclosures: Information for Organizations Exempt Under Section 501(c)(3)
Form 872-C

Letter 1045 (DO/CG)

Appendix I Determination Letters Recognizing Exemption

INFORMATION FOR ORGANIZATIONS EXEMPT UNDER SECTION 501(c)(3)

WHERE TO GET FORMS AND HELP

Forms and instructions may be obtained by calling toll free 1-800-829-3676, through the Internet Web Site at www.irs.gov, and also at local tax assistance centers.

Additional information about any topic discussed below may be obtained through our customer service function by calling toll free 1-877-829-5500 between 8:00 a.m. - 6:30 p.m. Eastern time.

NOTIFY US ON THESE MATTERS

If you change your name, address, purposes, operations or sources of financial support, please inform our TE/GE Customer Account Services Office at the following address: Internal Revenue Service, P.O. Box 2508, Cincinnati, Ohio 45201. If you amend your organizational document or by-laws, or dissolve your organization, provide the Customer Account Services Office with a copy of the amended documents. Please use your employer identification number on all returns you file and in all correspondence with the Internal Revenue Service.

FILING REQUIREMENTS

In your exemption letter we indicated whether you must file Form 990, Return of Organization Exempt From Income Tax. Form 990 (or Form 990-EZ) is filed with the Ogden Submission Processing Center, Ogden UT 84201-0027.

You are required to file a Form 990 only if your gross receipts are normally more than $25,000.

If your gross receipts are normally between $25,000 and $100,000, and your total assets are less than $250,000, you may file Form 990-EZ. If your gross receipts are over $100,000, or your total assets are over $250,000, you must file the complete Form 990. The Form 990 instructions show how to compute your "normal" receipts.

Form 990 Schedule A is required for both Form 990 and Form 990-EZ.

If a return is required, it must be filed by the 15th day of the fifth month after the end of your annual accounting period. There are penalties for failing to timely file a complete return. For additional information on penalties, see Form 990 instructions or call our toll free number.

If your receipts are below $25,000, and we send you a Form 990 Package, follow the instructions in the package on how to complete the limited return to advise us that you are not required to file.

If your exemption letter states that you are not required to file Form 990, you

Letter 1045 (DO/CG)

Appendix I Determination Letters Recognizing Exemption

are exempt from these requirements.

UNRELATED BUSINESS INCOME TAX RETURN

If you receive more than $1,000 annually in gross receipts from a regular trade or business you may be subject to Unrelated Business Income Tax and required to file Form 990-T, Exempt Organization Business Income Tax Return. There are several exceptions to this tax.

1. Income you receive from the performance of your exempt activity is not unrelated business income.

2. Income from fundraisers conducted by volunteer workers, or where donated merchandise is sold, is not unrelated business income.

3. Income from routine investments such as certificates of deposit, savings accounts, or stock dividends is usually not unrelated business income.

There are special rules for income derived from real estate or other investments purchased with borrowed funds. This income is called "debt financed" income. For additional information regarding unrelated business income tax see Publication 598, Tax on Unrelated Business Income of Exempt Organizations, or call our toll free number shown above.

PUBLIC INSPECTION OF APPLICATION AND INFORMATION RETURN

You are required to make your annual information return, Form 990 or Form 990-EZ, available for public inspection for three years after the later of the due date of the return, or the date the return is filed. You are also required to make available for public inspection your exemption application, any supporting documents, and your exemption letter. Copies of these documents are also required to be provided to any individual upon written or in person request without charge other than reasonable fees for copying and postage. You may fulfill this requirement by placing these documents on the Internet. Penalties may be imposed for failure to comply with these requirements. Additional information is available in Publication 557, Tax-Exempt Status for Your Organization, or you may call our toll free number shown above.

FUNDRAISING

Contributions to you are deductible only to the extent that they are gifts and no consideration is received in return. Depending on the circumstances, ticket purchases and similar payments in conjunction with fundraising events may not qualify as fully deductible contributions.

CONTRIBUTIONS OF $250 OR MORE

Donors must have written substantiation from the charity for any charitable contribution of $250 or more. Although it is the donor's responsibility to obtain written substantiation from the charity, you can assist donors by

Letter 1045 (DO/CG)

222

-5-

providing a written statement listing any cash contribution or describing any donated property.

This written statement must be provided at the time of the contribution. There is no prescribed format for the written statement. Letters, postcards and electronic (e-mail) or computer-generated forms are acceptable.

The donor is responsible for the valuation of donated property. However, your written statement must provide a sufficient description to support the donor's contribution. For additional information regarding donor substantiation, see Publication 1771, Charitable Contributions - Substantiation and Disclosure Requirements. For information about the valuation of donated property, see Publication 561, Determining the Value of Donated Property.

CONTRIBUTIONS OF MORE THAN $75 AND CHARITY PROVIDES GOODS OR SERVICES

You must provide a written disclosure statement to donors who receive goods or services from you in exchange for contributions in excess of $75.

Contribution deductions are allowable to donors only to the extent their contributions exceed the value of the goods or services received in exchange. Ticket purchases and similar payments in conjunction with fundraising events may not necessarily qualify as fully deductible contributions, depending on the circumstances. If your organization conducts fundraising events such as benefit dinners, shows, membership drives, etc., where something of value is received, you are required to provide a written statement informing donors of the fair market value of the specific items or services you provided in exchange for contributions of more than $75.

You should provide the written disclosure statement in advance of any event, determine the fair market value of any benefit received, determine the amount of the contribution that is deductible, and state this information in your fundraising materials such as solicitations, tickets, and receipts. The amount of the contribution that is deductible is limited to the excess of any money (and the value of any property other than money) contributed by the donor less the value of goods or services provided by the charity. Your disclosure statement should be made, no later than, at the time payment is received. Subject to certain exceptions, your disclosure responsibility applies to any fundraising circumstances where each complete payment, including the contribution portion, exceeds $75. For additional information, see Publication 1771 and Publication 526, Charitable Contributions.

EXCESS BENEFIT TRANSACTIONS

Excess benefit transactions are governed by section 4958 of the Code. Excess benefit transactions involve situations where a section 501(c)(3) organization provides an unreasonable benefit to a person who is in a position to exercise substantial influence over the organization's affairs. If you believe there may be an excess benefit transaction involving your organization, you should report the transaction on Form 990 or 990-EZ. Additional information can be

Letter 1045 (DO/CG)

-6-

found in the instructions for Form 990 and Form 990-EZ, or you may call our toll free number to obtain additional information on how to correct and report this transaction.

EMPLOYMENT TAXES

If you have employees, you are subject to income tax withholding and the social security taxes imposed under the Federal Insurance Contribution Act (FICA). You are required to withhold Federal income tax from your employee's wages and you are required to pay FICA on each employee who is paid more than $100 in wages during a calendar year. To know how much income tax to withhold, you should have a Form W-4, Employee's Withholding Allowance Certificate, on file for each employee. Organizations described in section 501(c)(3) of the Code are not required to pay Federal Unemployment Tax (FUTA).

Employment taxes are reported on Form 941, Employer's Quarterly Federal Tax Return. The requirements for withholding, depositing, reporting and paying employment taxes are explained in Circular E, Employer's Tax Guide, (Publication 15), and Employer's Supplemental Tax Guide, (Publication 15-A). These publications explain your tax responsibilities as an employer.

CHURCHES

Churches may employ both ministers and church workers. Employees of churches or church-controlled organizations are subject to income tax withholding, but may be exempt from FICA taxes. Churches are not required to pay FUTA tax. In addition, although ministers are generally common law employees, they are not treated as employees for employment tax purposes. These special employment tax rules for members of the clergy and religious workers are explained in Publication 517, Social Security and Other Information for Members of the Clergy and Religious Workers. Churches should also consult Publications 15 and 15-A. Publication 1828, Tax Guide for Churches and Religious Organizations, also discusses the various benefits and responsibilities of these organizations under Federal tax law.

PUBLIC CHARITY STATUS

Every organization that qualifies for tax-exemption as an organization described in section 501(c)(3) is a private foundation unless it falls into one of the categories specifically excluded from the definition of that term [referred to in section 509(a)(1), (2), (3), or (4)]. In effect, the definition divides these organizations into two classes, namely private foundations and public charities.

Public charities are generally those that either have broad public support or actively function in a supporting relationship to those organizations.

Public charities enjoy several advantages over private foundations. There are certain excise taxes that apply to private foundations but not to public charities. A private foundation must also annually file Form 990-PF, Return of Private Foundation, even if it had no revenue or expenses.

Letter 1045 (DO/CG)

Appendix I Determination Letters Recognizing Exemption

The Code section under which you are classified as a public charity is shown in the heading of your exemption letter. This determination is based on the information you provided and the request you made on your Form 1023 application. Please refer to Publication 557 for additional information about public charity status.

GRANTS TO INDIVIDUALS

The following information is provided for organizations that make grants to individuals. If you begin an individual grant program that was not described in your exemption application, please inform us about the program.

Funds you distribute to an individual as a grant must be made on a true charitable basis in furtherance of the purposes for which you are organized. Therefore, you should keep adequate records and case histories that demonstrate that grants to individuals serve your charitable purposes. For example, you should be in a position to substantiate the basis for grants awarded to individuals to relieve poverty or under a scholarship or education loan program. Case histories regarding grants to individuals should show names, addresses, purposes of grants, manner of selection, and relationship (if any) to members, officers, trustees, or donors of funds to you.

For more information on the exclusion of scholarships from income by an individual recipient, see Publication 520, Scholarships and Fellowships.

Letter 1045 (DO/CG)

225

Appendix I Determination Letters Recognizing Exemption

```
INTERNAL REVENUE SERVICE                    DEPARTMENT OF THE TREASURY
P. O. BOX 2508
CINCINNATI, OH  45201

Date:  MAY 17 2004                          Employer Identification Number:

                                            DLN:

C/O JODY BLAZEK                             Contact Person:
3101 RICHMOND STE 220                        JOHN J KOESTER              ID# 31364
HOUSTON, TX  77098-0000                     Contact Telephone Number:
                                             (877) 829-5500
                                            Accounting Period Ending:
                                             December 31
                                            Addendum Applies:
                                             No
```

Dear Applicant:

Based on information supplied, and assuming your operations will be as
stated in your application for recognition of exemption, we have determined you
are exempt from Federal income tax under section 501(a) of the Internal
Revenue Code as an organization described in section 501(c)(3).

We have further determined that, as indicated in your application, you
are a private foundation within the meaning of section 509(a) of the Code. In
this letter we are not determining whether you are an operating foundation as
defined in section 4942(j)(3).

If your sources of support, or your purposes, character, or method of
operation change, please let us know so we can consider the effect of the
change on your exempt status and foundation status. In the case of an amendment to your organizational document or bylaws, please send us a copy of the
amended document or bylaws. Also, you should inform us of all changes in your
name or address.

As of January 1, 1984, you are liable for taxes under the Federal
Insurance Contributions Act (social security taxes) on remuneration of $100
or more you pay to each of your employees during a calendar year. You are
not liable for the tax imposed under the Federal Unemployment Tax Act (FUTA).
However, since you are a private foundation, you are subject to excise taxes
under chapter 42 of the Code. You also may be subject to other Federal excise
taxes. If you have any questions about excise, employment, or other Federal
taxes, please let us know.

Donors may deduct contributions to you as provided in section 170 of the
Code. Bequests, legacies, devises, transfers, or gifts to you or for your use
are deductible for Federal estate and gift tax purposes if they meet the
applicable provisions of sections 2055, 2106, and 2522 of the Code.

Contribution deductions are allowable to donors only to the extent that
their contributions are gifts, with no consideration received. Ticket purchases and similar payments in conjunction with fundraising events may not
necessarily qualify as deductible contributions, depending on the circum-

                                            Letter 1076 (DO/CG)

Appendix I Determination Letters Recognizing Exemption

stances. See Revenue Ruling 67-246, published in Cumulative Bulletin 1967-2, on page 104, which sets forth guidelines regarding the deductibility, as charitable contributions, of payments made by taxpayers for admission to or other participation in fundraising activities for charity.

You are required to file Form 990-PF, Return of Private Foundation or Section 4947(a)(1) Trust Treated as a Private Foundation. Form 990-PF must be filed by the 15th day of the fifth month after the end of your annual accounting period. A penalty of $20 a day is charged when a return is filed late, unless there is reasonable cause for the delay. However, the maximum penalty charged cannot exceed $10,000 or 5 percent of your gross receipts for the year, whichever is less. For organizations with gross receipts exceeding $1,000,000 in any year, the penalty is $100 per day per return, unless there is reasonable cause for the delay. The maximum penalty for an organization with gross receipts exceeding $1,000,000 shall not exceed $50,000. This penalty may also be charged if a return is not complete, so please be sure your return is complete before you file it.

You are not required to file Federal income tax returns unless you are subject to the tax on unrelated business income under section 511 of the Code. If you are subject to this tax, you must file an income tax return on Form 990-T, Exempt Organization Business Income Tax Return. In this letter we are not determining whether any of your present or proposed activities are unrelated trade or business as defined in section 513 of the Code.

You are required to make certain returns available for public inspection for three years after the later of the due date of the return or the date the return is filed. The returns required to be made available for public inspection are Form 990-PF, Return of Private Foundation or Section 4947(a)(1) Nonexempt Charitable Trust Treated as a Private Foundation, and Form 4720, Return of Certain Excise Taxes on Charities and Other Persons Under Chapters 41 and 42 of the Internal Revenue Code. You are also required to make available for public inspection your exemption application, any supporting documents, and your exemption letter. Copies of these documents must be provided to any individual upon written or in person request without charge other than reasonable fees for copying and postage. You may fulfill this requirement by placing these documents on the Internet. Penalties may be imposed for failure to comply with these requirements. Additional information is available in Publication 557, Tax-Exempt Status for Your Organization, or you may call our toll free number shown above.

You need an employer identification number even if you have no employees. If an employer identification number was not entered on your application, a number will be assigned to you and you will be advised of it. Please use that number on all returns you file and in all correspondence with the Internal Revenue Service.

This determination is based on evidence that your funds are dedicated to the purposes listed in section 501(c)(3) of the Code. To assure your continued exemption, you should maintain records to show that funds are expended only for those purposes. If you distribute funds to other

Letter 1076 (DO/CG)

-3-

organizations, your records should show whether they are exempt under section 501(c)(3). In cases where the recipient organization is not exempt under section 501(c)(3), there should be evidence that the funds will remain dedicated to the required purposes and that they will be used for those purposes by the recipient.

If we have indicated in the heading of this letter that an addendum applies, the addendum enclosed is an integral part of this letter.

Because this letter could help resolve any questions about your exempt status and foundation status, you should keep it in your permanent records.

We have sent a copy of this letter to your representative as indicated in your power of attorney.

If you have any questions, please contact the person whose name and telephone number are shown in the heading of this letter.

Sincerely yours,

Lois G. Lerner
Director, Exempt Organizations
Rulings and Agreements

Letter 1076 (DO/CG)

Appendix J Chart of State Filing Requirements

State Sales Tax Exemptions

State	Exemption Information
Alabama	Use Form ST:EX-A1 to apply for exemption. Only certain types of organizations are granted exemption.
Alaska	Not applicable.
Arizona	Only currently approved organizations have exemption when making purchases, all nonprofits are exempt from collecting tax on sales.
Arkansas	Only currently approved organizations have exemption when making purchases.
California	You must file Form 3500 FTB with the California Franchise Tax Board.
Colorado	Automatic with 501(c)(3) tax exemption. Use Form DR 0715.
Connecticut	Automatic with 501(c)(3) tax exemption. Use CERT 119.
Delaware	Automatic with 501(c)(3) tax exemption.
District of Columbia	Automatic with 501(c)(3) tax exemption. Use Form 164 immediately but will not be finalized until IRS determination received.
Florida	Use Form DR-5 and attach IRS letter. Good for 5 years.
Georgia	Only certain types of nonprofits qualify for exemption. Send IRS determination letter with application.
Hawaii	Automatic with 501(c)(3) tax exemption. Use Form G-6.
Idaho	Only certain types of nonprofits qualify for exemption. Send IRS determination letter with application.
Illinois	Automatic with 501(c)(3) tax exemption. Apply to Department of Revenue to receive E-number.
Indiana	Use Form NP-20A and attach IRS determination letter.
Iowa	Only provate nonprofit educational institutions and museums can apply for exemption. Attach IRS letter.
Kansas	Only certain types of nonprofits qualify for exemption. Send IRS determination letter with application.

Appendix J Chart of State Filing Requirements

State Sales Tax Exemptions

State	Exemption Information
Kentucky	Use Form 51A125 and attach IRS determination letter.
Louisiana	Use Form R-1048 to apply for exemption from collection of sales tax during fundraising events. There is no exemption when making purchases.
Maine	Only certain types of nonprofits qualify for exemption. Send IRS determination letter with application.
Maryland	Use "Combined Registration Form" and attach IRS letter.
Massachusetts	Register with the Department of Revenue after you receive 501(c)(3) tax exempt status.
Michigan	Fill out Exempt Certificate and attach copy of IRS letter. Purchases made for fundraising activities are not exempt.
Minnesota	Use Form ST-16 to apply for exemption when making purchases. Attach IRS letter.
Mississippi	Only nonprofit schools are eligible for exemption.
Missouri	Use Form 1746 and attach IRS letter. Approval is not automatic for federally recognized exempt organizations.
Montana	Not applicable
Nebraska	File Form 4 with state, exemption is only extended to certain nonprofit organizations.
Nevada	Use APP 02.01 and attach IRS letter. Organization must conform to Nevada nonprofit statutes, not just federal.
New Hampshire	Not applicable
New Jersey	Use Form ST-5 and attach IRS letter. Exemption is for (c)(3)s making purchases only.
New Mexico	Use Form ACD-31050 and attach IRS letter.
New York	Use Form CT-247 and attach IRS letter.

Appendix J Chart of State Filing Requirements

State Sales Tax Exemptions

State	Exemption Information
North Carolina	After incorporation, the Department of Revenue will request a copy of your Articles and Bylaws in order to determine tax status.
North Dakota	Only certain types of nonprofits qualify for exemption. Send IRS determination letter with application.
Ohio	Automatic with 501(c)(3) tax exemption. Fill in exempt certificate.
Oklahoma	Use Form 13-16-A and attach IRS letter. Only certain types of organizations qualify.
Oregon	Not applicable
Pennsylvania	To obtain sales tax exemption complete Form Rev-72. It is not mandated that the organization be federally exempt.
Rhode Island	Use "Application for Certification of Exemption" and attach IRS letter.
South Carolina	Use Form ST-387 and attach IRS letter.
Tennessee	Use "Application for Registration" and attach IRS letter.
Texas	Use Form AP205 and attach IRS letter.
Utah	Use Form TC160 to apply. Organizations are exempt from paying sales tax on purchases of $1,000 or more. Must use TC-61N to get refund for sales taxes paid on smaller purchases.
Vermont	Use Form S-1 to register the organization. Attach IRS letter.
Virginia	Use NP Form and attach IRS letter.
Washington	There is no exemption for purchases or sales except for purchases made for resale.
West Virginia	Automatic with 501(c)(3) tax exemption. Fill in exempt certificate.
Wisconsin	Use Form S-103 to apply for exemption when making purchases. Attach IRS letter.
Wyoming	Separate state notification required but you must notify state after you receive 501(c)(3) tax exempt status.

Appendix J Chart of State Filing Requirements

Information on Annual Financial Reporting

As noted throughout the URS, most states requiring registration also require annual financial reporting. Although the URS CAN NOT BE USED FOR THIS PURPOSE, basic information on annual financial reporting for the URS cooperating states is presented below:

Alabama:
Due Date: Within 3 months of Fiscal Year end.
Fee: $25
IRS 990: Yes
Financial Report: Yes. May be submitted instead of 990.
Audit: No

Arkansas:
Due Date: By May 15th. If Fiscal Year other than calendar year, may file within six months after Fiscal Year end, upon request.
Fee: None.
IRS 990: Yes, if required to file with the IRS.
Financial Report: Yes, if no Form 990 to file and receive more than $10,000.
Audit: Yes, for organizations with gross revenue more than $500,000.

California:
Due Date: Within 4½ months after the close of the organization's fiscal or calendar accounting period.
Fee: $25 for organizations with assets or revenue exceeding $100,000 during Fiscal Year. Such organizations must submit Form RRF-1 due Within 4½ months after the close of the organization's fiscal or calendar accounting period.
IRS 990: Yes. (Note: Due within 4½ months of the close of the organization's fiscal or calendar accounting period. Extensions granted by the IRS will be honored)
Financial Report: Yes.
Audit: No.

Connecticut:
Due Date: Last day of the fifth month following the close of the organization's Fiscal Year end. Extensions of not longer than three months may be granted upon written request.
Fee: $25 if postmarked on or before the due date or extended due date, $50 if postmarked after the due date or extended due date.
IRS 990: Yes.
Financial Report: Yes.
Audit: Yes, for organizations with more than $200,000 in gross revenue (before any deductions) in the year of the report, excluding grants and fees from government agencies and revenue from trusts held by a trustee (usually a bank) for the benefit of the organization. Compiled or reviewed financial statements do not fulfill the requirement.

District of Columbia:
Due Date: September 1
Fee: $80
IRS 990: Yes.
Financial Report: Yes.
Audit: No.

Georgia:
Due Date: Within one year of filing but if Fiscal Year has ended within 90 days prior to date of filing, report may be dated as of end of preceding FY.
Fee: $10
IRS 990: Yes.
Financial Report: Certified annual financial statement required if proceeds are $500,000 or more; independent CPA review required for proceeds of $100,000 to $500,000; file Form 990 if proceeds are less than $100,000.
Audit: Yes, if revenue over $1 million.

Illinois:
Due Date: Within 6 months of close of Fiscal year.
Fee: $15 ($100 late fee if registration expires)
IRS 990: Yes.
Financial Report: Yes. (state form)
Audit: Yes, if gross revenue over $150,000 or professional fund raiser used and contributions exceed $25,000.

Kansas:
Due Date: Within 6 months of Fiscal Year end.
Fee: $20
IRS 990: Yes.
Financial Report: Yes. May be submitted instead of IRS Form 990.
Audit: Yes, if contributions in excess of $100,000.

Kentucky:
Due Date: Within 4 1/2 months of Fiscal Year end.
Fee: None.
IRS 990: Yes, unless Form 990 has not yet been filed with the IRS.
Financial Report: No.
Audit: No.

Louisiana:
Due Date: Anniversary of annual registration.
Fee: $25
IRS 990: Yes.
Financial Report: No
Audit: No.

Maine:
Due Date: November 30.
Fee: $100 plus $50 if raised more than $30,000
IRS 990: Yes.
Financial Report: Yes. May be submitted instead of 990.

Audit: Yes, if gross receipts are more than $30,000.

Maryland:
Due Date: Within 6 months of Fiscal Year end.
Fee: No fee if gross income from charitable contributions is less than $25,000; $50 if $25,000-$50,000; $75 if $50,001-$75,000; $100 if $75,001-$100,000; $200 if $100,001 or more.
IRS 990: Yes.
Financial Report: Yes, must be reviewed by an independent CPA if revenue is between $100,000 and $200,000.
Audit: Yes, if gross income equals or exceeds $200,000.

Massachusetts:
Due Date: Within 4 1/2 months of Fiscal Year end.
Fee: $35 if revenue under $100,000; $70 if $100,001-$250,000; $125 if $250,001-$500,000; $250 if over $500,000.
IRS 990: Yes.
Financial Report: Yes (Mass. Form PC),
Audit: Yes, if revenue exceeds $250,000. If revenue over $100,000 and not more than $250,000, CPA review required.

Michigan:
Due Date: 30 days prior to license expiration.
Fee: None.
IRS 990: Yes.
Financial Report: Yes.
Audit: Yes, if public support $250,000 or more. If between $100,000 and $250,000, reviewed financial statements required.

Minnesota:
FILERS MAY USE the URS in lieu of the state's own annual report FORM if the filer fulfills the audit requirement, below (See the Minnesota entry beginning on Page 4 of this Appendix for further information).
Due Date: If Fiscal Year ends December 31st, due on or before July 15th. Otherwise, due on or before the 15th day of the seventh month following the close of its fiscal year. Attorney General may extend the time for filing the annual report for a period not to exceed four months. File extension request in writing prior to due date.
Fee: $25 ($50 late fee)
IRS 990: Yes. Accepted in lieu of separate financial statement if it fulfills the requirements of Minnesota Statutes section 309.53 (2000).
Audit: Yes, if revenue exceeds $350,000. (Audit must be prepared in accordance with generally accepted accounting principles. Cash basis audit not acceptable)

Appendix J Chart of State Filing Requirements

Mississippi:
FILERS MUST USE THE URS AND CAN,
WITH A SINGLE FILING, BOTH RENEW
REGISTRATION AND EFFECT ANNUAL
FINANCIAL REPORTING
Due Date: Anniversary of registration
Fee: $50.
IRS 990: Yes.
Financial Report: Yes.
Audit: Yes, if gross revenues over $100,000
(or over $25,000 if a professional fundraiser is
used). Secretary has statutory authority to
request audits on a case-by-case basis for
registrants between $25,000-$100,000.

Missouri:
Due Date: Within 2 1/2 months of Fiscal Year
end.
Fee: $15
IRS 990: Yes.
Financial Report: Yes.
Audit: No.

New Hampshire:
Due Date: Within 4 1/2 months of Fiscal Year
end.
Fee: $50
IRS 990: Yes.
Financial Report: Yes.
Audit: No.

New Jersey:
Due Date: Within 6 months of Fiscal Year
end.
Fee: No fee if short form filer and less than
$10,000; $30 if short form filer and more than
$10,000. $60 if long form filer and less than
$100,000; $150 if long form filer and
$100,000- $500,000; $250 if long form filer
and more than $500,000. ($25 late fee if
submitted more than 30 days after due date)
IRS 990: Yes.
Financial Report: Yes and certified by
authorized officer of organization if revenue
under $100,000.
Audit: Yes, if revenue $100,000 and over.

New Mexico:
Due Date: Within 6 months of Fiscal Year
end.
Fee: None.
IRS 990: Yes.
Financial Report: Yes.
Audit: Yes, if total revenue is in excess of
$500,000.

New York:
Due Date: Within 4 1/2 months of Fiscal Year
end.
Fee: $10 if revenue between $75,000 and
$150,000; $25 if $150,000 or more.
IRS 990: Yes.
Financial Report: Yes. Must be reviewed by
CPA if revenue $75,000-$150,000.
Audit: Yes, if revenue $150,000 and over.

North Carolina:

Due Date: Within 4 1/2 months
after Fiscal Year.
Fee: $50 if revenue is under
$100,000. $100 if revenue
$100,001-$200,000. $200 if revenue
$200,001 or more.
IRS 990: Yes.
Financial Report: Yes. May be
submitted instead of 990.
Audit: No.

North Dakota:
Due Date: September 1.
Fee: $10.
IRS 990: No.
Financial Report: Yes.
Audit: No.

Ohio:
Due Date: Within 4 1/2 months of
Fiscal Year end.
Fee: $50 if revenue $5,000-
$24,999.99; $100 if $25,000-
$49,999.99; $200 if $50,000 or
more.
IRS 990: Yes or financial report.
Financial Report: Yes (on Attorney
General Form).
Audit: No.

Oklahoma:
Due Date: Anniversary.
Fee: $15.
IRS 990: Yes.
Financial Report: Yes (on a
designated state form).
Audit: No.

Oregon:
Due Date: Within 4 1/2 months of
Fiscal Year end.
Fee: $10 if $0-$25,000; $25 if
$25,000-$50,000; $45 if $50,000-
$100,000; $75 if $100,000-
$250,000; $100 if $250,000-
$500,000; $135 if $500,000-
$750,000; $170 if $750,000-$1
million; $200 if 1 million and over.
If $50,000-$10 million, subject to
percentage rate fee (1.18% of fund
balance rounded to whole dollar. If
less than .50 than drop but if .50 and
higher, round to next dollar.) ($20
late fee)
IRS 990: Yes.
Financial Report: Yes.
Audit: No.

Pennsylvania:
Due Date: Within 4.5 months of
Fiscal Year end.
Fee: $15 if $25,000 or less; $100 if
$25,001-$100,000; $150 if
$100,001-$500,000; $250 if
$500,001 and over.
IRS 990: Yes.
Financial Report: Yes. Must be
reviewed by CPA if contributions
$25,000-$100,000.

Audit: Yes, if gross contributions are
$100,000 or more.

Rhode Island:
Due Date: Anniversary of registration.
Fee: $75
IRS 990: Yes.
Financial Report: Yes
Audit: Yes, except no audit required when
proceeds are less than $500,000.

South Carolina:
Due Date: Within 4 1/2 months of Fiscal
Year.
Fee: $50.
IRS 990: Yes.
Financial Report: Yes. May be submitted
instead of 990.
Audit: No.

Tennessee:
Due Date: Within 6 months of Fiscal Year
end.
Fee: $100 if annual gross receipts $0-
$48,999.99; $150 if $49,000-99,999.99; $200
if $100,000-$249,999.99; $250 if $250,000-
$499,999.99; $300 if $500,000 or more.
IRS 990: Yes, if revenue between $25,000 and
$100,000. Organizations with more than
$100,000 in revenue must submit audited
financial statements.
Financial Report: Yes, audited statements
required when revenue is more than $100,000.
Audit: Yes if gross revenue exceeds $250,000.

Utah:
Utah requires initial registration and annual
renewal of registration only.

Virginia:
Due Date: Within 4 1/2 months of Fiscal Year
end.
Fee: $30 if revenue less than $25,000; $50 if
revenue is $25,000-$50,000; $100 if $50,000-
$100,000; $200 if $100,000-$500,000; $250 if
$500,000-$1 million; $325 if 1 million or
more. ($100 late filing fee)
IRS 990: Yes (or audit) if revenue of $25,000
or more. Certified treasurer's report for
proceeds less than $25,000.
Financial Report: Yes.
Audit: Yes (or 990) if revenue $25,000 or
more.

Washington:
Due Date: Within the 15th day of the 5th
month of Fiscal Year end.
Fee: $10.
IRS 990: Yes.
Financial Report: Yes.
Audit: No.

West Virginia:
Due date: Anniversary of registration.
Fees: $15 if gross revenue is less than $1
million; $50 if gross contributions $1 million
or more.
IRS 990: Yes.
Audit: Yes if contributions exceed $50,000.

233

Appendix J Chart of State Filing Requirements

Wisconsin:

Due date: Registration renewed July 31st. Annual financial report within 6 months of Fiscal Year end.

Fee: $15

IRS 990: Yes, plus Wisconsin supplement, Form 1952, or may file Wisconsin form #308 instead of IRS Form 990.

Financial Report: Yes. If contributions from Wisconsin amount to more than $5,000 organizations must file either Wisconsin form #308 or IRS Form 990.

Audit: Yes, if charitable organizations receive contributions in excess of $100,000, except this level is raised to $175,000 if all revenue received is from one contributor.

Appendix J Chart of State Filing Requirements

Checklist for Initial Registrations©
(URS v. 2.31)

State	Fee	State Forms	IRS Det. Lttr	Fndrsr Cntr	Bylaws	Cert/Arts Inc	Form 990	Audit	Notarized
Alabama	✓								✓
Arkansas	✓	✓	✓	✓		✓		✓	✓
California	✓		✓		✓	✓	✓		
Connecticut	✓								
D.C.	✓		✓	✓	✓	✓	✓		✓
Georgia	✓	✓	✓				✓	✓	✓
Illinois	✓		✓	✓	✓	✓	✓	✓	
Kansas	✓		✓				✓	✓	
Kentucky	✓					✓	✓		✓
Louisiana	✓			✓			✓		
Maine	✓		✓	✓	✓	✓	✓	✓	
Maryland	✓		✓	✓	✓	✓	✓	✓	
Massachusetts	✓		✓	✓	✓	✓	✓		
Michigan	✓		✓	✓	✓	✓	✓	✓	
Minnesota	✓		✓	✓		✓	✓		
Mississippi	✓	✓	✓	✓		✓	✓	✓	✓
Missouri	✓	See Appendix	✓	✓		✓	✓		✓
New Hampshire	✓		✓		✓	✓	✓		✓
New Jersey	✓		✓	✓	✓	✓	✓	✓	✓
New Mexico	✓		✓	✓		✓	✓	✓	
New York	✓		✓		✓	✓	✓		✓
North Carolina	✓	See Appendix		✓	✓	✓	✓	✓	✓
North Dakota	✓	✓		✓	✓	✓	✓		✓
Ohio	✓		✓		✓	✓	✓		✓
Oklahoma	✓			✓			✓		✓
Oregon	✓		✓		✓	✓		✓	
Pennsylvania	✓		✓	✓	✓	✓	✓	✓	
Rhode Island	✓		✓	✓			✓		
South Carolina	✓		✓	✓			✓		
Tennessee	✓	✓	✓	✓	✓	✓	✓	✓	✓
Utah	✓	See Appendix	✓	✓	✓	✓	✓	✓	✓
Virginia	✓		✓	✓	✓		✓		✓
Washington	✓	See Appendix	✓	✓			✓		
Wisconsin	✓		✓		✓	✓	✓	✓	✓

Appendix K Form 8734, Support Schedule for Advanced Ruling Period

Form **8734** (Rev. January 2004) Department of the Treasury Internal Revenue Service	**Support Schedule for Advance Ruling Period** Please refer to the separate instructions for assistance in completing this schedule. For additional help, call IRS Exempt Organizations Customer Services toll free at 1-877-829-5500.	OMB No. 1545-1836

For tax years beginning **11/15/2004** , and ending **12/31** , 20 **08**

Print or type. See Specific Instructions.	Name of organization **Sample Organization**		Employer identification number 55 : 5555555
	Number and street (or P.O. box number if mail is not delivered to street address) **1111 Main Street**	Room/Suite	Telephone number (**555**) **555-5555**
	City or town, state, and ZIP + 4 **Any Town, XX 77777**		E-mail address **info@sample.org** Fax number (**555**) **555-5556**

Note:
- Get **Schedule A (Form 990 or 990-EZ)**, *Organization Exempt Under Section 501(c)(3)*, and its separate *Instructions* before you complete this form.
- If you did not receive any support for a given year, show financial data for the year by indicating -0- or none.
- Year 1 should reflect support received as of the date legally organized, unless otherwise specified in the determination letter.
- Organizations that filed Form 990 or 990-EZ will be able to use information reported on Schedule A, Part IV-A, to complete this form.

Calendar year (or fiscal year beginning in) ▶	(a) Year 5 2008	(b) Year 4 2007	(c) Year 3 2006	(d) Year 2 2005	(e) Year 1 (See **Note** above.)	(f) Total of Years 1 through 5
1 Gifts, grants, and contributions received. (Do not include unusual grants. See line 14.)	270,000	100,000	330,000	74,000	0	774,000
2 Membership fees received	0	0	0	0	0	0
3 Gross receipts from admissions, merchandise sold or services performed, or furnishing of facilities in any activity that is related to the organization's charitable, etc., purpose	83,500	73,500	21,000	45,500	0	223,500
4 Gross income from interest, dividends, amounts received from payments on securities loans (section 512(a)(5)), rents, royalties, and unrelated business taxable income (less section 511 taxes) from businesses acquired by the organization after June 30, 1975	1,700	1,275	1,250	925	0	5,150
5 Net income from unrelated business activities not included in line 4	0	0	0	0	0	0
6 Tax revenues levied for your benefit and either paid to you or expended on your behalf	0	0	0	0	0	0
7 The value of services or facilities furnished to you by a governmental unit without charge. Do not include the value of services or facilities generally furnished to the public without charge	0	0	0	0	0	0
8 Other income. Attach a schedule. Do not include gain (or loss) from sale of capital assets	0	0	0	0	0	0
9 Total of lines 1 through 8	355,200	174,775	352,250	120,425	0	1,002,650
10 Line 9 minus line 3	271,700	101,275	331,250	74,925	0	779,150
11 Enter 1% of line 9	2,717	1,013	3,313	749	0	

For Paperwork Reduction Act Notice, see page 6 of separate instructions.   Cat. No. 10010S   Form **8734** (Rev. 1-2004)

See Appendix D for corresponding public support information.

Appendix K Form 8734, Support Schedule for Advanced Ruling Period

12 If you are an organization that normally receives a substantial part of your support from a governmental unit or from the general public, complete lines **12a** through **12f.** (Sections 509(a)(1) and 170(b)(1)(A)(vi)). **If you want the IRS to compute your public support test as a section 509(a)(1) and 170(b)(1)(A)(vi) organization, complete only lines 12a and 12b.**

a	Enter 2% of amount in column (f), line 10 . . . . ▶	**12a**	15,583	
b	Attach a list showing the name of and amount contributed by each person (other than a governmental unit or publicly supported organization) whose total gifts for Year 5 through Year 1 exceeded the amount shown in line 12a. Enter the total of all these excess amounts . . . . ▶	**12b**	272,168	
c	Total support for section 509(a)(1) test: Enter line 10, column (f) . . . . ▶	**12c**	779,150	
d	Add: Amounts from column (f) for lines: 4 5,150 5 0 8 0 12b 272,168 . . . . . . ▶	**12d**	277,318	
e	Public support (line 12c minus line 12d total) . . . . ▶	**12e**	501,832	
f	**Public support percentage (line 12e (numerator) divided by line 12c (denominator))** . . . ▶	**12f**	64.41 %	

13 If you are an organization that normally receives: **(1)** more than 33⅓% of your support from contributions, membership fees, and gross receipts from activities related to your exempt functions, and **(2) no more than** 33⅓% of your support from gross investment income and net unrelated business taxable income from businesses acquired by the organization after June 30, 1975, complete lines **13a** through **13h.** (Section 509(a)(2)). **If you want the IRS to compute your public support test as a section 509(a)(2) organization, complete only lines 13a and 13b.**

a For amounts included in lines 1, 2, and 3 that were received from a "disqualified person," attach a list showing the name of, and total amounts received in each year from, each "disqualified person." Enter the sum of such amounts for each year:

(Year 5) . . . . (Year 4) . . . . (Year 3) . . . . (Year 2) . . . . (Year 1) . . . .

b For any amount included in line 3 that was received from each person (other than "disqualified persons"), attach a list showing the name of, and amount received for each year, that was more than the **larger** of **(1)** the amount on line 11 for the year or **(2)** $5,000. (Include in the list organizations as well as individuals.) After computing the difference between the amount received and the larger amount described in **(1)** or **(2)**, enter the sum of these differences (the excess amounts) for each year:

(Year 5) . . . . (Year 4) . . . . (Year 3) . . . . (Year 2) . . . . (Year 1) . . . .

c	Add: Amounts from column (f) for lines: 1 2 3 6 7 . . . ▶	**13c**		
d	Add: Line 13a total and line 13b total . . . . . . ▶	**13d**		
e	Public support (line 13c total minus line 13d total) . . . . ▶	**13e**		
f	Total support for section 509(a)(2) test: Enter amount from line 9, column (f). ▶ **13f**			
g	**Public support percentage (line 13e (numerator) divided by line 13f (denominator))** . . . . ▶	**13g**	%	
h	**Investment income percentage (line 4, column (f) (numerator) divided by line 13f (denominator))** ▶	**13h**	%	

14 **Unusual Grants:** For an organization described in line 12 or 13 that received any unusual grants during Year 5 through Year 1, attach a list showing for each year the name of the contributor, the date and amount of the grant, and a brief description of the nature of the grant. **Do not include these grants in line 1.**

List the amount of unusual grants excluded for each year below.

(Year 5) . . . . 0 (Year 4) . . . . 0 (Year 3) . . . . 0 (Year 2) . . . . 0 (Year 1) 0

15 Please list the name and telephone number of an officer, director, or trustee who can be contacted during business hours if we need more information. If someone other than an officer, director, or trustee will represent the organization, attach a properly completed **Form 2848,** Power of Attorney.

Name: **A.B. Sample, President**
Type or print name and title.

Phone: (**555**) 555-5555   Fax Number (if available): (**555**) 555-5556

Please Sign Here	I declare under the penalties of perjury that I am authorized to sign this form on behalf of the above organization and that I have examined this form, including the accompanying attachments, and to the best of my knowledge it is true, correct, and complete.
	▶ Signature of officer, director, or trustee Date
	A.B. Sample, President
	Type or print name and title or authority of signer

✸   Form **8734** (Rev. 1-2004)

Appendix K Form 8734, Support Schedule for Advanced Ruling Period

Sample Organization
Form 8734

Question 12b

Amount on line 12a of the Support Schedule (2% limitation) $15,583

**Contributors whose total gifts from Year 5 through Year 1
were in excess of the 2% limitation**

(a) Name	(b) Year 5	(c) Year 4	(d) Year 3	(e) Year 2	(f) Year 1	(g) Total	(h) Excess contributions (col. (g) less the 2% limitation)
Major Donor 1	50,000	-	50,000	-	-	100,000	84,417
Major Donor 2	7,500	5,000	10,000	2,000	-	24,500	8,917
Major Donor 3	20,000	10,000	5,000	-	-	35,000	19,417
Major Donor 4	50,000	25,000	50,000	50,000	-	175,000	159,417
Total							$ 272,168

The Silent Partner Behind America's Foundations

Compliance Monitoring at the Point of Transaction

By Jeffrey D. Haskell, senior vice president, Foundation Source

Ideally, private foundations should endeavor to monitor all activity at the point of transaction to ensure compliance with the Internal Revenue Code and Treasury Regulations. By reviewing transactions as they occur, problematic issues can be identified and swiftly addressed before they cause public embarrassment or result in the imposition of penalties. Generally, the earlier a problematic transaction is identified, the easier it is to correct and more likely to have penalties abated.

In our experience, most compliance issues arise because the foundation's family and directors are not well acquainted with the provisions governing private foundations set forth in the Internal Revenue Code ("Code") and Treasury Regulations. This is hardly surprising, given that most individuals who start private foundations are not Chapter 42 experts. Their desire is simply to practice philanthropy – to give back to society and to support causes that are important to them. For the largest foundations, one solution is to hire specialized staff that monitors compliance continually. However, this is cost prohibitive for most foundations. Instead, they rely on professional advisors, such as attorneys, CPAs and outsourced administrative service companies that understand the rules and regulations.

The following discussion demonstrates a key compliance area private foundations should monitor regularly:

Verification of Grantee's Status as a Public Charity Prior to Every Grant

Prior to making a grant, foundations need to make certain that potential grantees are considered public charities in good standing with the IRS if they wish to avoid exercising expenditure responsibility. Many foundations assume that once the final tax status of a grantee has been established as a public charity, the foundation need not verify the grantee's tax status each time a grant is made to it. Foundations must be aware that the IRS may revoke a grantee's status at any time subsequent to the first grant. If a foundation makes a grant to an organization that has had its status as a public charity revoked, the grant may constitute a taxable expenditure and result in the imposition of a penalty under Code Section 4945. The first tier tax penalty assessed for a taxable expenditure is 10% of the taxable expenditure; if uncorrected, a second tier tax penalty of 100% of the taxable expenditure could be imposed. Accordingly, a foundation should not complacently accept the determination letter as definitive proof of an organization's current qualification as a public charity. Treasury Regulations Sections 1.170A-9(e)(4)(v)(b) and 1.509(a)-3(c)(1)(iii)(a).

To verify the current tax status of a grantee, a foundation should check IRS Publication No. 78, which, among other things, identifies organizations that are classified as public charities and governmental units. Publication No. 78 is updated and reissued annually and additions are published in cumulative quarterly supplements. When the IRS withdraws recognition of status or recognizes a change in an organization's status, such changes are published by

Appendix L Compliance Monitoring at the Point of Transaction

announcements in the Internal Revenue Bulletin. The extent to which foundations may rely on the listing of organizations in this publication for purposes of grant making is set forth in Revenue Procedure 82-39, 1982-2 C.B. 759.

Generally, Revenue Procedure 82-39 provides that where an organization has lost its status as a public charity but is still listed as such in the publication, a grant made to it by a foundation will not constitute a taxable expenditure under Code Section 4945 if the foundation: (1) was unaware of the change in the organization's status at the time the grant was made; (2) was not responsible for or aware of the activities on the part of the organization that gave rise to the loss of its status; and (3) made the grant prior to the date of publication of an announcement in the Internal Revenue Bulletin that contributions to the organization were no longer deductible.

Electronic versions of Publication No. 78 and the Internal Revenue Bulletins are accessible from the IRS's website. Many practitioners take the following steps to verify an organization's public charity status online:

- First, they access Publication No. 78 by going to the IRS's website at www.irs.gov, clicking on "Charities and Nonprofits," then "More Topics," and then "Search for Charities." Publication No. 78 is presented as a researchable database regularly updated every three months.

- Second, they find the Internal Revenue Bulletin for each week since Publication No. 78 was last updated to see if the organization's public charity status has been withdrawn by going to http://www.irs.gov/irb. The Internal Revenue Bulletins are available in both .pdf and html formats.

The online version of Publication No. 78 is convenient to access and search but it has its drawbacks. For example, a user may search by an organization's name, city and state but is unable to execute a pinpoint search by an organization's employer identification number (EIN) or tax classification. This can be frustrating where the user knows the organization's EIN, but has to sift through a search result listing hundreds of organizations with similar names. Further, some organizations are listed in the publication but cannot be found because they operate under and are commonly known by a name different than that listed in the publication. Indeed, certain modest organizations not required to file a Form 990 are not listed in the publication at all.

Another reliance problem arises after a new organization's advance ruling period has expired but before it has received a final determination letter. Treasury Regulations Section 1.170A-9(e)(5)(iii)(b) provides that a new organization's status as a public charity may be relied upon for the period beginning with its inception and ending 90 days after the advance ruling date. If an organization submits Form 8734 within 90 days of the end of the advance ruling date, however, the regulation states that the organization's status as a public charity will continue without interruption until the IRS has made a final determination. Although Publication No. 78 shows an organization's advance ruling date, neither the publication nor the Internal Revenue Bulletin indicates if, in fact, the IRS has ever received Form 8734 from such an organization.

Appendix L Compliance Monitoring at the Point of Transaction

In the not-so-distant past, a toll-free call to the IRS's exempt organization hotline at (877) 829-5500 would quickly resolve this factual question. An IRS customer service representative in the Cincinnati determination group would check the IRS's records and provide a simple yes or no answer. However, in my personal experience, for the past several months the IRS consistently has refused to disclose to an outsider whether or not it has received a given organization's Form 8734. When asked why they have refused to disclose this vital information, they uniformly have responded that this particular taxpayer information is confidential.

Many experienced practitioners in this area believe that, per Revenue Procedure 82-39, foundations may continue relying upon an organization's listing in Publication No. 78 as a public charity for grant making purposes, even after the 90-day window following the advance ruling date has closed, so long as that organization remains listed in the publication and its public charity status has not been withdrawn in an Internal Revenue Bulletin. In fact, this belief is mistaken. Revenue Procedure 82-39 cites Treasury Regulations Section 1.509(a)-7(a), which states:

> Once an organization has received a _final_ ruling or determination letter classifying it as an organization described in section 509(a)(1), (2), or (3), the treatment of grants and . . . the status of grantors . . . to such organization under sections . . . 4942 [and] 4945 . . . will not be affected by reason of a subsequent revocation by the Service of the organization's classification as described in section 509(a)(1), (2), or (3) until the date on which notice of change of status is made to the public . . . . (emphasis added).

As illustrated by the above regulation, the general rule set forth in Revenue Procedure 82-39 is meant to apply _only_ to those organizations that have received _final_ determination letters. No explicit reference is made to new organizations caught in that awkward "twilight period" beginning at the close of the 90-day window following the advance ruling date and ending on the date the IRS has made a final determination. Thus, a foundation may not rely upon an organization's mere listing in Publication No. 78 to protect grants made by it to that organization during the twilight period from being recharacterized as taxable expenditures. A foundation can avoid making a taxable expenditure with certainty during this period by (1) exercising expenditure responsibility or (2) knowing that the IRS has received the organization's Form 8734 within the 90-day period following the advance ruling date.

However, these options may be impractical or impracticable for the following reasons: First, many foundations are unwilling to assume the administrative burden associated with the exercise of expenditure responsibility, especially where the grant amount is not very large. Second, the IRS steadfastly refuses to disclose whether or not it has received a given organization's Form 8734. Accordingly, during this time frame, many foundations do not make grants to such organizations at all, unwilling to incur the risk associated with making such grants.

Just this past summer, one particular foundation wished to make a sizable grant to a small charity located in South Carolina. Prior to making the grant, we reviewed Publication No.

Appendix L Compliance Monitoring at the Point of Transaction

78 and recent Internal Revenue Bulletins. Although the charity was listed in the publication and its status as a publicly-supported charity had not been withdrawn, we noticed that its advance ruling date had expired several years ago. Predictably, the IRS representative refused to indicate whether or not the charity had submitted Form 8734.

I pointed out to the representative that a new organization could find its efforts to garner the required public support hampered or blocked because of the risk associated with making grants to it while its tax status remains in limbo. The representative ruefully conceded that the IRS's refusal to reveal whether or not it had received an organization's Form 8734 to protect confidentiality may, ironically, prove detrimental to that very organization. Thereafter, I contacted the charity's president, a retired Southern gentleman, who, unfortunately, told me that he had never even heard of Form 8734. After explaining the purpose of that form and advising him to get in touch with the charity's tax advisor or to call the IRS's exempt organization hotline, I contacted the foundation's Board and described the risks and options open to them if they wished to proceed with the grant.

This episode spurred me to contact a TE/GE official in Washington, D.C. and make the following recommendation: Further revise Form 1023 to provide an organization applying for recognition as a publicly-supported charity with the option of authorizing the IRS to disclose whether or not the organization submits Form 8734 within the 90-day period following the advance ruling date. If selected, this option would permit IRS customer service representatives to disclose this vital information to outsiders. Further, if an organization submits Form 8734 within the 90-day period following the advance ruling date, its listing in Publication No. 78 could be modified to reflect this fact; for example, an asterisk might appear beside the advance ruling date, signifying that Form 8734 had been submitted to the IRS in a timely fashion. The official said he would consider the recommendation and discuss it with his associates.

Conclusion

Compliance monitoring at the point of transaction is a highly effective way to avoid potential problems. The old adage, "an ounce of prevention is worth a pound of cure" is certainly applicable here. By implementing systems and processes to monitor a foundation's activities, the foundation can focus its time and energy on its philanthropic mission.

About the Author

Jeffrey D. Haskell is senior vice president of legal affairs for Foundation Source. He is responsible for the company's product architecture and legal issues around the foundations the company creates. Prior to joining Foundation Source Mr. Haskell was an associate at the law firm of Kronish Lieb Weiner & Hellman LLP and Olshan Grundman Frome Rosenzweig & Wolosky, in the Tax and Trusts and Estates departments. Prior to joining Olshan Grundman, Mr. Haskell worked at Coopers & Lybrand for several years in the Business Tax Planning Group. Mr. Haskell holds a B.A. in political science from Yeshiva University. He is a graduate of the Benjamin N. Cardozo School of Law, where he was a staff member of Cardozo Law Review. He received a Masters of Law in Taxation from New York University School of Law and was a staff member of N.Y.U. Tax Law Review. Mr. Haskell is an adjunct lecturer at Baruch College of Accountancy, where he teaches corporate tax.

Appendix M Proposed Methodology for Part IX

November 28, 2004

Jeffrey D. Haskell
Senior Vice President
Foundation Source

PROPOSED METHODOLOGY

FOR PREPARATION OF REVISED FORM 1023, PART IX

STATEMENT OF REVENUE & EXPENSE AND BALANCE SHEET

Appendix M Proposed Methodology for Part IX

SCENARIO 1 – EXISTED MORE THAN 4 YEARS (NO SUGGESTED MODIFICATION)

Facts:

Foundation has a calendar year and is incorporated on 04/17/00; the 1023 is prepared on 04/05/05.

Problem:

Where the applicant has been in existence for more than four years, how should it complete columns (a) through (d) of Part IX., A., Statement of Revenue and Expenses (the "Revenue Statement") and what date should be used to prepare Part IX., B., the Balance Sheet?

Solution:

Column (a) would provide financial information regarding the applicant's most recently completed year, 2004, from 01/01/04 - 12/31/04.

Column (b) would report the tax year 2003, from 01/01/03 – 12/31/03.

Column (c) would report the tax year 2002, from 01/01/02 – 12/31/02.

Column (d) would report the tax year 2001, from 01/01/01 - 12/31/01.

DIAGRAM SCENARIO 1

Revenue Statement
Part IX. A.

Balance Sheet
Part IX. B.

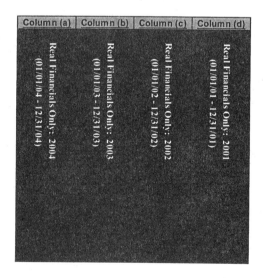

The Balance Sheet would be prepared using balances as of 12/31/04.

Analysis of Scenario 1:

This memorandum makes no suggested modifications with respect to the preparation of the revised 1023 where the applicant has been in existence for four years or more.

The adjacent diagram, however, does clarify how columns (a) through (d) of the Revenue Statement should be prepared.

1

Appendix M Proposed Methodology for Part IX

SCENARIO 2 – EXISTED MORE THAN 1 YEAR, LESS THAN 4 YEARS

Facts:

Foundation has a calendar year and is incorporated on 12/01/04; the 1023 is prepared on 07/15/05.

Problem:

Where the applicant has been in existence for more than one year but less than four, how should it complete columns (a) through (d) of the Revenue Statement and what date should be used to prepare the Balance Sheet?

Solution:

<u>Column (a)</u>, the current tax year, would report the period from 01/01/05 - 7/15/05. This column would reflect only "real" financial information for the date range specified at the top of the column; it would <u>not</u> project financial information through 12/31/05.

<u>Column (b)</u> would report the short tax year from 12/01/04 - 12/31/04. This column would reflect only real financial information for the specified date range.

<u>Column (c)</u> would report the period from 01/01/05 - 12/31/05. This column would combine real financial information from 01/01/05 – 07/15/05 and projected financial information from 07/16/05 – 12/31/05.

<u>Column (d)</u> would report the period from 01/01/06 - 12/31/06. This column would provide a financial projection for the entire calendar year 2006.

DIAGRAM SCENARIO 2

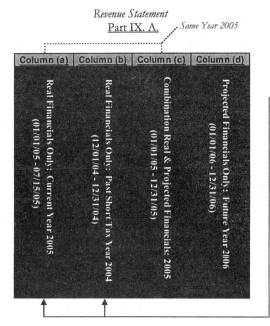

Revenue Statement
Part IX. A. ⸱⸱ *Same Year 2005*

Balance Sheet
Part IX. B.

The Balance Sheet would be prepared using balances as of 7/15/05.

The sum of line 24 column (a) and line 24 column (b) of the Revenue Statement would be equal to the applicant's total net assets reflected on line 18 of the Balance Sheet.

2

Appendix M Proposed Methodology for Part IX

Analysis of Scenario 2:

Proposed Methodology

Under the proposed methodology, the Revenue Statement would provide financial information regarding the applicant's first taxable year, 2004, its current year, 2005, and its next year, 2006, for a total of three full years of financial information. Of key importance is the fact that the applicant would provide a full year's worth of financial data regarding its current year, 2005, and the IRS would be able to distinguish at a glance between real and projected financial information for that year by comparing columns (a) and (c).

The Balance Sheet would reflect balances as of July 15, 2005, the end of the date range specified in column (a) of the Revenue Statement. Consequently, the sum of line 24 column (a) and line 24 column (b) of the Revenue Statement would equal the applicant's net assets reflected on line 18 of the Balance Sheet. The proposed methodology would provide a simple, fast and accurate means to validate the financial information.

Comparison with Methodology of 1023 Instructions

Where an applicant has been in existence for more than one year but less than four, both the proposed methodology and the 1023 instructions would require three full years of financial information for the same period, 2004 through 2006.

However, the 1023 instructions would require the applicant to combine the actual and projected financial information for 2005 in column (a). Accordingly, the IRS would have had no means of discerning where the real financial information for the current year had left off and the projected financial information had begun. In addition, the sum of line 24 column (a) and line 24 column (b) of the Revenue Statement would not equal the applicant's net assets reflected on line 18 of the Balance Sheet. Accordingly, the Revenue Statement and Balance Sheet would not "tie out."

Additionally, where the applicant has been in existence for more than one year but less than four, the 1023 instructions would require the applicant to prepare the Balance Sheet using balance information from its most recently completed year. Here, that would mean preparing the Balance Sheet as of December 31, 2004 rather than as of July 15, 2005, reflecting balances over six months out of date. Although the 1023 instructions would require the applicant to explain any substantial changes in its assets and liabilities since the date reflected on the Balance Sheet, such an explanation would be wholly unnecessary if the applicant simply used current—rather than stale—balance information per the proposed methodology.

3

Appendix M Proposed Methodology for Part IX

SCENARIO 3 – EXISTED LESS THAN 1 YEAR

Facts:

Foundation has a calendar year and is incorporated on 01/08/05; the 1023 is prepared on 03/02/05.

Problem:

Where the applicant has been in existence for less than one year, how should it complete columns (a) through (d) of the Revenue Statement and what date should be used to prepare the Balance Sheet?

Solution:

Column (a), the current tax year, would report the period from 01/08/05 - 03/02/05. This column would reflect only real financial information for the date range specified at the top of the column; it would <u>not</u> project financial information through 12/31/05.

Column (b) would report the period from 01/08/05 - 12/31/05. This column would combine real financial information from 01/08/05 – 03/02/05 and projected financial information from 03/03/05 – 12/31/05.

Column (c) would report the period from 01/01/06 - 12/31/06. This column would provide a financial projection for the entire calendar year 2006.

Column (d) would report the period from 01/01/07 - 12/31/07. This column would provide a financial projection for the entire calendar year 2007.

DIAGRAM SCENARIO 3

Revenue Statement
Part IX. A.

Balance Sheet
Part IX. B.

ame Year 2005

The Balance Sheet would be prepared using balances as of 03/02/05.

Line 24 column (a) of the Revenue Statement would be equal to the applicant's net assets reflected on line 18 of the Balance Sheet.

4

Appendix M Proposed Methodology for Part IX

Analysis of Scenario 3:

Proposed Methodology

Under the proposed methodology, the Revenue Statement would provide financial information regarding the applicant's first and current year, 2005, as well as financial projections for its next two years, 2006 and 2007. As in Scenario 2, the applicant would provide a full year's worth of financial data regarding its current year and the IRS would be able to distinguish between real and projected financial information for that year simply by comparing columns (a) and (b).

The Balance Sheet would reflect balances as of March 2, 2005, the end of the date range specified in column (a) of the Revenue Statement. Consequently, the amount appearing on line 24 column (a) of the Revenue Statement would equal the applicant's net assets reflected on line 18 of the Balance Sheet. As in Scenario 2, the proposed methodology would provide a simple, fast and accurate means to validate the financial information.

Comparison with Methodology of 1023 Instructions

Where an applicant has been in existence for less than one year, both the proposed methodology and the 1023 instructions would require three full years of financial information for the same period, 2005 through 2007. Also, both methodologies would require that the Balance Sheet be prepared using the most recent balance information.

However, the 1023 instructions would require the applicant to combine the actual and projected financial information for 2005 in column (a). By contrast, the amount appearing on line 18 of the Balance Sheet would reflect only real—not projected—balance information[1]. Accordingly, the Revenue Statement and Balance Sheet would never balance. Moreover, column (a) of the Revenue Statement would reflect a muddle of real and projected financial information, providing the IRS with no clear means of distinguishing between fact and fiction.

Conclusion:

This memorandum makes no suggested modifications to the 1023 instructions where the applicant has been in existence for four years or more. In connection with Scenarios 2 and 3, however, the proposed methodology would provide the IRS with the same financial information presently required by the 1023 instructions, but would separate real and projected financial information for the current year into different columns. Consequently, the Revenue Statement in Scenarios 2 and 3 would be presented much more precisely. Further, in connection with Scenario 2, the proposed methodology would require that the Balance Sheet be prepared using up-to-date rather than outdated financial information. Finally, in Scenarios 2 and 3, the Revenue Statement and Balance Sheet would balance, providing a simple means of validating the accuracy of the financial data presented in Sections A. and B. of Part IX.

---

1 Confusing matters further, the instructions explicitly state that the applicant should enter the year-end date for the information provided on the Balance Sheet (e.g., December 31, 2005) rather than the actual date used to compile the financial information reflected thereon (e.g., March 2, 2005).

5

Index